NOEL 'RAZOR' SMITH

The Criminal Alphabet

PENGUIN BOOKS

PENGUIN BOOKS

UK | USA | Canada | Ireland | Australia
India | New Zealand | South Africa

Penguin Books is part of the Penguin Random House group of companies
whose addresses can be found at global.penguinrandomhouse.com.

First published by Particular Books 2015
Published in Penguin Books 2016
001

Typeset in Chaparral Pro 10.75/14 pt
Printed in Great Britain by Clays Ltd, St Ives plc

A CIP catalogue record for this book is available from the British Library

ISBN: 978-0-141-03856-8

www.greenpenguin.co.uk

Penguin Random House is committed to a
sustainable future for our business, our readers
and our planet. This book is made from Forest
Stewardship Council® certified paper.

Contents

This book is dedicated to the memories of Bernadette Mary Smith, Joseph Stephen Smith, Elizabeth Christine McClean, Edward Joseph Regan and my old mate Rockin' Oz. Never forgotten.

Introduction

I have spent almost thirty-three of the last fifty-four years in and out of prison, but mainly in. I was a juvenile offender back in the mid-1970s and went on to become an adult prisoner in the 1980s and beyond. My shortest prison sentence was seven days (for criminal damage) and my longest sentence was life (for bank robbery and possession of firearms). I have fifty-eight criminal convictions, for everything from attempted theft to armed robbery and escape from prison, and I was a career criminal for most of my life. What I do not know about criminal and prison slang could be written on the back of a postage stamp and still leave room for the Lord's Prayer.

For example, take the word 'slang' itself. It's a mix of the words 'secret' and 'language' and perfectly encapsulates the whole reason for slang. Slang has always been a way of communicating in secret, a way to exclude the uninitiated, so it is particularly useful for criminals, who, by the very nature of their deeds, must keep secrets from the police and the general public. A large portion of criminal slang is either rhyming slang (sometimes referred to as cockney rhyming slang, because it's thought that it was invented by the people of the East End of London in the 1840s) or a corruption of it, and market and street traders as well as criminals from all over the UK tend to use it.

It's said a cockney is somebody who was born within the sound of Bow Bells, and some people believe this refers to the area of Bow in the East End of London. The saying actually refers to the bells of St Mary-le-Bow in Cheapside. There was a church on this site over a thousand years ago, and later versions were destroyed in the Great Fire of London in 1666 and then bombed by the Luftwaffe during the Blitz of 1941. The bells of St Mary-le-Bow fell silent on 13 June 1940 and didn't ring again until 1961, therefore during this time no 'true' cockney could be born. I was born in the old Charing Cross Hospital on the Strand on 24 December 1960, as they were transporting the new bells to St Mary-le-Bow, and I like to think that if those bells made any sound at all during this time then I am possibly the only true cockney born in the twenty-one years that the bells were otherwise silent. Perhaps that's why I've always liked rhyming slang.

The use of rhyming slang, in particular, is usually misunderstood by amateur practitioners. The whole idea is to exclude the casual listener, so it's always best to be concise. For example, if I were to say in conversation that 'I was going down the frog and toad in my jam jar when I got a John Bull from the **ducks and geese** because I don't have any beeswax' I would be using rhyming slang. But it wouldn't take a genius to break that particular code ('I was going down the road in my car when I got a pull from the police because I don't have any road tax'). The same statement but using only the first part of each phrase would be much harder to crack: 'I was going down the frog in my jam when I got a John from the ducks because I don't have any bees.' This is the way rhyming slang is intended to be used. It's so extensively spoken, even today, that some slang words and phrases have more than one meaning, which is why context is so important. Take 'bees', for instance. In the example above, 'bees' is slang for 'tax', as in beeswax = tax. But 'bees' is also rhyming slang for 'money', as in bees and honey = money. A better example of how one slang word can have many different meanings is the word 'bottle'. The original rhyming slang is 'Aristotle' (a Greek philosopher) = **'bottle'**. So the words 'aris' or 'bottle' can mean 'arse' (but a later rhyming slang is bottle and glass = 'arse'). It can also mean 'courage', or lack of it ('He's got no bottle'); to follow someone or be behind them ('He's on your bottle'); the action of smashing someone over the head with a glass bottle ('He got two years for bottling a geezer in the pub'); pick-pocketing ('to be out on the bottle'); and a hiding place (up the anus) for criminal contraband ('He's got five grams of heroin bottled').

Some time ago I was telling a friend of mine (who has never been a criminal) a 'joke'* about **skagheads** and **crackheads**, and he didn't have a clue what I was talking about. Looking bewildered, he asked what a skaghead was, and I had to explain that a skaghead is a heroin addict and a crackhead is someone addicted to crack cocaine. This made me think about how little the ordinary person in the street knows about criminal, drug or prison slang. Words and phrases I've taken for granted all of my life are like a foreign language to the vast majority of people. Ignorance of this sort of slang may not affect the ordinary man or woman in the street – 'straight-goers', as they're known by criminals – but sometimes a misunderstanding of such language can lead to dangerous or frightening situations. Many years ago a street-trader friend of mine was selling overpriced cigarettes and cold drinks at an open-air reggae concert on Clapham Common, and got into an argument with a man who objected to paying £5 for a can of lukewarm lemonade fished out of a plastic dustbin full of water in the back of a van. After words were bandied back and forth for a few minutes my pal decided to give the man a fifty-pence refund to shut him up. Business was good and there was no shortage of 'tobys' (Toby jug = mug) willing to shell

* What's the difference between a skaghead and a crackhead?
 Answer: They'll both steal their mother's purse, but the crackhead will help her look for it.

out for his goods, so he just wanted the man to leave his pitch. He realized that he didn't have any loose change on him and shouted to me to 'get the rifle out of the bag in the front of the van so I can pay this fucking idiot out'. I moved swiftly to comply but noticed a look of abject fear cross the customer's features as he backed away from the pitch. I watched in amazement as he dropped his can of lemonade and pegged ('pegged' is a slang word made popular by an old music-hall ditty called 'Jake the Peg', about a three-legged man) it across the common and into the crowd as fast as his legs would carry him. Me and my pal looked at each other and burst out laughing. We both realized why he'd bolted. He thought I was going to pull a rifle from the van and shoot him for arguing! In fact, my pal had been asking me to get the money bag with the loose change in it from the footwell. In rhyming street-trader slang the word 'rifle' means 'change', as in rifle range = change. The poor sap thought he was going to get shot, all over fifty pence!

The above story shows how a simple misunderstanding in language can cause a bit of 'agg' for the unwary. Even for the experienced face, or **boat**, criminal slang changes so quickly that mistakes can inadvertently be made. So even though this book will be as up-to-the-minute as I can possibly make it, some words and phrases will still be out of fashion by the time you read it. New rhyming slang is really dependent on popular culture and what happens to be in vogue on the day. For example, a few years ago James Blunt was a particularly popular singer and, for a while, both the female genitalia and a stupid person were being called a '**James**'. . . I'm sure you can work it out for yourself. Some celebrities fall out of vogue and the connection of their name to rhyming slang becomes lost in the mists of time. At one time, trainers were known as '**Claires**' ('Nice pair of Claires, mate') after the late *Daily Mirror* agony aunt Claire Raynor. With all the changes it goes through, the study of rhyming slang is never going to be an exact science.

A lot of criminal and prison slang is obscure, and false etymologys are given for some slang words and phrases. For example, many people say that the word 'kettle', meaning a watch, comes from the phrase 'kettle of scotch', which was supposedly a measure of scotch. But I've never been able to find 'kettle' being used as a measurement of whisky or any other alcoholic beverage. I prefer to believe the explanation I got from an old cockney villain whom I met during my first incarceration, in Wormwood Scrubs back in the early 1980s, which is that early watches were carried in a suit or jacket pocket (wristwatches didn't come into use until the 1920s) known as the 'fob' pocket, so such watches were called 'fob watches' or 'fobs'. So the rhyming slang for a watch became 'kettle' (kettle and hob = fob), a hob being where you put your kettle to heat the water in it). But there are some people who will swear blind to this day that the rhyming slang for watch is 'kettle of scotch'. Incidentally, the word 'kettle' for watch is still used a lot in certain circles today. Bear in mind when you're reading what follows that when I'm not completely sure of the etymology of certain words and phrases I've gone with what I consider to be the most likely and logical choice.

I'm no language expert. What I know mainly comes from the practical experience of using slang in my everyday life. In the criminal and prison worlds slang is just another tool for survival, another safeguard for the cautious, who rightly believe that someone may be listening in and hoping to take advantage, sometimes to the cost of their liberty. Being a resident of what the more lurid tabloids love to call 'the underworld' meant that I got to hear and use criminal slang from all over the UK and beyond.

Criminals don't play at using slang; it's an integral part of their world and so common as mostly to go unnoticed by the people who speak it. I've always loved slang, loved hearing about the origins of a word or phrase, and if I heard something that was new to me, I'd make it my business to find out how it had come about. Of course, I was no student or academic, and the idea of researching anything – other than the details of my next bank job, that is – was anathema to me. If I wanted to know something about a slang word or phrase, I'd go straight to the knowledgeable people in my world and ask them for an explanation. After all, the people who were using this language on a daily basis were ideally situated to answer my queries. That's why you'll find no real 'evidence' cited for the etymology I give a word or phrase, no names of authors who've written about slang, for example, because I haven't read any of their books. This is what *I* know about slang – the language I've used all my life. I don't need the internet, Google or Wikipedia to tell me about it; it's my second language. Many people look up slang words on the internet and, though I imagine what they find there might be interesting, there's also a lot of 'ollocksbay' (back slang for 'bollocks'; back slang is a simple slang once called pig Latin, in which the first letter of the word is transferred to the end of the word and an 'ay' sound is added) written by people who don't really understand slang. An example is the explanation of '**nonce**', meaning a sex offender, you find on Wikipedia (the one word I did look up on the internet, just to see if anyone had the right explanation). It mentions that the etymology for 'nonce' is unknown but that it's believed to be a corruption of 'nancy boy', as in 'nance'. Excuse me while I wipe the tears of laughter from my eyes! The word 'nonce' originated in Wakefield Prison in the 1900s. Before every prison had a 'protection wing' for sex offenders and others who might be in danger from their fellow prisoners, these undesirables would be kept on the same wings as the other prisoners but could only be let out of their cells when the other cons were locked up to protect them from being injured. The staff would mark their door card with the acronym NONCE (Not On Normal Courtyard Exercise) so that unwary staff would not open the doors of the sex offenders' cells while those of the rest of the prison population were unlocked. As far as I'm concerned, this is the true etymology of 'nonce'.

It isn't only rhyming slang that I concern myself with here. Criminal and prison slang is an eclectic mix of words, dialects and languages. These days, the slang you hear on prison landings and among young gang members is likely to be a mix of American street slang and West Indian (in particular, Jamaican) patois.The modern young criminal will chat about **paper**, jacking and **man dem**, just as their predecessors used to 'rabbit' about 'dosh', blagging and **chinas**. On a recent visit to a young offender prison to speak to the YPs about writing and language, I was asked by one of the USLAs (prisoners under school-leaving age) how he could make paper from writing. When I told him that he'd need a lot of discipline and to do a lot of hard work, he got a bit **vex** and told me he would rather get his 'strap' and 'move someone up'. I replied that he didn't look **hench** enough to be chatting that kind of 'coup'. The conversation became a bit heated, and he got 'screwface' and started 'getting all up in my grille', so I had to'step up' and put the 'kibosh' on the 'convo'. As you can imagine, the screws were getting worried, as they couldn't understand a word we were saying! But if you read the rest of this book you'll understand perfectly.

While the modern young criminal mainly prefers American and West Indian words and slang, they can't help but also use some of what has gone before, such as rhyming slang, back slang, Romani, Yiddish and variations on their own geographical dialect. Mixed in with the modern slang are old favourites that never seem to go out of fashion. A lot of Romany Gypsy words are still in use, the prime example these days being 'chav', which means 'boy' but has come to mean something entirely different to different sets of people. Gypsies and old cockneys still use 'chav' in its original meaning, as in 'Ah, he's a good chav' or 'I need a few quid to get a present for my chav's birthday'. Other people now use it to describe young people from the 'lower classes', and the 'lower class' youths use it to describe a certain mode of dress and behaviour. But 'in the death', it just means 'boy'.

This book isn't purely about language and slang, it's also an overview of the demographic that uses slang in their daily life – the history, events, the people and the lifestyle – so think of it not as a dictionary but as a journey through a world I have known almost from birth.

Page numbers for cross-references have been supplied only when the entry referred to is in a different chapter.

Origins

I was born in the old Charing Cross Hospital on the Strand on Christmas Eve 1960, which makes me a Londoner, but both of my parents are from Ireland – my father from the rough and ready North of Dublin and my mother from the more genteel Southside of the city – which, under Section 2 of the Irish constitution, makes me Irish. So, right from the start, I was exposed to the rich dialect of two capital cities. Until the age of nine I lived in North London. We tended to move around a lot, as my parents could usually only afford to rent rooms, so at various times we lived in Paddington, Camden Town, Finsbury Park and Holloway. As a kid on the streets of North London in the early 1960s I heard the slang and banter of street-market traders around Angel Market as well as the accents and dialects of my schoolmates, who were a mix of Londoners, Irish, Scottish and Jamaicans. The mix of Dublin and London slang I was exposed to as a child could sometimes be confusing. For example, the Irish call a cupboard a 'press', and they call dishes and cups 'delft' (only, with the Dublin accent, the 't' in 'delft' is silent). So when my mother told me to 'wash the delft and put it in the press' I knew what she was talking about, though my English pals wouldn't have a clue. In Irish slang, a number of anything is a 'rake' ('a rake of delft to wash'). Also, anything you can't remember the name of is a 'yoke', as in 'Where's that yoke that fits on the end of the carpet sweeper?'. So, from a young age, I had to learn to translate in my own head what was being said both inside and outside of the home. Pretty typical for the child of immigrants in what was, to them, basically a foreign country, but this may have been where my love for words and language was first ignited. I remember once I told the teacher that I was going home for a 'coddle' that evening and she tried to correct me – 'No, Noel, it's pronounced "cuddle",' she said, emphasizing the 'u'. I was actually talking about an Irish stew made from sausage, bacon and potatoes. Dublin coddle was, in my young mind at least, world famous.

Very early on I learned to adapt my language to the situation. Those were the days when it wasn't uncommon to hear kids in London exclaiming 'Gor blimey!' or 'Gertcha!' (today, the only time you hear these expressions is in old black-and-white films or in Chas and Dave songs): we really did talk like this. Of course, we didn't know that the phrase 'Gor blimey!' was a corruption of the ancient exclamation 'God blind me!', an exhortation to God to take away the power of sight when you are faced with something terrible or horrifying. And 'Gertcha!' was a shortened version of 'Get the fuck away from me, you!', usually growled and with the added emphasis of a raised hand. When we were scrumping apples from local gardens, running round the stalls in Angel Market or just generally acting like kids, there was always some old geezer who would raise a hand and shout 'Gertcha!' in our direction. And we copied what we heard.

When I was nine my family got their first real home, a council flat in Balham, South London, and off we went to the badlands of 'sarf', as North Londoners would say. Living in South London meant learning a whole new set of words and phrases. For example, in North London playing truant from school was known as 'hopping the wag', but in South London it was called 'bunking it'. In Dublin it was called 'mitching'. So when my mum asked if I'd been 'mitching school' I could honestly reply that I hadn't, because in my mind I was 'bunking it'. It's no wonder I was a confused kid!

South London slang differs from the slang used in other parts of London, and indeed in the country as a whole.

Bermondsey, in particular, used to have its own language, which even people in other parts of South London found hard to decipher. A 'stone ginger' was a certainty, as was the word 'million', as in 'Yeah, he's a million for parole since he's behaved himself'. Once I became a teenager and involved in a life of crime, my language expanded further. The language of borstal and juvenile jails is littered with slang, some of it dating back to Victorian times. For example, in **borstal** there was a tradition for boys in the last fortnight of their sentence to count down the days like this – '14 and a **brek** . . . 13 and a brek . . . 12 and a brek' and so on – 'brek' being short for 'breakfast', because on the morning you leave custody you're not released until the institution has served breakfast. In the last ten days of the sentence the tradition was to cough into your hands and then show via your fingers how many days and a brek you had left. (Of course, it could be very annoying to others, who were only just starting their sentences, to have people openly and gleefully counting down the days to their release, and this sometimes led to violence.)

The borstal system was a hotbed of slang. If someone was misbehaving, they would be told to 'toe it', meaning to toe the line. I found out years later that the expression 'toe the line' dates back to the early days of bare-knuckle fighting, when a line would be drawn on the ground and, after a knockdown, each fighter would start again, with their toes on this line. So to 'toe it' meant to get up and get ready for what was coming. Insults in the borstal system were rife, and if you weren't the brightest spark in the box you would be referred to as a **Plum** (apparently a reference to a dim-witted Red Indian character featured in *The Beano*, Little Plum). 'Sap' was also big as an insult in borstal. This word has its origins in American slang: it was a small cosh carried by police and criminals, a blunt instrument. It was also used to describe a soppy or stupid person, and borstal boys picked up the word from old Hollywood films. Borstal society was basically split into two separate factions: you were either a **chap** or a sap. Chaps were tough guys, future career criminals, and not to be messed with – the leaders. And the majority of borstal boys were the saps, sheep to be bullied and taken advantage of.

My entry into the world of the professional criminal and adult prison was an eye-opener when it came to slang. An old expression that was still in vogue among criminals when I started out was 'wearing the paper hat', meaning to be 'mugged off' or put in a compromising position with no gain, or to end up behind bars, and it's still heard today in some circles. If a group of criminals is committing a crime and one of them gets caught while the rest get away, the one who's caught is said to be left 'wearing the paper hat'. Nobody wanted to be in that position. I entered the world of the police **fit-up** (tailoring of evidence by the police to fit the suspect), the sweatbox (prison transport) and the **mattress job** (a beating by police in which a cell mattress is put over the prisoner before they are given a kicking), of **verbals** (made-up statements supposedly said by the suspect at the time of arrest and recorded in the arresting officers' notebooks as gospel) and 'mags' (magistrates' court). The slang was coming fast and hard, and I barely had time to learn it all before I found myself serving a lengthy sentence.

At the age of sixteen I appeared at the Old Bailey, having forsaken the juvenile crimes of TDA (Taking and Driving Away), **hoisting** (shoplifting) and 'scrumping' (stealing fruit from gardens or orchards) in order to pursue a career in the more adult environment of blagging and GBH (Grievous Bodily Harm). I stood in the dock and was sentenced to a three-stretch (three years) for my indiscretions, and though I was still legally a juvenile offender, I was treated like an old **lag**. My life was now set out for me – crime, detention centre, crime, borstal, crime, prison, old age, die was what I was heading for. Having read a report written by a prison governor in 1976, when I was fifteen, I have no reason to believe that 'the system' (what most criminals and prisoners call the criminal justice machine) had any faith in me pulling out of the life I'd chosen. The report said, 'Smith has been identified as one of a small group of boys who will spend their lives in and out of institutions.' Nice to know that I was written off at the age of fifteen! But, it must be said, I was a terrible little **scrote** who couldn't stop **half-inching** 'the prize' (proceeds of robbery) whenever the opportunity presented itself.

Armed robbery, the criminal offence that became my *raison d'être*, is a game that is littered with slang. Sometimes known as the **heavy** (because of the heavy prison sentences it attracts), or 'pavement work' (when it's robbing security vans in the street), or just **work** (because professional robbers class themselves as working men; it just so happens that robbing at gunpoint is their job). In order to carry out an armed robbery, you need certain tools of the trade, such as a 'shooter' (gun), a **smother** (mask), **turtles** (gloves), a **happy bag** (the bag used to carry firearms to and the cash from the job) and a 'jam jar' (getaway car). Once you have the tools, you'll do a 'recce' (reconnaissance) on your target, whether it be a 'jug' (bank – from the days when people buried their money in a pot or jug) or the **corey** (security vehicle), unless, that is, you are just going out on 'spec' (speculation). You must keep your eyes open for police **obbo posts** (observation points) or a **ready-eye** (police ambush) by **the Sweeney** (the Flying Squad). Once you go **across the pavement** (start a robbery) you must be on guard for any 'have-a-gos' (members of the public who want to be heroes) and go for the prize.

JAM JAR/GETAWAY CAR

Of course, once I took up armed robbery as a career it was odds-on that I'd be spending some time in prison, and prison is a place that is rich in slang. When in prison, doing **bird** (bird lime = time) or serving your stretch, whether it be a **shit and a shave** (a very short sentence), a **carpet** (three months; the time it takes a prisoner to make a rug for his cell), or even 'the big L' (a life sentence), you need to switch on and tune in, or you'll be the one left wearing the paper hat.

The Out

1. *The Language of Crime*

The *Concise Oxford English Dictionary* defines crime as 'an offence against an individual or the state which is punishable by law'. Very concise. But that definition hardly begins to scrape the surface of the myriad crimes that exist in this country alone. And for every crime there is a whole language of slang that, in the criminal world, relates to it. The successive governments of Tony Blair and Gordon Brown introduced over four thousand new laws in just over ten years, which, in effect, means that these days you can end up with a criminal record without even breaking a sweat. But let us suppose, just for the sake of simplicity, that you have found yourself on the wrong side of the law or, even worse, been convicted and sent to prison. To survive in this environment, you must, at the very least, understand the language. Of course, it may be that you're determined to make crime your career (a lot of people do, but it isn't something I'd recommend). In that case, you'll have to start somewhere, and that would be choosing the sort of criminal activity that appeals to you and which you might be good at. And to know exactly what is on offer for the novice criminal, it's important to understand the language. For example, there'd be no point asking you to 'get your boys, **turtles** and **smother** for a bit of **aggy**', as you, at this stage, would have no idea what was being said. If you're going to be **at it**, you'll have to be familiar with the world and language of crime, even if you're coming in at the ground floor, so to speak. All criminals, petty or professional, casual or career, are after what is known in criminal circles as the 'prize'. The prize can be cash, jewels, gold, silver or any other item worth stealing. No thief – with perhaps the exception of joyriders and kleptomaniacs – will go out stealing just for the fun of it: everybody is after something. The prize is, however, not to be confused with 'the big one'. The big one is the ultimate prize, enough loot to allow the criminal to retire to sunnier climes. Very few criminals ever manage to pull off the big one, though it has been known – think of the Great Train Robbery (1963: £2.6 million), the Brink's-MAT Robbery (1983: £26 million in gold; worth £75 million today) and the Tonbridge Securitas Robbery (2006: £53 million), to name but a few. But it's even rarer for those who manage to take down the big one to get away with it: most end up in prison for many years, or abroad and on the run in places that don't sell Watneys Red Barrel or Marmite (not that you can get Watneys Red Barrel even in this country any more, but hopefully you'll know what I mean).

If you choose the drug game as your criminal career, then you'll have to learn a completely different way of speaking. When I say 'choose the drug game', I don't mean choosing to take drugs – though if you do choose to consume illegal drugs, you'll still have to touch the criminal world – I mean choosing to deal, smuggle or supply drugs as a criminal enterprise. The problem with the drug game, as far as a lot of professional criminals are concerned, is the amount of otherwise 'straight-goers' who get involved because of the large profits that can be made. The perfect example is cocaine. In its country of origin a kilo of pure cocaine can cost as little as £2,000, but once it's smuggled into Britain that same kilo is worth around £40,000. Once it's been cut several times and has made its way into street deals of a gram a piece, it can be worth as much as half a million pounds. With money like that on offer, it stands to reason that a lot of people who normally wouldn't have much to do with organized and major crime get greedy and are tempted by the big profits. Businessmen put up 'front money' to buy and smuggle the cocaine, then leave the distribution to a criminal network and sit back and wait for the **paper** to roll in. The trouble starts when the investors end up getting nicked. Now, I'm not saying that criminals are all stand-up guys (honourable men), to use the American vernacular, but there is some honour amongst professional villains, and being a **grass** is a big no-no which, in extreme cases, is punishable by death. All professional criminals know this; they've entered the criminal world with their eyes wide open and know that if they don't follow the rules they're putting themselves in line for serious grief. Professional criminals have usually come up through the ranks and served their time in remand centres, detention centres, borstal and prison. They know not to talk to the authorities and how to behave under interrogation, i.e. ask for your brief and then keep 'schtum' (*stumm* is the German word for 'silent'). Threats by police interrogators should be like **oil off a stone** to the professional law-breaker. However, the businessman who dabbles in the drug game has no such grounding in the criminal ethos and therefore doesn't know how to act when confronted by **Plod**. He is liable to panic and sob out the names and details of everyone involved. Blinded first by the anticipation of great riches for little effort and then by the fear of ending up in prison, these former straight-goers will turn over faster than a turtle in a waterfall.

That's one reason why many professional criminals now shun the drug game in favour of crimes in which they don't have to rely on straight-goers. As for the language of the drug game, like any other criminal slang, it's very eclectic and changes constantly. For example, the smuggling and distribution of drugs rely heavily on phone calls and messages so, as police and customs crack each drug code, it has to be replaced. There are dozens, maybe hundreds, of words to describe heroin and cocaine alone. Heroin can be H, horse, tar, tackle, skag, **the naughty**, nikki, gammynock, **brown**, the dragon, **China white**, Afghan . . . to name but several. And Charlie, Chaz, hooter, beak, oats, white, snozz, trumpet, sniff and YaYo are just a few names for cocaine. So you can see how complicated it can be. All drugs are now commonly known as 'food' by street dealers.

There is a theory of progression in criminal activity, that there are various 'gateway' crimes that will inevitably lead to more serious offences. For example, a lot of shoplifters and sneak thieves go on to become burglars. The clue is in the furtive nature of these crimes: they appeal to people who like to keep their offending low-key and under some kind of cover, as opposed to, say, armed robbers, who commit their crimes out in the open and usually in full view of their victims. However, not all shoplifting is done by men or women wearing huge coats with secret pockets; these days, shoplifters are a lot more blatant.

As an aside, I find it interesting when slang words and phrases that began life in the crime-and-punishment sphere end up being used, unknowingly, by straight-goers. For example, a lot of people know the phrase 'to be left in the lurch', but not many know its origins. In the days of public executions in Britain the prisoners who were due to be executed were picked up from the prison in a caged wagon known as a 'lurch'. They were then paraded through the streets to their place of execution, as crowds jeered and pelted them with stones and rotten food. If a particular miscreant was hated by the crowd, they would have a whip-round to get a few pennies to give to the driver of the lurch so he could go and have a drink and something to eat. He would then leave the prisoners 'in the lurch' and at the mercy of the crowd.

So now let's move on to the crimes themselves. We'll start with the **tea leaves**. Thieving has been with us for as long as people have lived on this earth. The act of taking something that doesn't belong to you is almost natural – watch a bunch of toddlers interacting with each other at play and you'll see how quick we humans are to snatch anything that takes our fancy, even at that age. Some people never learn the lesson that taking things that don't belong to you is bad, or choose to ignore it. Section 1 of the Theft Act 1968 states that 'a person is guilty of theft if he dishonestly appropriates property belonging to another with the intention of permanently depriving the other of it'. The maximum penalty in the UK is seven years' imprisonment. Many people confuse 'theft' with 'robbery' and, while they are both crimes covered by the Theft Act, there are major differences. According to the act, 'a person is guilty of robbery if he steals, and immediately before or at the time of doing so, and in order to do so, he uses force on any person or puts or seeks to put any person in fear of being then and there subjected to force'. To explain it in simple terms, a thief is someone who will creep into your premises and take your property without you knowing it, whereas a robber will tell you he is stealing your property and do it right in front of your eyes by use of threats or force. Under the Theft Act 1968 there are many varied definitions of the act of theft and, in real life, thieves come in every shape, size, hue and creed.

ACROSS THE PAVEMENT

To go **across the pavement** is criminal parlance for robbing banks and security vans. If someone tells you that he likes to go across the pavement, it means he is active in armed robbery. It comes from the modus operandi of serious armed robbery. When robbing a bank or any other premises, the method is usually to pull up outside, emerge from the vehicle as quickly as possible, then go across the pavement to the premises without attracting too much attention. The 'pavement' can be compared to the Rubicon as, once it has been crossed, there is usually no going back. When robbing security vans (money in transit) you will 'take the pavement', which means to control the stretch of street immediately around the target by means of threats and threatening gestures, usually with a firearm, to keep the public at bay while the robbery is being carried out.

The Wembley Mob (a gang of bank robbers from the late 1960s and early '70s led by Derek 'Bertie' Creighton Smalls) pioneered the MO of driving the getaway vehicle up on to the pavement outside the target bank and blocking the entrance to passers-by. It was what became known as a 'crash-bang gang', in that they would rely on the element of surprise by 'crashing' the bank doors open and then firing ('bang!') a shotgun into the ceiling in order to elicit fear and compliance. 'Bertie' Smalls was eventually caught for the robbery of £237,736 in cash from the Wembley branch of Barclays Bank and, faced with the prospect of a twenty-five-stretch in the 'big house', he decided to give up his confederates in a deal with the DPP (Director of Public Prosecutions) that saw him walk free without serving a single day in prison for his numerous crimes. Billed as the first ever supergrass, and the only one never to serve any time, Bertie gave evidence against dozens of his former mates and criminal partners in return for complete immunity from prosecution. The men he grassed on were sentenced to a total of 414 years in prison. Only two men came out of the Bertie Smalls deal with smiles on their faces: one was Bertie Smalls himself, and the other was a man named Jimmy Saunders. Saunders had been **fitted up** by the police for a robbery in Ilford in 1970 and had been jailed for twelve years, despite his protestations of innocence. If the police and the DPP were going to accept the word of Smalls in order to jail nearly fifty major criminals, then it stood to reason that when he gave up the team for the 1970 Ilford robbery and Saunders wasn't in it, they had to accept that Saunders was an innocent man.

See Rice Shots (p. 64)

ACTIVE

Active is a word used by police and prison officers to describe a criminal or prisoner they suspect of carrying out illegal activities ('He's keeping a low profile at the moment but we know he's active'). Often the major police squads will carry out intermittent surveillance on criminals who they think are active in order to try to get some intelligence on exactly what they are up to. The active criminal will be followed, filmed and recorded, and all their contacts will be marked as suspect. This is the police version of trawling in the hope of making a catch, and sometimes they'll get lucky and come across a crime that is being planned or one that's in progress. In prison, the Security Department will do the same with active prisoners who they suspect of drug dealing, planning escape or sedition. The easiest way for the prison Security Department to find out who's dealing drugs on a prison wing is to introduce a couple of **clucking** junkies (drug addicts who need their fix) into the environment and then just watch who they go to or talk to. Clucking junkies will find a drug dealer on a prison wing within minutes of landing.

AGGY/AGGY MERCHANTS

Section 10 of the Theft Act 1968 states that 'a person is guilty of aggravated burglary if he commits any burglary and at the time has with him any firearm or imitation firearm, any weapon of offence, or any explosive; and for this purpose (a) "firearm" includes an airgun or air pistol, and "imitation firearm" means anything which has the appearance of being a firearm, whether capable of being discharged or not; and (b) "weapon of offence" means any article made or adapted for use for causing injury to or incapacitating a person, or intended by the person having it with him for such use; and (c) "explosive" means any article manufactured for the purpose of producing a practical effect by explosion, or intended by the person having it with him for that purpose. A person guilty of aggravated burglary shall on conviction on indictment be liable to imprisonment for life.'

Aggy, or aggravated burglary, is the most violent crime in the burglary genre. It involves forcing your way into premises while they are occupied, usually by way of threat or violence, in order to steal from those premises. Often, **aggy merchants** will go armed and with the intention of inflicting injury on their victims if they do not comply. Most of the time, the aggy merchant relies on the element of surprise, either by knocking on the door of the premises and then forcing their way in when the door is answered by the unsuspecting occupant, or by effecting an entry in secret and then pouncing on the occupants. The occupants are quickly overpowered and secured before being questioned as to the whereabouts of cash and valuables. In the criminal pecking order, aggy merchants are viewed with a patina of distaste by other serious criminals, but particularly by armed robbers, or the **heavy** mob. Aggy is classed as a very personal crime, because the perpetrators often enter someone's home, rather than commercial or banking premises, in order to ply their trade, which goes against the code of the serious criminal. Also, some aggy merchants have rather unsavoury reputations for sexually abusing or torturing their victims, which doesn't sit well with the professional robber's ethos of it 'just being a job'. A lot of psychopaths and other sick people are attracted to the aggy game.

One of the most infamous aggy merchants was the legendary highwayman Dick Turpin. Before becoming the dashing highwayman of story, song and fable, Turpin worked with a gang of aggravated burglars called the Essex Gang. They specialized in forcing entry into isolated farmhouses and torturing the occupants for their loot. In one case, Turpin and his gang sat a sixty-five-year-old woman on an open fire in order to get her to reveal the whereabouts of her valuables. Aggy merchants are particularly nasty people who will stop at little in their hunt for the prize.

See Cat Burglars, Commy Burgs, Creeper

AT IT

If someone is deemed to be **at it**, it means they are engaged in criminal activity on a regular basis. A typical conversation between criminals planning a criminal venture will be about who might be at it, in other words, who is still committing crime and who is no longer available to take on the the job because they are 'on their toes' (on the run from police or prison) or in 'shovel' (shovel and pick = nick). Career criminals are constantly at it. Though used originally by criminals, this phrase is now often used by the police to describe prolific offenders: the police will be well aware of who is at it on their particular patch. Of course, like much other slang, it has more than one meaning in the criminal world. For example, to 'get someone at it' means you are pulling a stroke on them, i.e. spinning elaborate lies or tales in order to sucker them in ('I had John checking his car for listening devices after I told him I saw someone bugging him. I got him right at it!').

BILKING

Bilking is the practice of eluding payment for goods or services by making a quick getaway. These days, it is mostly the preserve of motorized bandits and car thieves, who will pull into a petrol station, fill their tank with fuel and then drive off without paying. There are also a few hard-core bilkers who make it their business to eat in top restaurants and leave without paying. If arrested, a bilker will be charged with theft. It is believed that the word 'bilk' may be a form of the word 'balk', which is a term used in the card game cribbage.

THE BIRD GAME

The bird game added a new dimension to **hoisting**, in that the thieves were after a bit of livestock. Some bored sadist with time on his hands discovered that parrots, cockatiels and other expensive birds were susceptible to ether. One spray of the stuff and they would keel over and be spark out for a number of minutes before waking up none the worse for wear. There is a spray you can buy from most petrol stations called Easy Start which you squirt into a diesel engine on a cold morning to aid the ignition, and this spray contains ether. Spray it into the face of a bird, and the bird will go to bye-byes long enough for it to be stolen without the usual struggle, squawks and pecking that would result from manhandling a conscious bird. Now parrots, in particular, are not cheap – some go for upwards of a thousand pounds – and to the desperate little junkies of Bermondsey, a parrot was drug money for the taking. So, usually in teams of two, the thieves would enter a pet shop that sold these expensive birds and go to work. One would wear a puffa jacket, the kind that has plenty of room in the sleeves, and while their companion distracted the shop staff with inquiries about the care of his non-existent aardvark or chinchilla, the other would give a couple of parrots a blast of the ether spray and slip their unconscious bodies down each sleeve of the jacket before walking nonchalantly out of the shop. By the time the birds came to, they'd be in a cage in the getaway car, heading towards a dealer who would facilitate their sale for heroin or crack, or both. The bird game was a real money spinner for a while, until the market was flooded with exotic birds – every drug dealer in South London had at least two African Greys sitting in their front room – and pet shops started beefing up their security.

BOOSTING

Boosting is American criminal slang for stealing. To boost something is to take it without paying. To boost an item is to grab it and go, as in 'giving it a boost'.

BOOT BURGLARS

A **boot burglar** is a petty, motorized thief who will cruise car parks and quiet streets looking for likely targets, that is, any half-decent-looking car or van that might have something of value in it that can be quickly sold on. The main items targeted for theft by the boot burglar are spare wheels – always good for £20 a piece if in good condition – tools and anything else that people might be tempted to keep in the boot of their car. Most car boots can be opened by the experienced boot burglar in less than a minute, using the blade of a large pair of scissors to **jiggle** the lock. If this doesn't work, then there are cruder methods of entry, such as jemmying the boot lid or breaking a quarterlight and getting inside the car to release the boot lock. Sometimes a boot burglar can get lucky and hit the jackpot. A friend of mine once jiggled the boot of a Ford Cortina and found a bag with £20,000 in cash in it. But, to counter that, I also know someone who got caught jiggling a boot at three o'clock one morning and had his arm broken by the owner, who crept from his house wielding a golf club when alerted by the noise. On the whole, boot burgling is the breadline of the criminal world and not a way of getting rich and being able to retire. It becomes a high-risk enterprise when you do it for a living, because of the sheer amount of crimes you have to commit in order to make any money. In reality, a boot burglar would be better off getting a straight job, as even road sweeping would pay more.

See Jiggling and Scissoring

THE BULL

The bull is the nickname given by pickpockets to the plain-clothes Metropolitan Police pickpocket squad. Quite often they would jump on and manhandle suspected pickpockets quite roughly, and this led to them being called bullies, or the bull for short. On the London Underground, a major hunting ground for pickpockets back in the 1970s and '80s, you would often hear warning cries of 'Bull! Bull!' from the gangs when one of the pickpocket squad was spotted.

BURGLARY

Section 9 of the Theft Act 1968 states that 'a person is guilty of **burglary** if (a) he enters any building or part of a building as a trespasser and with intent to commit any such offence as is mentioned in subsection 2 below (stealing anything in the building or part of the building in question, of inflicting on any person therein any grievous bodily harm or raping any person therein, and of doing unlawful damage to the building or anything therein) or (b) having entered into any building or part of a building as a trespasser he steals or attempts to steal anything in the building or that part of it or inflicts or attempts to inflict on any person therein grievous bodily harm. A person guilty of burglary shall on conviction on indictment be liable to imprisonment for a term not exceeding (a) where the offence was committed in respect of a building or part of a building which is a dwelling, fourteen years, and (b) in any other case, ten years.'

CAT BURGLARS

Cat burglars are the elite of the burglary game. These are the people who will climb the outside of buildings in complete darkness and silently break into luxury flats in order to steal cash and jewels. The cat burglar can be in and out with your goods long before you know they've been there. Perhaps one of the most infamous British cat burglars of the twentieth century was Peter Scott, known as the 'Human Fly'. Scott described some of his more glamorous exploits in his memoirs, *Gentleman Thief* (1995), in which he took sole credit for the previously unsolved theft of film star Sophia Loren's jewellery in the raid on her Elstree hotel room in 1960. However, recent revelations by the man who supposedly 'trained' Scott have thrown doubt on this claim. Ray 'The Cat' Jones now claims that, though Scott planned the raid, it was he, Jones, who carried out the job. Sophia Loren was in England that year making *The Millionnairess* and brought her jewels, worth £185,000 (a hell of a lot of money in 1960), with her. Jones claims he broke into Loren's bedroom as Scott kept watch downstairs. He sold the jewels to an underworld **fence** for £44,000 and had to pay a £6,000 'fee' to the policemen who had supplied the inside information. Whatever the truth of the story, underworld opinion is that Ray 'The Cat' Jones was probably the best cat burglar who ever pulled on a pair of gloves.

Probably the most notorious cat burglar of the nineteenth century was Charles Peace, one of the few real criminals to be mentioned by Arthur Conan Doyle's fictitious detective Sherlock Holmes (in his short story 'The Adventure of the Illustrious Client'). Charles Peace was a highly skilled musician, a violin virtuoso described as the 'modern Paganini' (having taught himself on a violin with only one string), but it was his skills as a cat burglar that led to his notoriety and brought him wealth and fame. Peace was what Victorians called a 'portico thief' (because their method of entry was to climb the portico of a house and enter by an upstairs window or skylight), which later in the twentieth century became known as a cat burglar. He was once described, by the Earl of Birkenhead, Solicitor General of Britain, as an 'arch-criminal, a curious mixture of sordid villainy and artistic tastes'. Charles Peace was perhaps the first man to turn burglary into a serious business, as he invented a set of special tools with which to gain entry to premises, his 'burglary kit', which consisted of a skeleton key, two pick-locks, a centre-bit, a gimlet, a gouge, a chisel, a vice jemmy, a knife, a portable ladder, a revolver and a life preserver (a heavy piece of cane about a foot long with a six-ounce lead ball on one end and a leather or catgut loop to go around the wrist on the other, which was used as a cosh and much favoured by nineteenth-century 'gentlemen'). He also found time to invent a few other things. Along with a man named Brion, Charles Peace patented a device for raising sunken vessels, and worked on a smoke helmet for firemen, an improved brush for washing railway carriages and a form of hydraulic tank. Peace was arrested during a burglary in Blackheath, after trying to shoot the arresting officer, and was eventually hanged in 1879, for the murder of a police officer during an earlier burglary and the murder of a love rival. But, like the **creeper** Flannel Foot, Charles Peace took burglary to a more sophisticated level.

See Creeper

COMMY BURGS

Commy burgs, or commercial burglars, are the people who will break into warehouses, shops or factories in their pursuit of ill-gotten gains. Commy burgs are unlikely to come across anyone during their crime, so theirs is seen as an entirely impersonal crime, acquisitive rather than violent. Commy burgs are usually highly organized and will know exactly what they're after and sometimes have a buyer lined up before they even start. In the twenty-first century a lot of the commy burgs at the top end of the scale steal technology, such as microchips and circuit boards, which can be worth a small fortune. Others prefer to raid warehouses and steal lorry loads of goods; anything with a quick resale value is the order of the day. Nowadays, with the price of metal so high, a lot of commy burgs are targeting scrapyards or anywhere that may hold unmarked metals that can quickly be weighed in at a scrap merchant's. *See Cat Burglars*

CRACK CONVERTERS

In recent years in most cities and towns in the UK there has been an influx of shops that buy or lend money on things of value such as jewellery, electrical goods and other household items. Perhaps the best known of these is the ubiquitous Cash Converters – known to the thieving junkie contingent as **Crack Converters**, because it's usually here that they convert their stolen goods into cash for crack cocaine and other drugs. Funnily enough, Cash Converters usually offers less than a third of the retail price for the goods they buy, i.e. less than the criminal **fence** has traditionally offered for stolen goods. These type of businesses normally try to safeguard themselves by demanding various forms of identification from the sellers, but thieves, and in particular thieving junkies, have little trouble stealing or forging ID – it's part of the life.

See Crack, Fence, Fencing, Roger (pp. 325)

CREEPER

Creeping is the exact opposite to the **walk-in**. A **creeper** is the type of burglar who enters dwellings while the occupants are in bed and creeps around the premises looking for items to steal. The object of the creeper is to get in and out, with the valuables, without anyone knowing they've been there until the escape has been made. Some people get creepers confused with **cat burglars**, but they are slightly different animals. The cat burglar is a climber, whilst the creeper usually enters by the ground floor of a premises. Perhaps the most infamous creeper was a fella called Flannel Foot, a burglar and jewel thief in the 1930s. The legend goes that, during his time in solitary confinement in Dartmoor Prison, Flannel Foot spent his entire time training to move in complete silence so as to become a better creeper on release. He would scatter various objects around the cell floor, blindfold himself and tie cloths around his feet and hands, then try to make his way around the cell without disturbing anything or making a noise. In this way, he taught himself to move silently in complete darkness so he would never need a light while he was committing a burglary and was unlikely to wake the occupants.

See Sneak Thief

DIP/DIPPER

A **dip** or **dipper** is a pickpocket. The name comes from the
Elizabethan era, when the punishment for pickpockets was
to be tied to a ducking stool and immersed in water until
they were near death. The art of picking pockets has been
around for a very long time, probably since we first had
pockets, but this crime enjoyed something of a renaissance
in the early 1970s. It became the career choice of many
young criminals, perhaps due to the popularity of the
musical film *Oliver* (1968), which starred Jack Wild as the
Artful Dodger, Ron Moody as Fagin and Oliver Reed as Bill
Sikes. *Oliver* turned a whole generation of kids on to the
delights of picking a pocket or two. (Interestingly, at one
stage, the punishment for theft, including pickpocketing,
was death by hanging. These executions were held in public
as a deterrent to thieves and pickpockets and would often
feature a large scaffold that could hang up to ten thieves
in one go. However, as a deterrent, these public hangings
were a complete failure, as pickpockets would be working
the crowds that gathered to watch. Some people will steal
no matter what the penalty if caught – nobody commits
crime thinking they will have to pay the price for it. That's
why the death penalty has never been, nor ever will be, a
deterrent.)
See Whizzer, Whiz mob

DRUMMER

Drummer is a word dating from the 1920s for a burglar
who can get into places, even when they are 'as tight as a
drum'. Houses are sometimes referred to as 'drums', as in
'I went up to his drum but he wasn't in'. If someone in
prison were to tell you he was in for 'drumming', you

shouldn't therefore assume that he's a criminal percussionist. (Unless, that is, you're in a Northern Irish prison, where drums and violent parades can sometimes lead to imprisonment.)

See Burglary, Creeper, Housebreaking

FENCE/FENCING

Section 22 of the Theft Act 1968 states that 'a person handles stolen goods if (otherwise than in the course of stealing) knowing or believing them to be stolen goods he dishonestly receives the goods, or dishonestly undertakes or assists in their retention, removal, disposal or realization by or for the benefit of another person, or if he arranges to do so. A person guilty of handling stolen goods shall on conviction on indictment be liable to imprisonment for a term not exceeding fourteen years.'

Fencing, or handling and purchasing stolen goods with a view to selling them on, is a criminal trade for someone who has the cash to buy goods and the contacts to sell them on. The term dates back to when dockers would bring items snaffled from the cargo holds of ships up to the fence of the docks to pass to a buyer or accomplice. It's often said that, without a **fence** to buy their loot, thieves and burglars would be in trouble, which is why the courts tend to take a dim view of receivers of stolen goods. But the truth is that there are more than enough so-called straight-goers who are willing to part with money even if they know that the goods are stolen. The usual price paid by a professional fence is one-third of the retail value of the item, which is the acknowledged rule in the criminal world. The average £100-a-day-habit drug-addicted thief will therefore have to steal at least £2,400 worth of goods every week in order not to get 'sick'. Multiply that by the amount of addicts on the thieve in the major cities alone and you can see that a lot of fences must be absolutely coining it. Apart from the serious and professional criminal fences, there's also a whole network of amateur buyers who, though they wouldn't class themselves as criminals, make a nice profit from stolen goods.

See Crack Converters, Jekyll (p. 81), the Snide game (p. 84)

GAS-METER BANDIT

On a par with the **boot burglar** is the **gas-meter bandit**. This dates back to the days when most households had gas and electricity meters which you had to feed with coins in order to have heat, light and cooking facilities. Even burgling a council flat would guarantee the burglar a quantity of cash from the meters, as well as whatever other goods they could carry. The most I ever heard of anyone getting from a coin meter was around £70 – all in ten-pence pieces! Those burglars who broke into gas and electricity meters were classed as petty amateurs by 'real' criminals, and the terms boot burglar and gas-meter bandit were insults. No criminal worth his salt wanted to be known as either. Of course, these days, there are no coin-operated meters in houses and flats, and the modern-day equivalent of the gas-meter bandit is the house burglar who special-izes in crude entry – usually by smashing a window or kicking a door through – and stealing jewellery and elec-trical goods from council houses. Many major criminals start out as gas-meter bandits and then progress through the ranks.

See Cat Burglars, Commie Burgs, Creeper

HAND-OVER MAN

A **hand-over man** is an essential part of a **dipping**, or pickpocketing, team. The dip, or finger man, will do the actual stealing by dipping his hand into someone's pockets and then whatever he takes from the pocket will be handed to his accomplice, the hand-over man. The hand-over man will walk quickly away from the scene of the crime so that even if the dip is challenged, the finger man will have no evidence of the theft about his person.

See On the Bottle

HOISTING

There is in fact no such criminal charge as shoplifting (**hoisting**): if you steal from a shop, you will be charged with theft. In the past, hoisting was considered more a crime perpetrated by female criminals, but in recent years it has mainly become the preserve of junkies, who have taken it to another level. Forget the old image of the shady character hanging about in the aisle of a supermarket in a big coat, nervously stealing glances at the shop staff as he fingers the packets of rump steak. For the modern hoister, speed and daring are of the essence. Hoisters normally work in teams of two or three people: one person to wait outside the shop in a vehicle with the engine running for a quick getaway; one to do the actual hoisting; and sometimes a third, who will cause a commotion in order to distract the shop staff. The favourite tool of the modern-day hoister is the laundry bag – those huge fabric bags you can buy in laundrettes. Armed with their laundry bag, the hoister will pick his shop carefully – no point robbing something like an estate agent's or a Burger King; not much to throw into your bag – and sometimes recce his target. What they are after are small, portable, high-value items such as razor blades, perfume, aftershave or batteries. The hoister will march into the target shop, shaking out the laundry bag, go directly to the items they intend to steal, then sweep the whole stock off the shelf and into the bag before marching swiftly from the shop and jumping into the getaway car. Most times it happens so quickly the security staff have no time to react. This is also known as **blitzing** or 'going on a mission'. This type of shop theft was pioneered by a bunch of junkies from the Caledonian Road (or **Cali**) area of North London in order to fund their drug habits, but has now become popular all over the country.

Back in the day, there was no more prolific a gang of female hoisters than the Forty Elephants, also known as the Forty Thieves. Hailing from in and around the Elephant and Castle area of South London, they were closely allied with the male Elephant and Castle mob, who were thieves and hard men. The Forty Elephants were prolific professional shoplifters who raided the quality shops in London's West End but also ranged all over the country in the biggest organized shoplifting operation this country has ever witnessed. The Forty Elephants gang was in existence from 1873 until the late 1950s. During the early twentieth century the gang was led by a woman called Alice Diamond, an accomplished thief and fighter known variously as 'the Queen of the Forty Thieves' or 'Diamond Annie'. At one time, in the 1960s, 'Mad' Frankie Fraser's sister Eva was a prominent member.

The word 'hoisting' could come from the fact that women would 'hoist' up their outer garments and secrete the goods under them, or it could refer to the even older practice of hoisting up the side of a tent in order to steal its contents.
See Hoisting bag

HOUSEBREAKING

Housebreaking and burglary are two sides of the same crime. Housebreakers are burglars who specialize in breaking into houses during daylight hours, whereas burglars will break into any building, but usually during the night. On the whole, housebreakers are more random and disorganized than night-time burglars, though most of them will dress smartly in order to blend into the areas where they plan to commit their crimes. Unless they're working on inside information, which is rare for housebreakers, they'll simply pick an area and walk or drive around it looking for a likely target before knocking on the door to see if anyone is home. If no one answers the door, the housebreaker will do his job and break in. A lot of housebreakers will enter via the front of the house, either by breaking a window or kicking or otherwise forcing the front door open, and they'll go through the premises in a matter of minutes looking for valuables. The first room a housebreaker will head for is the master bedroom, as they know this is where most people will keep jewellery, cash and other items of value. Housebreakers are looking for quick cash and easily saleable items that are not too bulky. Housebreakers rely on speed and can be in and out of a house within five minutes.

See Aggy/Aggy Merchants

JIGGLING AND SCISSORING

These days, most car thieves and those who steal from vehicles tend to cause a lot of damage in pursuit of the prize. Because of the sophisticated security systems now fitted as standard on most vehicles, the only way in is normally to break a window or jemmy the boot or doors. Though some commercial vehicles can still be scissored, this is mainly used by **jump-up** merchants. **Scissoring** is using a large pair of stainless-steel scissors to open a lock. You insert the point of the scissors into the lock, wrench them up and down to break the tumblers, then give them a quick twist, and the lock should spring open. This whole process should take no more than a few seconds. **Jiggling** can be used on older vehicles, and this involves using a car key (pretty much any key will do) in the lock to work it open. You have to move it in a fast up-and-down and side-to-side motion in order to catch the tumblers in motion and then give it a sharp twist when you get a bite. *See Draggers* (p. 71), *TDA Merchants* (p. 75), *Twockers* (p. 76)

THE JUMP-UP

Another crime that has now become associated with desperate junkies is **the jump-up**. In the jump-up, a thief follows delivery trucks and vans in their **smoker** and waits until the target vehicle is left unattended. The thief then jumps up on to the back of the delivery vehicle and throws off as many goods and parcels as possible. Usually working in pairs, jump-up merchants will steal anything that might have even the slightest resale value. Back in the 1940s and '50s, the jump-up was a respectable crime for any aspiring professional criminal wanting to get into the game on the ground floor. All you needed was a smoker and a bit of bottle when it came to nabbing the prize. Nowadays, the jump-up is mostly the preserve of junkies and petty thieves, some of whom have no embarrassment or compunction about doing a jump-up on a bread van or milk float in order to feed their habit. (If the doors of a delivery van are locked, the jump-up merchant has to open them quickly, and this is done by **jiggling and scissoring**.) *See Clipboarding* (p. 79), *On the UPS*

LAY

Lay is an old-fashioned word dating from the late 1700s. As a criminal, your lay is the crime you specialize in. For example, if you break into houses during daylight hours, then your lay is housebreaking. A lot of professional criminals (that is, those who do it for a living) will try their hand at any sort of crime that will bring the shekels in, but usually have one form of crime which they are best at, and that would be their lay. The origins have been lost but I have been told that it comes from the fact that each day petty criminals would set out to steal enough money to get a bed for the night, so what they stole first was their 'laying-down money'. This became shortened to 'lay'.

ON THE BOTTLE

To be **on the bottle** is to be out and about picking pockets, so-called because the most common place that men keep their wallets is in the back pocket (bottle and glass = arse). Stealing from a back pocket is also the easiest pickpocketing move, as the thief is behind the victim (on the bottle) so cannot be identified and can make an unseen getaway. *See Hand-over man*

ON THE KNOCKER

To be **on the knocker** is to be out and about in residential areas knocking on doors in order to facilitate a con. A lot of conmen go on the knocker, as people feel safe in their own homes and don't expect to be conned on their own doorstep. The most common con games perpetrated on the knocker are **the sharp, the sparkle, the sponsor game** and selling **swag**. *See – the Sharp, the Sparkle, the Sponsor game, Swag*

ON THE UPS

One of the most common forms of **the jump-up** is going **on the UPS**. This is stealing from the vans of parcel couriers UPS (United Parcel Service). At one time, these vans relied on the traditional van lock for security, but this can be easily **jiggled** or **scissored** by professional thieves, so now they also padlock the doors shut. This makes stealing from UPS slightly more difficult, although most professional thieves will have a pair of bolt-croppers in their tool bag for just such a problem. The thief going on the UPS will usually have a vehicle and drive around until they spot a UPS van, then follow it until it stops and the driver enters whichever premises he's delivering to. Then the thief will leap from their vehicle and get to work breaking through the back door of the van to grab however many parcels they can and get back to the vehicle for the getaway. This is a simple but audacious theft that's carried out many times a day on the streets of the UK. Going on the UPS is a particular favourite with drug addicts who need a constant cash flow to feed their habit.

See the Jump-up

PONY BAG

A **pony bag** is the security bag or box carried across the pavement by cash-in-transit guards. The bag (contained inside an alarmed metal box) is only insured to contain up to £25,000 and this is why criminals refer to it as a pony bag – a **pony** being twenty-five. A lot of armed robbers who go out on spec are looking for guards transporting pony bags across the pavement and into financial institutions. The most dangerous time for the guard is when he has to walk across the stretch of open ground from the security of the armoured van to the institution he is delivering to. This is the window of opportunity for a robber or thief to strike.

SHOULDER SURFER

Shoulder surfers are criminals who peep over the shoulders of people using cashpoint machines, either to note the PIN number of the card or to see if there is enough cash coming out of the machine to be worth snatching. It's a very modern crime. There are also distraction teams, who specialize in thefts at cashpoint machines. The most common form of distraction involves two or three thieves, one of whom (the shoulder surfer) stands directly behind the victim and drops a £5 note by the victim's feet just as he or she presses the button to withdraw cash. Another of the team, pretending to walk by, taps the victim on the shoulder and points out the banknote at his feet. As the victim bends down to pick up the £5, the shoulder surfer will reach over and take the cash coming out of the machine, or the card, or both. The thief then walks briskly away with the prize, leaving the victim standing at the machine waiting for his cash to appear. More sophisticated shoulder surfers are after the details of the card or the card itself but work in much the same way.

SLEEVING

Sleeving is the lower end of the market in the **hoisting** game and is done mainly by youngsters and petty thieves. It involves going into a shop or a supermarket wearing a jacket with elasticated cuffs (much like perpetrators of **the bird game**) and, while reaching into a fridge or chill cabinet, slipping a can or bottle of drink up your sleeve.

The 'sleeper' will then casually walk out of the shop as though they have decided against buying anything. This method is usually used to steal alcoholic drinks for personal consumption rather than as a commercial exercise. Another form of sleeving is used by professional hoisters, and this involves stuffing high-value items which still have the security tags attached up both sleeves and then lifting your arms over the top of the alarm sensor on the way out, thus avoiding setting off the alarms. (Most sensor alarms in large shops reach only to shoulder height.)

See the Bird game, Hoisting

SMASH-AND-GRAB MERCHANTS

Smash-and-grab merchants are criminals who specialize in the theft of valuable items from shop windows. A heavy object is used to break the glass and the goods are snatched before the criminals make a quick getaway. This crime is usually carried out in broad daylight and is reliant on the elements of speed and surprise. The main targets are jewellery shops. These days, smash and grab has all but disappeared, as tougher safety glass has been fitted to shops with expensive goods displayed in the window. Criminals are nowadays more likely to drive a vehicle through the windows of a shop than waste their time throwing bricks. In the mid-2000s, there was a short-lived vogue for smashing jewellery-shop windows with a Hilti-gun (a tool used in the construction industry, which fires nails) and a sledgehammer before snatching very expensive jewellery. This kind of crime came to a head on 7 November 2000, when a gang of thieves tried to snatch the Millennium Star diamond (203.04 carats, and worth £200 million) from the De Beers diamond exhibition in the Millennium Dome in Greenwich, London. The thieves tried to break into the display case using a Hilti-gun but the police were lying in wait and the gang members arrested. Smash-and-grab has all but been replaced by **ram-raiding**, but there is an element of this old crime in the modern one of smashing the windows of shops and banks then using a vehicle to drag out a cashpoint machine. Smash-and-grab will always be with us in one form or another.

THE SMOTHER GAME

The smother game is picking pockets or stealing from handbags using a coat draped over the arm to hide your actions; it's often practised on public transport during the rush hour. The **stiks** or **stiks men** of the 1970s even had certain named moves for stealing using a smother.
See Stiks/Stiks man

SNEAK THIEF

The sneak thief is classed as perhaps the lowest of the low amongst the **tea-leaf** fraternity. A sneak thief will steal anything from anyone – family, friends, the disabled, the weak and frail – they have no conscience. They will enter premises, ask to use the toilet and, while pretending to do so, will rifle through the victim's goods looking for anything of value. The modus operandi of the sneak thief is to leave as little evidence of their thieving as possible so that the victim might blame someone else for it when it is finally discovered. But they also specialize in stealing charity boxes from public places. Nothing is sacrosanct to the sneak thief.
See Tea leaf

SNOWDROPPERS

A **snowdropper** is someone who makes a living by stealing clothes from washing lines (as opposed to someone who steals only underwear from lines and is known as a pervert!). This crime was particularly prevalent in the Victorian era, when cotton and linen sheets stolen from the washing lines of the rich and well-to-do was a pretty lucrative **lay**. These days, snowdroppers usually go for designer clothing and sell the items in pubs and markets. Though it can be a fairly profitable crime if you steal the right snowdrops, it is still well down on the scale of serious theft and practised mainly by kids and the desperate amateur.

See Lay

STIKS/STIKS MAN

The re-emergence of the pickpocket in the 1970s meant a change in the name **dipper**, which had become too well known, to **stiks** or **stiks man**, from the line in the nursery rhyme 'Five, six, pick up sticks'. (This is used mainly by young West Indian pickpockets.) In the 1970s a lot of thriving pickpocket gangs used distraction techniques in order to steal. Typically, a stiks gang would consist of three members: the **dip** or 'feeler', who sticks their hand into pockets and bags; the 'front man', who bumps into the victim and pretends to be confused and flustered, all the better to confuse and fluster the victim as they brush them down and apologize profusely while the dip goes to work; and, lastly, the 'pass-off' man, to whom the prize will be passed once it has been retrieved. The stiks gangs work with great speed, which is why the pass-off man is essential. If the victim feels or senses that their pocket has been picked, then by the time they raise the alarm and point the finger, the prize will have been deftly palmed off to the innocent-looking pass-off man, who will have quickly walked away. Even if the dip and front man are grabbed by passers-by and held for **the bull**, nothing will be found on them.

The stiks gangs had their own slang, such as 'the bull' for police, which was short for 'bullies'. The 'bull squad' or 'dip squad' in London usually operated out of West End Central Police Station and had a reputation amongst the dippers and stiks men as being a bit heavy-handed and very sneaky. Members of the bull squad would disguise themselves as tourists or tramps, or even dress up as women in their constant quest to nick the dips. The squad had a fairly constant turnover because as soon as they'd made four or five nickings they would be easily recognizable to the dips.

If a stiks man were to say, 'I've been under the earth looking for beagles and practising my back-off,' it would be translated as 'I've been working the London Underground looking for wallets and purses and practising stealing from back pockets'. The London Underground was the main hunting ground for stiks men, as there were very few CCTV cameras in the 1970s and '80s and, in the rush-hour crowds, it was easy to get close to someone in order to steal from them. A wallet or purse was known as a 'beagle', but nobody seems to know why. Stiks men and dips had various tried-and-tested methods of stealing, such as the 'back-off' (lifting the prize from the victim's back pocket by gripping with the fingertips and then kneeing the victim lightly behind their knee to make them bend slightly so the wallet, or whatever it was, comes out of the pocket easily), the 'breast-off' (putting a coat or newspaper under the victim's chin or in front of their face while the dip hand reaches for the inside jacket pocket), or the 'slide' (quickly sliding the hand into a side pocket, as though it were an accident). Picking pockets using distraction techniques is known as working **the smother game**. Pickpocketing is also known as going out **on the bottle**, from the action of getting behind the victim.

See On the Bottle, the Bull, the Smother game

TEA LEAF

If you are **at it**, then the chances are better than good that you're a **tea leaf**. In the original cockney rhyming slang, a tea leaf means a thief. There are many forms of thieving or 'tea-leafing', from pickpocketing to commercial burglary. In some 'manors', or districts, being a tea leaf is a fairly honourable profession, and sometimes a way of life and a means of survival. In the 1800s there were lots of 'thieves' dens', particularly in London, where all the tea leafs lived with their families and from where they would set out to rob the rich, or the richer. Some areas of London still have a hangover of that reputation today and are viewed as 'criminal manors', such as Bermondsey in South London, or **the Cali** (Caledonian Road) in North London. Former assistant commissioner in charge of the CID Gilbert Kelland states in *Crime in London* that, from the 1970s until the '90s, 'ninety-seven per cent of the armed robberies committed in England were carried out by a small group of robbers from one small corner of South London.'

See the Cali (p. 348)

TILL-HOPPING

Till-hopping is a specialist form of theft involving the robbing of cash registers in large shops and department stores. I met a fella called Kevin while on remand in HMP

Latchmere House in 1976 who went on to become one of the most prolific till-hoppers in Europe in later life, serving time in Germany, France, Switzerland and the UK for theft of cash from tills. When Kevin was twelve years old he sometimes worked in his uncle's shop and noticed how simple the key to the till was. He decided to try his uncle's till key in the till of another local shop and, when the owner was distracted, he managed to open the till and walk out with a handful of half-crowns. That was the start of a criminal career that has spanned almost four decades and shows no sign of slowing down. Kevin discovered that till locks could be opened by any of three generic types of till key, and that was him off and running. His first modus operandi was to walk into a supermarket and make his way to the staff changing room, where he would steal a shop coat with the store's logo on it. He'd then slip on the shop coat, make his way to one of the tills that wasn't being used, casually unlock it and help himself to the cash inside. In a busy supermarket, nobody would even give him a second look; the shop uniform was as good as camouflage. He'd keep the shop coats he stole to use in different branches of the same shop. Kevin would hit five or six shops a day and was earning a nice few quid from his endeavours, but it wasn't long before the supermarkets started to notice the thefts and decided to take steps. What you have to remember is that all this was happening in the 1970s, before there was CCTV in every nook and cranny and when shop security usually consisted of a series of mirrors set in strategic spots and a retired copper as a less-than-invisible store detective. Eventually, one of the major supermarkets set up a watch on its unused tills and Kevin was nabbed red-handed removing a bundle of notes from the till.

Getting nicked was really no drama for Kevin – he was

only charged with theft and it was his first offence. He was given a conditional discharge and walked out of the court determined to become more professional – giving up his lucrative activities never even occurred to him. As he perfected his operation, he recruited a couple of like-minded young criminals from his small corner of South London and set about ripping off the cash registers of the capital in a big way. Kevin would still use a shop coat and his **jigglers** (keys) to steal from the till, but with the help of his two new partners in crime, he could now steal more than ever. His new method of operation involved his partners either starting a fight in the shop or 'accidentally' knocking down a display so as to attract the attention of shoppers and staff. While the victims were engaged in the 'show' created by his colleagues in crime, Kevin would be doing three or four tills in the same shop. To use the criminal vernacular of the time, Kevin absolutely rinsed every major supermarket and department store in London and the home counties over a period of five years. Sometimes he and his parters in crime would be caught and have to serve short periods in prison, but the money was so good that they would immediately go back to it once they were released. They travelled the British Isles carrying out their till thefts and, finally, when it became too **hot** for them to work in the UK (their pictures were on the watch list of most major retailers), they applied for passports and took their thieving road show to Europe. Kevin kept right up to date on any technology to do with tills and cash registers, and whenever a new till went on the market, he'd purchase one direct from the company, along with more keys to add to his theft kit. In Europe they took to setting light to slug pellets, which creates a lot of thick, foul-smelling smoke, and then raising the fire alarm so that everyone had to evacuate the premises, leaving Kevin to rifle every till in the shop. Till-hopping now seems to be a dying crime but is still carried out by some 'distraction' thieves who use the old trick of creating a diversion pioneered by Kevin and his gang.

THE TOM GAME

The term **tom game** originated in the 1930s and is still widely used by criminals today. Usually carried out by at least two perpetrators, the tom game, also known as 'the ring game', is no more than a slightly sophisticated 'snatch'. A motor vehicle is essential in order to carry out this crime, unless the perpetrators are very fast runners (and that would be highly unlikely, as most of the firms that carry out this sort of crime nowadays are made up of drug addicts using the loot to fund their habits). The driver pulls up outside a good-quality jeweller's and leaves the engine running while his companion, suitably suited and booted, appears as a customer at the door of the premises. Once he has been buzzed in, the front man asks to look for example, at diamond rings, chooses the most expensive ring on the tray, takes it in his hand and turns towards the window of the shop as if to examine it in the light. This is the signal for the driver to leave the car and make their way to the door. The driver waits for the shopkeeper to buzz the door open then holds the door wide while the front man makes a hasty exit. Both then jump into the vehicle and make their getaway, leaving the shocked shopkeeper minus an expensive diamond ring. The team will usually then take their prize to a dealer and cash it in for drugs.

WALK-IN

A **walk-in** is an audacious theft usually committed in broad daylight which requires the perpetrator to have plenty of front and an air of entitlement – someone a bit like a Tory minister. The typical walk-in thief is well dressed and confident, so that they can enter large office buildings without attracting suspicion. The thief breezes into an office block, usually carrying a large briefcase in which to load the loot, and walks around, casing the building, looking out for valuable items that are easy to steal. This could be the personal property of those working in the building or equipment belonging to the company. Laptop computers are a favourite – they're portable and high value – as are handbags, wallets, purses and mobile phones. It is rare that anyone will know everyone who works in their building so, unless there are vigilant security guards, anyone who looks the part can walk in, take what they want, then walk right out again. There are criminals who make a decent living at the walk-in and travel up and down the country and abroad to do it. Front is everything in the walk-in game.

See Creeper

WHIZZER/WHIZ MOB

Whizzer as slang for a pickpocket has largely fallen out of vogue since its heyday in the 1940s and '50s. **Whiz mobs** used to work the crowds at racecourses, picking pockets then blending into the throng of race-goers. The origin of the word 'whiz' is uncertain, but some people say it's to do with the speed with which these criminals could **dip** a crowd – they would whiz right through.

See Dip, Stiks/Stiks man

2. *Going Equipped for Crime*

Section 25 of the Theft Act 1968 states that 'a person shall be guilty of an offence if, when not at his place of abode, he has with him any article for use in the course of or in connection with any burglary, theft or cheat. A person guilty of an offence under this section shall on conviction on indictment be liable to imprisonment for a term not exceeding three years.' This is the crime of going equipped.

In order to commit most crimes, you will need certain tools of the trade. For example, without a weapon, or something that resembles a weapon, you'd be very hard pressed to carry out an armed robbery. That said, I have robbed two banks with nothing more than my pointed fingers inside a paper bag. But I digress. It stands to reason that if you set out to do a job or **bit of work**, you'll need the kit to carry it out. Some crimes, obviously, don't require any tools. I mean, take the crime of Actual Bodily Harm (ABH): in order to commit ABH all you need is your fists, feet, head, elbows or knees, because ABH is causing someone harm with blows or kicks. It's very rare, though, that the law will class any part of the human body as a tool for the purposes of going equipped for crime. There have been cases of certain boxers and martial arts experts registering their hands or feet as deadly weapons, but this is more hype than anything else, and it would create serious problems were the courts to order the confiscation of these 'weapons' after they had been used in crime.

There are many tools used by the criminal and prison fraternity and some of them have no uses other than criminality. The sawn-off shotgun, or **nostrils**, is specific to armed crime, as a shotgun is only ever shortened in order to make it easy to conceal. There is actually a criminal charge of shortening the barrels of a firearm, which carries a maximum prison sentence of four years. I was charged with just that in 1993 and received the maximum sentence. I wonder if people are aware that you can be put into prison for years for wielding a junior hacksaw.

Other tools used specifically by criminals and prisoners include the **chiv** – a home-made stabbing and slashing weapon for inflicting injuries on rivals (used only in prisons), the **strip**, a flattened piece of flexible metal used in car theft, and the **cosh**, a hand-held, weighted implement used for hitting people. However, if you are in possession of any of the weapons mentioned above, it will inevitably lead to the more serious charge of possession of offensive weapons. There are many more, and you'll come across them sooner or later in this book. But even the most common household implement can be used in crime. Scissors are great for opening car locks and, in prison, a scissor blade is a common stabbing tool; you can use a fishing rod to poke through letter boxes and hook house and car keys; and common spark plugs can be used to break glass, as can a centre punch. Some professional burglars even use newspaper and jam or marmalade to gain entry to a building. They smear a window with the preserve and slap a few sheets of newspaper over it before giving it a whack with a hammer. This deadens the sound, which is especially useful if you're working at night, and an added advantage is that the glass sticks to the newspaper, enabling the burglar to 'peel' the window out, again without making much noise.

At one point in the 1970s the police, ever eager for convictions, used 'creative' thinking when arresting people for going equipped. I know of at least one person who was sent to **borstal** for being in possession of a sock! The police claimed he was going to smash a shop window in order to steal, then put the sock over his hand to avoid leaving fingerprints. He spent eighteen months in a closed borstal for this. Being stopped by the police and having a pair of gloves was a sure-fire way of getting arrested, especially at night, hence the substitution of socks, and hence the police and the courts moving the goalposts and making it an offence to be caught in possession of a sock.

Prisoners in British jails, and probably in jails the world over, are expert at creating weapons out of mundane objects. Knives can be made from the lids of tin cans, the handles of plastic toilet brushes or toothbrushes – in fact, just about anything. Spears and arrows capable of piercing human flesh can be made from tightly rolled paper, and coshes can be fashioned from anything from batteries in a sock to bars of soap in a pillow case. The tools of crime and violence are all around us in our everyday lives – but particularly in prison. Boiling water has become a favourite weapon in prison. Scalding a fellow prisoner is known as **wetting up** or **jugging**. The perpetrator will fill a plastic jug or bucket with boiling water from the hot-water boiler (there is one on most prison wings so that prisoners can make tea and coffee) and mix in a pound of sugar. They'll stir the sugar until it has partly melted, making the water more like a syrup, then throw the liquid in the face of the victim. The part-melted sugar will cling to the flesh and burn to the bone. This is a 'punishment' reserved mainly for sex offenders and informers, but even a minor argument can lead to action of this sort when you live in an environment of brutality, fear and paranoia like the British prison system.

APRIL

An **April** is a weapon, as in April fool = tool. If a villain tells you he is going to sort you out with his April, don't think, 'Well, it's only June now so I've got plenty of time'; it means they are going to get a weapon and intend to inflict serious injury on you. An April can be anything from a cosh to a machine gun. In prison, you should be aware of Aprils in the showers that come your way!
See Chiv (p. 257), *Cosh* (p. 258), *Tooled up*

BOYS

Boys is slang for 'keys' but, in a common twist when it comes to criminal slang, it is slang for what is already a slang word: keys were once known as **twirls** (from the 'twirling' action used when opening a lock) in the criminal fraternity (boys and girls = twirls = keys). Some criminal and prison slang has become convoluted over the years, either because it has fallen into common usage and been 'translated' by the enemy and the general public, or because a more modern word has replaced it. As a result, there can be several levels of slang before you get to the original words. Sometimes, working out the etymology of slang is like being an archaeologist, as you have to dig very deeply in order to uncover the word that is the basis for a couple of hundred years' worth of slang. Skeleton keys, which were once a mainstay of the burglary kit, are known as 'bones', for obvious reasons.

HAPPY BAG

In serious armed robbery circles, the **happy bag** is an essential piece of kit. It is the bag, or bags, used to keep and transport the weaponry needed to carry out the act.

Guns, masks, tools and gloves will be stored in it before and after the robbery, and the bag will also be used to carry the cash away, hence the 'happy' tag. When they mount surveillance operations the Flying Squad are always pleased to see a happy bag, as it means that a robbery is imminent.

See *Across the Pavement* (p. 26)

HOISTING BAG

A **hoisting bag** is usually a large laundry bag lined with tinfoil. The foil allows the hoister to walk out of any shop with a bag full of stolen items still with their security tags on and not set off the sensor alarms at the doors – essential for the modern hoister, who relies on speed and surprise rather than secrecy and guile. The hoisting bag will allow the villain that extra precious couple of minutes to get to the getaway vehicle before all the hue and cry.

See *Hoisting, Space Blanket*

KEEPING DOG

Keeping dog is to be the lookout, or warning man, when a crime is being committed (doggy's eye = spy). If someone were to ask you to keep dog, they wouldn't be inviting you to become the owner of a canine but rather to keep an eye out while something is going down. In public schools the person keeping dog would shout a warning of '*Cave!*' if someone in authority were to approach, Latin for 'beware'. The more common criminal warning cry is 'On top!', meaning that someone is close.

See *Have It Up!* (p. 79)

DOGGY'S EYE/SPY

NOSTRILS

'Taking **nostrils** for a walk' is a phrase meaning to be out and about with a sawn-off double-barrelled shotgun for the purposes of crime, 'nostrils' being slang for this type of gun, for obvious reasons.

RICE SHOTS

Rice shots are sometimes used by professional armed robbers in order to frighten their victims into compliance, but also as a non-lethal alternative to a gunshot. The robber will take a live shotgun cartridge, saw the top off the plastic cartridge case then empty out the lead shot. They will replace it with grains of uncooked rice and stick the top of the cartridge back on with superglue. If it's a double-barrelled shotgun, the robber will have the rice cartridge in one barrel and a live lead-shot cartridge in the other. The gun will still fire the rice cartridge, however, as the detonating cap in the base of the cartridge remains untouched, and it will sound just like a real shot. During the course of a robbery, the robber knows that he can now let off a shot without the danger of killing or seriously injuring anyone. Some robbers will fire a rice shot into the ceiling of the target premises in order to grab attention and frighten people into doing what they say. Hard, uncooked rice hitting a ceiling sounds very much like lead shot. Some robbers will only use the rice cartridge if someone 'has a go'. The force of the rice and cartridge wadding will seriously sting and bruise anybody it's fired at and will definitely discourage any have-a-go-hero.

SMOTHER

In general criminal terms, a **smother** is a mask, or disguise. In prison parlance, to 'create a smother' is to distract the screws while something illegal is carried out – usually a drug deal or an act of violence. There is a form of **dipping** that is known as **the smother game** because it is all about using various items to mask the act of pickpocketing. But, on the whole, to smother up is to disguise yourself for the purpose of crime.

See Dipper, Stiks/Stiks man, Whizzer/Whiz mob

SPACE BLANKET

A **space blanket** is a lined piece of tinfoil which, when wrapped around the head and body, will allow the wearer to walk right through any sensor alarms without setting them off. They are particularly loved by commercial burglars, especially those who target social and working men's clubs, which is where you often find such alarms. The sensors seek heat or movement, but the foil fools them, enabling the foil-clad thieves to empty tills and fruit machines.

See Burglary, Hoisting Bag

THE STRIP, SCAFF, SLIDE HAMMER AND HOT-WIRING

Some professional car thieves use a **strip**, a length of flat, flexible metal (usually aluminium) that can be forced through a small gap between the window and the frame and used to hook the handle up from the inside. Once inside the vehicle, the professional thief will **scaff** the car: put a length of scaffolding tube into the steering wheel and apply pressure until the steering lock snaps. They will then either use the scaffolding tube to snap off the ignition barrel, or a **slide hammer** or panel puller – a short steel pole with a heavy weight that slides easily up and down it, and into the end of which a self-tapping screw slots. They'll insert the screw into the ignition lock and give it a couple of turns until the threads bite into the softer metal of the lock, then twist it in as far as it will go and use the weight to exert pressure on the screw, pulling backwards. The ignition lock will pop out of its housing quite easily, exposing the ignition wires. Then the professional car thief will stick a flathead screwdriver into the hole and twist. They now have ignition. Another way of getting ignition is to strip the wires and then connect them together; this is commonly known as **hot-wiring**, as the car thief is looking for the 'hot' wire, the one with the power running through it.

See Draggers (p. 71), *TDA merchants* (p. 75), *Twockers* (p.76)

TOOLED UP

To be **tooled up** is to be equipped for a crime, but particularly for a crime of violence. If someone asks you if you are tooled up, they are usually enquiring whether you are carrying any weapons on your person. Tooling up usually means obtaining a firearm. In prison, to be tooled up is to be carrying a weapon for the purpose of violence.

See April

TURTLES

If you are going to commit any sort of crime, the minimum you are going to need in order to avoid detection, arrest and imprisonment is a decent pair of **turtles** (turtle doves = gloves). Gloves are of course used by criminals to avoid leaving fingerprints behind at the scene of the crime, but they are also useful if your theft requires you to smash something made of glass (a window usually) in order to gain entry. Not only do they prevent your hands being cut, but also, should that happen, they enable you to avoid leaving behind an incriminating drop of blood from which DNA can be extracted. However, in recent years, forensic experts have been able to take glove prints from the scene of a crime, and if the perpetrator is caught with the same gloves in their possession, they can be matched.

TWIRLS

Twirls is old-fashioned slang for 'keys'. The word derives from the fact that, once you put the key in the lock, you then have to spin, or twirl, it in order to open the lock. At one time (up until the 1960s) twirls referred specifically to skeleton keys, or 'bones', which are used in crime and, in particular, burglary. Car twirls were a set of double-edged FS keys that would fit almost any car, up until car security began to improve in the 1980s. To be 'out on the twirl' was slang for thieving of any sort.
See Boys

WORK

As a professional or full-time criminal you will class your criminal activities as **work**, because this is what you earn your living from. Work used to be a word that applied only to armed robbery. Robbers would talk of 'having a bit of work' or 'going to work'. In recent years the word has come to be applied to most criminal activity from which the criminal earns enough to avoid real work.

3. *Transport*

Section 12 of the Theft Act 1968 states that 'a person shall be guilty of an offence if, without having the consent of the owner or other lawful authority, he takes any conveyance for his own or another's use or, knowing that any conveyance has been taken without such authority, drives it or allows himself to be carried in or on it. A person guilty of an offence shall be liable to . . . a fine . . . or to imprisonment for a term not exceeding six months, or both.' This is the crime of taking a motor vehicle or other conveyance without authority.

Transport is essential to most criminals, not only for getting to and from the job but also as a way of carrying off the loot. Since the early days of the twentieth century, motorized vehicles have been used extensively by criminals in order to commit crime or to make a swift getaway. In America, criminals were quick to spot the potential of the motor vehicle, in particular the V8 Ford. Clyde Barrow, of Bonnie and Clyde fame, even wrote a letter to Henry Ford praising his cars for being great at outrunning the police. The Prohibition era led to the use of vehicles such as trucks for transporting illegal liquor, as well as big, fast cars as outriders to protect the loads. By the 1920s, all over America motor vehicles were being used for crime, from the store-robbing antics of Bonnie and Clyde to the bank-robbing sprees of John Dillinger, 'Machine Gun' Kelly, et al. In Chicago, they would 'bullet-proof' their cars by filling the door panels with copies of the Chicago phonebook. It was so thick it would slow down and absorb gunfire. In the UK, too, criminals were discovering the benefits of motorized transport. One famous case occurred as early as 1927, when PC George Gutteridge was shot dead in a quiet village in Essex by a team of shop-breakers when he tried to stop their car in the early hours of the morning (a disturbing aside to this case is that the criminals shot PC Gutteridge through both eyes after his death, as they believed the last image seen by a victim was imprinted on their retinas). By the late 1940s in the UK cars were regularly being used as getaway vehicles by snatch gangs who specialized in the wages snatch. In those days, many firms and businesses paid their employees in cash, and this meant that someone from the firm would have to pick the money up from a bank (this was before the rise of cash-in-transit vehicles) and they would be a target for robbers. The modus operandi of the old snatch gangs of the 1940s and '50s was to jump the employee with the cash bag, **cosh** him over the head, usually with a lead pipe, snatch the cash bag and then jump into a car driven by an accomplice. Simple, but effective.

Vehicles were also a target of crime. There are many reasons why vehicles are stolen: for example, joyriding, to sell on, for parts, or to use in a crime. Lorry hijacking has been going on the world over for almost as long as lorries have been around. It has been said that the word 'hijack' comes from the American Prohibition era, when those who wished to steal a lorry's cargo would approach the driver while he was taking a driving break and greet him with a friendly 'Hi, Jack' in order to allay his suspicions.

The latest uses of motorized vehicles to commit crime are the practices of using powerful motorbikes to carry out smash-and-grab raids on prestigious stores and designer shops and the raiding of cargo lorries at stops and in lay-bys, during which the thieves will cut straight through the canvas sides of the vehicles in order to get to the goods inside.

Of course, the police have kept up their own use of motorized vehicles in their war against crime and criminals. The infamous Flying Squad was so named because it was the first group of Metropolitan Police officers to use motor vehicles.

ALLOWING YOURSELF TO BE CARRIED . . .

If you enter a stolen vehicle, knowing or suspecting it to be stolen, you are liable to a charge of **allowing yourself to be carried** in a stolen vehicle. This crime can net you up to two years' imprisonment. It is perhaps the least serious of all the charges involved with the theft of motor vehicles, but still not to be taken lightly.

See Draggers

AVT (AGGRAVATED VEHICLE TAKING)

Section 12A of the Theft Act 1968 states that 'a person is guilty of aggravated taking of a vehicle if (a) the vehicle was driven dangerously on a road or other public place; (b) owing to the driving of the vehicle, an accident occurred by which injury was caused to any person; (c) owing to the driving of the vehicle, an accident occurred by which damage was caused to any property, other than the vehicle; and (d) damage was caused to the vehicle. A person guilty of an offence under this section shall be liable on conviction under indictment to imprisonment for a term not exceeding two years or . . . if it is proved that the accident caused the death of the person concerned, fourteen years.'

Aggravated vehicle taking is what you will be charged with if you use threats or actual violence while stealing a vehicle. The American term is 'carjacking', sometimes shortened to 'jacking', which is creeping into British usage, mainly through youngsters who have been exposed to an almost constant diet of American films and TV shows.

DRAGGERS

A **dragger** is a professional car thief. The Romany word 'drag' dates from the days of horse-drawn vehicles, when the horse would drag the vehicle behind it. Hence, a place where cars race is known as a 'drag strip' and a main road as the 'main drag'. Draggers steal vehicles for a variety of reasons. Low down on the car-theft totem pole is the joyrider – kids and amateurs who steal cars for the pure pleasure of driving, and sometimes in order to annoy the police and entice them to chase the stolen car. These people are not really criminals in the professional sense of the word, more thrill seekers and car enthusiasts who cannot afford or are too young to buy their own cars. In the old days, when car security was not really up to much, the perfect way for a dragger to go equipped was with a set of **twirls** – double-edged FS car keys that would fit almost any motor. You could normally get these from a friendly, or bent, garage or a breakers' yard. It was simply a matter of going through your keys until you found one that would fit the door. This would inevitably fit the ignition, too. Any car was fairly easy to steal, but the sure-fire winners with a set of twirls were Fords and Austins. Motorbikes were also pretty easy to steal, though more often than not the potential thief needed to do a bit of **hot-wiring** in order to start the ignition. The professional dragger will steal cars to order, sometimes for armed robbery teams. Professional draggers also make good money by stealing a vehicle, stripping down all the removable parts and selling them on.

See Boys (p. 60), Hot-wiring (p. 65), Twirls (p. 67)

RAM-RAIDING

Some say that the crime of **ram-raiding** originated in the north of England, around Tyneside, in the 1990s, but it has actually been around since the 1930s and is prevalent all over the world. The first use of this term to describe it was, however, in Belfast in the late 1970s. The crime involves using a vehicle as a battering ram to smash into shops in order to steal goods. Most ram-raiders are opportunistic thieves who plan no further than driving a stolen car through the window of their local supermarket in order to steal cigarettes and alcohol, but there are also professional thieves who take ram-raiding very seriously and make it a very lucrative form of crime. Professional ram-raiders target high-end shops that sell designer items and jewellery. The 'ram car', usually a heavy SUV, is driven at speed through the front of the target premises, smashing a way in so that the thieves can jump out and grab the loot. The perpetrators then transfer the stolen goods to a couple of 'clean' vehicles parked outside and make their getaway, leaving the ram car blocking access to the premises. Speed and surprise are the main elements in this crime, and the typical professional ram raid will take no more than three or four minutes. Alarms are no deterrent. The only way to combat ram-raiders is by placing bollards or concrete blocks in front of your premises so that raiders cannot get their vehicle close enough to it. Whereas the amateur ram-raider tends to work at night and favours premises that are empty, the professional will target open premises during the day. This is particularly the case when the target is a jewellery shop, as it will have its wares out on display during opening hours but locked up in a safe when the shop is closed.

A version of ram-raiding that has become popular among serious criminals is the stealing of cashpoint machines. This does not use traditional ram-raiding techniques and is usually carried out in the small hours of the morning, but it does rely on speed and surprise. Thieves find premises with a cashpoint and a clear pavement outside, then steal a tractor, JCB or similar vehicle, drive it right up to the target premises and smash straight into the cashpoint, knocking it loose and loading it on to the back of a pick-up truck, which is then driven away at speed. The crime seems worth it to criminals because of the large amount of ready cash that is held in these machines. This crime usually causes thousands of pounds' worth of damage to the machines and the surrounding premises, and wakes up the whole neighbourhood, but by the time the police arrive there is only rubble left behind.

Ram-raiding can also take place on an industrial scale, with large trucks used to smash into the warehouses of technology companies to steal high-value equipment to sell on the black market.

See Commy Burgs, Draggers

RINGERS AND CLONES

Ringers and clones are pretty much two sides of the same coin. Both involve changing the identity of a vehicle for criminal purposes, but ringing is more involved and professional than cloning.

In order to ring or clone a car you must first nick the car! Let's assume you have a red-hot Range Rover Vogue in your possession. Obviously, you won't be able to drive a stolen car for long without attracting the attention of the police, so you need to **smother,** or disguise, the car. Step one is to find a similar car: same model, same colour, not necessarily the same year but as close as possible. You don't even have to touch this second car, just write down what the number plate is. Next, get a friendly/bent garage to knock you up a set of number plates using this number and you replace the plates on your stolen car with the new ones. Using a golf-ball typewriter (it produces the typeface favoured by the DVLA), fill in your stolen or fake log book (blank log books for vehicles can be picked up for as little as £50) and advertise your new car. Lock it up for a week or so while you place an advert in the free press. Your advert might say 'FOR SALE, BLUE RANGE ROVER VOGUE' and give the year of the new plate and a mobile phone number (usually a cheap, 'throwaway' phone bought specifically for this purpose). Give it a few days, then drive your new Range Rover out on to the street. The car will now withstand a cursory police check (although, if you get a pull and they start going under the bonnet and checking the VIN (Vehicle Identity Number), all bets will be off!) and, if you do nothing to attract the attention of the police, you can probably (and some people do) drive this car for years without any comeback. If you do get a pull and the police discover that your car is a clone, you can point out that you bought the car after seeing the advert – there will be a record of it – and that you were even given a log book! This will be enough to raise reasonable doubt over whether you purchased the vehicle in good faith. At worst, the car will be confiscated, in which case you just move on to the next one.

Ringers are a much more involved and professional proposition. A professional vehicle ringer will work only on the most expensive vehicles – ones that are worth the effort, usually luxury sports cars or prestige vehicles, often exported to oil-rich countries for large amounts of cash. A good ringer will first erase all sign of the target vehicle's true identity. This includes removing VIN plates from the bodywork and engine, grinding out any numbers on the chassis or engine, replacing any glass that had identification numbers on it. They will then make and fit their own VIN plates and identification numbers for the car and put in new glass, attach new number plates and sometimes even respray the vehicle to match the details on the new (fake) logbook. They will also replace the tax disc (and, if necessary, the MOT certificate) so that everything on the car matches up. Most good ringers can pass any roadside test. It's only if the police take the car in and give it a thorough ramp inspection that it might be discovered to be a ringer.

SMOKER

One of the things that most thieves and, in particular, those who practise **hoisting**, need in order to get about is transport. This normally comes in the form of a **smoker** – a cheap second-hand car usually purchased for under £100 from a breaker's yard or the side of the street. As most criminals have opted out of straight society, they don't bother themselves with such niceties as having a driver's licence, MOT, tax or insurance. As long as the vehicle runs reasonably well and won't attract too much adverse attention, it'll do. Smokers are also used by burglars, car thieves, **boot burglars** and **gas-meter bandits**. The joy of a smoker for the criminal is that, because the car is not registered, none of the crimes committed in it can come back to the criminal once he scraps it or sells it on. You can park where you like and not worry about tickets or fines, and you can cane the vehicle into the ground and just buy another. Police estimate that there are over ten thousand smokers on the roads at any one time.
See Ringers and Clones

TDA MERCHANTS

TDA merchants are basically car thieves, usually of the juvenile variety.
See Touching dogs' arses, Twockers

TOUCHING DOGS' ARSES

The charge of stealing cars used to be called TDA (Taking and Driving Away a motor vehicle), and young criminals found it amusing to insult amateur car thieves by saying they were into **touching dogs' arses**. Amateur car thieves are the ones who steal cars just for the fun of it, with no financial gain – so-called joyriders.

TWOCKERS

Twockers are car thieves, usually of the teenaged joyriding variety. On the whole, they are amateurs who will use any method to steal a car but will usually rely on crudely smashing a window, either with a sparkplug, centrepunch or by hitting it with a hammer. They aren't interested in selling the car on, although if a buyer is available they will usually sell easily removable parts such as the stereo, battery and, sometimes, the wheels. The car will be driven around until it gets too **hot**, then dumped or used for further crimes, such as ram-raiding, or to attract the attention of the police in order to initiate a chase for the sheer excitement of it.
See Ram-raiding, TDA merchants

4. *Working the Con*

The Fraud Act 2006 states that the crime of obtaining property by deception is committed by 'a person who by any deception dishonestly obtains property belonging to another, with the intention of permanently depriving the other of it. Penalty – not exceeding ten years' imprisonment'.

'Working the con' is to be engaged in spinning stories in order to part gullible people from their money. 'Con', in this instance, is short for 'confidence trick', which is all about making people believe one thing while the reality of the situation is something completely different. You build up the person's confidence in what you are saying and then take their money. For example, you might tell someone that you have some **hot** jewellery for sale when, in reality, what you have is **snide**, or fake, worthless junk. It will be of no comfort to anyone who has had the con game worked on them, but it relies almost entirely on the greed of the victim. Most people, if they think they're getting a great bargain, won't question, or will be willing to overlook, where the bargain is coming from. Con men thus rely on the basest of human emotions. There are many small-scale cons being worked all over the country every day – from sponsored swims to doorstepping **sharps**. Most straight-goers don't even realize that they have been conned until afterwards, and some will never know.

THE BRICK GAME

In the mid-1980s old yellow-stock bricks became very popular with yuppies doing house conversions and renovations (they needed the old bricks to blend in with the existing buildings), and prices went through the roof. Builders were paying up to

£1.25 per brick, which made the theft of yellow-stock bricks a very lucrative prospect. Some thieves would even move into empty buildings and demolish them from the inside in order to steal them. Others would **clipboard** the bricks from building sites. Wearing a hard hat, a high-visibility vest and carrying a clipboard, they would either divert deliveries to places where they could easily be lifted and driven away, or wait until the bricks were delivered and reload them on to their own vehicle. The **smother** of the clipboard, high vis and hard hat meant that passers-by were fooled into thinking the workers loading the bricks were legitimate. Some brick thieves even had the brass neck to pull up on sites and brazen it out, telling the workers or owners that they were from the brick company and were taking the bricks back, as they had been delivered to the wrong place by mistake, and that the correct order was on its way. A van loaded with old yellow-stock bricks was as good as money in the bank.

See Clipboarding, Smother (p. 65)

BUJO/THE BAG GAME

Bujo, or **the bag game**, is a Gypsy fortune-telling con that goes back at least two hundred years. It involves convincing the **mark** that their money has been cursed. They are told to seal it in a cloth bag and bring it to the elder, or shaman, in order for it to be blessed and have the curse lifted. During the 'blessing' the money is secretly removed from the bag and replaced with worthless paper or stones. The victim is told that the 'spirit' of the curse changed the money out of spite. This is a ruse still being extensively used by African conmen.

See Mark

CLIPBOARDING

Clipboarding is an old con that made a big comeback in London in the late 1980s. Basically, it's a misdirection con in which the con merchant poses as an official or somebody connected to the chosen target premises. Clipboarders usually wear shop coats or overalls and, obviously, carry a clipboard and pen. They position themselves at the rear of a commercial premises and watch for delivery vans and lorries delivering goods, sometimes working on inside information about delivery times, loads and so on.

Once they spot a van or lorry pulling in to deliver a load, they will approach the driver even before he gets out of the cab, waving the clipboard as if it gives them authority, tell them that there's been some kind of hitch and redirect them either to premises nearby which they have rented or entered illegally, or to another quiet yard or parking space in the vicinity. The clipboarder helps the driver to unload the goods, waves them off and immediately loads the goods into their own vehicle and heads off to sell them. The delivery driver is used to seeing men in overalls waving clipboards and will usually be completely duped. Anything stolen in this way is pure profit and can be sold on for ridiculous prices. If the delivery driver grows suspicious and starts asking questions, the clipboarder usually just shrugs and walks away. Clipboarding is a low-risk/high-value piece of thievery.
See The Brick Game

HAVE IT UP!

In the typical illegal street-trading team there will be the trader himself, the one who has the patter and does the selling, and the lookout, or 'doggy's'(doggy's eye = spy). The doggy's will hump the gear about, help set up the pitch, then keep an eye out for police and trading standards officers. The traditional warning cry of the doggy's is '**Have it up!**', which means pack everything fast, the cops are coming. A cry of 'Have it up!' on any criminal enterprise is cause for concern and will result in an unseemly scatter.

HEDGE

Illegal street traders and purveyors of dodgy goods like nothing better than a large **hedge** of customers around them as they spin their fanciful yarns in order to sell their **swag**. It's well known that pretty much everyone loves a bargain, and it would seem that some members of the general public are quite happy to shell out their hard-earned cash for non-kosher goods just as long as the person they are buying from, even if he does look a bit shifty, has a nice line in patter. A lot of street traders like to pretend that the goods they are selling are stolen property, as in 'This gear didn't fall off the back of a lorry, ladies and gentlemen, I had to climb up on the lorry and push it off meself!!!', but in reality most of the stuff peddled by street traders is legally bought 'tutt' (poor-quality items). One way in which illegal street traders do break the law when it comes to what they sell is by intimating, either very directly or by insinu-ation, that the goods are something they are not. For example, commercial wholesalers will sell boxed yellow metal earrings *and* strips of stickers marked '9ct gold' – all quite legal. Of course, if you were to take the printed stickers and put them on the boxes of yellow metal earrings, you would be breaking the law, and this is quite common practice among illegal street traders.

See Toby (p. 310)

JEKYLL

If something is classed as **Jekyll**, it means it is false, a fake, not the real thing. Like **boys**, it is second-level rhyming slang: Jekyll and Hyde = **snide** = fake. It came into usage during the Victorian era with the popularity of the novella *Strange Case of Dr Jekyll and Mr Hyde* by Robert Louis Stevenson (1886), which tells the story of a doctor who creates a potion that he hopes will suppress his evil urges but which instead turns him into his most evil self, and is still in use in many parts of London today.
See The Snide game

THE LONG FIRM

One long and fairly complicated example of working the con is **the long firm**. This is where you set up a seemingly legitimate business and pay for your first couple of stock orders promptly to give the impression that your enterprise is well run. Once you've built up the confidence of your supplier, you hit them for large orders on credit, which you sell out of the back door for a fraction of the value, then you abandon the business. This was very popular up until the 1970s and is by no means dead in the water today. Many people still work the long firm in various ways, and legitimate businesses are regularly ripped off in this way. The most infamous practitioners of the long firm in Britain were the Richardson brothers of South London. Described as a South London 'Torture Gang' in the media for their treatment of slow payers and business rivals, before being jailed for up to thirty years at the Old Bailey in 1966, Charles and Edward Richardson and their gang were pretty accomplished long-firm merchants. The proceeds of the long firm are sometimes used to finance other criminal ventures.

MARK

The **mark** is the victim of a con, a **Toby**. The con game, much like the racecourse gangs of the 1930s, had its own slang words and phrases, and 'mark' is one of them. The mark was so called because the con man would put a chalk mark on the victim so that their partners in the con would know who they were to target. The word has now found favour with younger criminals, who use it to describe any victim, and has been popularized in the lyrics of American rappers, where it is used to mean a stupid person or victim.

THE RAFFLE GAME

The **raffle game** is a simple con that can be practised by con merchants of all ages. It involves setting up a fake raffle with a desirable prize, or prizes, and selling tickets to punters who feel they may be in with a chance of winning. This con can be played in many ways and with as many prizes as you like. A sophisticated version will have a visible prize with which to tempt the punters – a car, say, or something of similar value. Sadly, as the raffle is fixed, nobody will ever get their hands on it! The rule in this con is 'the bigger the prize, the more expensive the ticket'. You can pick up books of raffle tickets at any stationery shop for less than a pound, and that is all you need. Selling the tickets for a pound a piece and claiming the prize is worth £200 will bring in customers all day long. As the tickets are sold to loads of different people, no one will ever know who won (or that nobody won, in fact). Most people, especially in pubs when they've had a few drinks, will buy a handful of raffle tickets and forget all about them. If they do remember, the majority will merely shrug and assume that someone else has won. It's a perfect con, guaranteed to bring the money rolling in and carrying little danger of the perpetrator being sussed.

THE SHARP

The sharp is a little-known con game extensively used by Gypsies and Travellers. It involves going from door to door offering to sharpen household implements – knives, chisels, shears, scissors, the blades of lawn mowers, secateurs, and so on. Basically, it's a simple con which involves charging cash for a service that will never be provided. In order to carry out the sharp all you need is a small metal file, a can of oil and some old newspapers. You knock on the doors of houses, preferably in middle-class residential areas, offering to sharpen a variety of household and garden tools and implements. If a householder hands over, say, a set of knives, the con artist carries them out of sight of the owner (saying that they are taking them to the sharpening wheel in the back of their vehicle) and either gives the blades a rub with the file or, if you don't have a file, runs the blades up and down a lamp post or kerb to get a burr on them. They then smear oil over them, wrap them up in newspaper, take them back to the owner and charge around £65. When handing the 'sharpened' tools back, the con man will say something like 'Careful there, my love, those blades are now so sharp you could have your fingers off!' and tell the victim that they should leave the oil on the blades for at least a couple of hours, which will give the con merchant plenty of time to vacate the area. If the victim asks to come and watch the blades being sharpened, they'll generally be told that insurance forbids anyone being in the vicinity of the sharpening wheel because of flying slivers of metal, and that the work is done in the back of a truck with the doors closed so there is nothing to see. As in all cons, cash is king; anyone involved in the sharp will refuse a cheque, perhaps by saying that several have bounced in recent years. Some sharpeners can earn up to £1,000 a day with little or no outlay or overheads.

See On the Knocker

THE SNIDE GAME

The snide game became quite popular in London around the late 1970s and involved fake jewellery that had been stamped with a hallmark. The jewellery itself – heavy rings, bracelets, chains, watches, and so on, all without hallmarks – would be bought cheaply and a forger would mark them using a set of metal dies and a hammer. Once marked, the jewellery would pass as genuine under any quick visual examination. Any jeweller would be able to spot the fakes immediately, of course – but that's why you would never sell to a jeweller! Selling snide depends entirely on the greed and gullibility of the buyer. Those at the sharp end – the street sellers, usually young criminals – would buy several items from the supplier, paying pretty low prices, i.e. £5 per item, and then go into shops, markets and factories with a story about the items being **hot** – very similar to the way illegal street traders work – and needing to offload them quickly at half price. The rule was that you could charge whatever the market could stand. For example, a bracelet marked '9ct gold' for which you had paid £5 might go for as much as £40 to the right customer, but would, in reality, be worth about 6 pence in scrap. It's surprising how many law-abiding citizens will part with their cash if they think they're getting a bargain. Of course, if they tried to sell the piece on to a legitimate buyer, they would quickly find out they had been conned. The beauty of this crime, for the criminal, however, is that there is no comeback from the buyer. Who's going to go to the police and explain that they have paid cash for an item that they know, in their heart of hearts, is stolen? 'Snide' is also used as an insult for a false or sneaky person.

See Hedge, Jekyll, Swag, Toby

THE SPARKLE

The sparkle is pretty much the same as **the snide game**, except it's a little bit more sophisticated. It still involves selling fake jewellery to the **Tobys**, but first you supply them with a real piece, usually a diamond ring, to convince them to part with big money, maybe even going with them to a jeweller to have it valued. What the punter doesn't know is that cheap, fake copies of it have been made. Just before the punter hands over the cash the sparkle merchant makes the switch and the toby ends up with a brass-and-paste ring. A version of this con is also played in legitimate jewellery shops: the con man asks to look at an expensive item of jewellery and replaces it with a fake as a colleague distracts the shopkeeper. An easy distraction con that works every time if it is done well, this is known as 'the switch'.

Another pretty common con that is worth mentioning here is 'the lost ring'. A woman pulls into a petrol station and starts searching on the ground, looking for something. She goes up to the counter (having made sure that everyone inside has seen her frantically searching) and says that she's lost her diamond engagement ring. She tells the cashier, and whoever else may be listening, that the ring is worth £12,000 and that she'll pay £5,000 in cash, no questions asked, to whoever finds it. She then says that she has to go but will be back in two days to see if her ring has been handed in. Later that day a young man (the woman's partner in crime) goes into the petrol station with a fake diamond ring, claiming to have found it by the pumps. The cashiers know they can get five grand for it from the woman who lost it, so they offer to buy it from him. He pretends to be dubious but says it looks like a nice diamond and he might give it to his girlfriend. They offer him £3,000 cash, safe in the knowledge that, even if the woman who lost the ring doesn't come back, it's worth £12,000. The young man reluctantly takes the cash, the woman never comes back and the buyer is left with a worthless piece of paste.

THE SPONSOR GAME

The sponsor game is a very simple con, usually played by kids or teenagers. It involves printing up forms that say you will be swimming/running/walking, etc., a number of lengths or miles for a well-known charity. The teenager then knocks on doors asking people to sponsor them per lengths or mile, and after the proposed date of the sponsored event, enters a number of lengths or miles on the form and goes back knocking on doors to collect the loot.

See On the Knocker

SWAG

Swag is the proceeds of crime, or fake, shoddy or illegal goods sold to unsuspecting punters. The letters stand for 'Sold Without A Guarantee', and the term has long been a fixture in the lexicon of the illegal street trader. It has also come into usage as an insult, as in 'That car you drive is a load of old swag' or 'This meal is fucking swag'. Many people who go **on the knocker** will be selling swag to unsuspecting punters.

See Have it up!, Hedge, Toby (p. 310)

Interlude

Interlude

5. *Get Your Strides On, Chummy, You're Nicked!*

In recent years the reputation of the British police force among the general public has become somewhat tarnished, to say the least. Gone are those halcyon days of **bobbies** on bicycles, armed only with a stout truncheon, of fine, upstanding men and women you could ask for directions or even the time of day – the modern-day British **copper** is dressed in more body armour than RoboCop, barely steps outside of his car or armoured vehicle, carries a sub-machine gun and is more likely to shoot you, beat you up or plant evidence on you than give you the time of day. But even back in the so-called good old days the police had a terrible reputation for violence, bribery and corruption – though it was only really known by professional criminals, hence the criminal motto (found on many a cell wall or tattooed villain) 'All Coppers Are Bastards' (or **ACAB** for short). Let's not be too harsh on the boys in blue, though; the majority of police officers are still decent, hardworking, honest people who do a great job.

When you take up crime as a profession you will inevitably go up against the police at some stage – unless, that is, you are some kind of 'super-crook', a criminal genius who commits only perfect crimes. I have never met or heard of such a crook, but then, I suppose if any did exist, by definition no one ever would find them out! So, let's assume that the majority of criminals are not super-crooks and will come to the attention of the police at some point. The first thing you'll learn is that just as you, the criminal, do not play by the rules, neither do the police. A law-abiding citizen might be quite shocked to receive a few digs from a policeman, should they be unlucky or careless enough to get arrested. They might also find it shocking when police officers blatantly lie on oath and rearrange the evidence to make you look guilty, or pull you to one side and tell you that if you 'make a contribution' (offer a bribe) the worst of the evidence against you can 'disappear'. But, to professional criminals, that kind of behaviour from the police is standard and expected. Personally, I've been more shocked when, on rare occasions, I've been dealt with by a 'straight' copper who is only interested in truth and justice.

I've had many dealings with the police over the years and I feature very prominently on the PNC (Police National Computer), but it always amuses me when I get stopped by uniformed officers for a 'routine check' when I'm walking or driving (usually around South London). They start off politely enough – 'Excuse me, sir, is this your car?' But when they run my details through the PNC I suddenly cease to be 'sir' and become 'sunshine'! It's 'All right, sunshine. Where do you think you're going?'. It's amazing how the thin veneer of respect shown by police to the ordinary man on the street leaches away when they find out you have a criminal record. I've witnessed many incidents of corruption, racism and brutality from the police over my three decades as a criminal, as well as a great big dollop of stupidity.

Some years ago I was working a con called the credit game, which involves using false ID to obtain goods from shops on credit and having no intention to pay, and got arrested in possession of some false ID by a uniformed officer from Earlsfield station. Before I was charged I was told that the CID 'wanted a word'. I was approached by a rather dapper CID sergeant who told me that he knew from my record that I was involved in the **heavy** (armed robbery) and he was interested in 'nicking some blaggers' (armed robbers). He was obviously very ambitious and saw that nicking people for serious crimes was his way up the ladder. At first he tried putting on the pressure, telling me that he knew I was **at it** and that the credit game was just a sideline. He intimated – in fact, insisted – that because there was a trilby hat on the back seat of my car I was obviously out on a 'recce' to find places to rob, using the hat as a disguise. Notwithstanding the fact that he was right, I casually denied it and laughed him off. He knew the evidence against me was flimsy so, next, he offered inducement. If I were to give up the names of a couple of likely lads who were at the heavy, he would make sure the false ID charge disappeared – and there might even be a few quid in it for me! Not wanting to ruin my chance of bail I told him I'd certainly give it some consideration, though he'd have had more chance of growing another head than of getting any information out of me. If I wouldn't name my accomplices at the Old Bailey when facing eight life sentences, I certainly wasn't going to cough up names in order to get bail on a petty false ID charge! But I strung him along, saying I'd consider it and be in touch. As I was leaving the station he had an afterthought that illustrates the casual corruption and racism of a lot of police in the 1980s. 'Listen,' he says, 'what would be ideal would be a couple of spade robbers, and if we could catch them in the act, that would be great! Juries are more likely to convict darkies with guns!' Then he gave me a big, shit-eating grin and walked back into the station.

So, talking as a criminal, dealing with the police is sometimes no different from dealing with other criminals.

100-YARD HERO

100-yard hero is how police refer to anyone who shouts insults or obscenities at police cars or police officers in the street, and implies, usually quite correctly, that the perpetrators are not so mouthy up close. In some areas of the country it's the done thing to shout insults at the police, especially on 'problem' estates, where the police are hate figures.

1664

1664 is police code for a female who looks sixteen years old from behind but sixty-four from the front.
See Three Ns

ACAB

ACAB is an acronym for the well-known and well-used criminal phrase 'All Coppers Are Bastards'. It is often seen as graffiti in prison, in police and court holding cells and it's also a tattoo popular among young lawbreakers. The big problem with tattooing the legend ACAB on to your body is that, whenever you're arrested, the police will check and record all distinguishing marks, and this includes tattoos. Needless to say, they're never best pleased to see their legitimacy called into question so indelibly, especially on the flesh of someone they consider to be a **scrote**. At the very least, you may 'trip' several times on your way to the cells. Or, if you're under eighteen, you might be given a 'good clip around the ear' (a police euphemism for a good kicking).
See the Bizzies, Borstal dot, The Filth

ACTON POST OFFICE ROBBERY

On 15 December 1988 an armed robbery took place at the main post office in Acton, West London, which was to have far-reaching consequences for both the police and armed robbers. The four men, armed with semi-automatic weapons, had been under police surveillance, and on this occasion the Flying Squad were lying in ambush. At this time the Flying Squad were still using the standard police-issue Smith & Wesson .38 five-shot revolver, despite having repeatedly asked for an upgrade to bigger and better guns. The ambush turned into something like the shoot-out at the OK Corral. Two police officers were shot, one in the hand and the other in the leg, and officers then emptied their guns at the robbers. One was shot several times but carried on running and firing his semi-automatic pistol at the police. He was eventually brought down by an officer who stepped from a doorway and hit him across the shins with a baseball bat. Detective Sergeants Stephen Thomas and Alan Knapp, the injured officers, received the George Medal in recognition of their bravery. Two of the robbers, Brian Beckford and Andrew Clark, were convicted at the Old Bailey of robbery and shooting at a police officer in 1989. The police used this to bolster their case for more effective firepower and, in the early 1990s, the Flying Squad were issued with semi-automatic weapons.

AFO

AFO is a police acronym for Authorized Firearms Officer. The AFO is the policeman who is going to shoot you if called on to do so. Back in the 1980s and early '90s there was a unit of firearms officers known as PT17, but, after a few well-publicized police shootings, they changed their name to SO19 (Special Operations 19). I was told by a Flying Squad sergeant that SO19 were all 'trigger-happy bastards who spend their down time dribbling over Rambo movies' – and this was from a man who had shot dead at least two armed robbers himself! There were also AFOs in the Regional Crime Squads (RCS) and Flying Squad, officers who were designated carriers and authorized users of firearms in the event that SO19 were unavailable. These days, there are a lot more armed police on our streets and, instead of five-shot Smith & Wessons, they're carrying more weaponry than most Third World dictatorships.

AT LARGE

This is a phrase used by the police to describe anyone who has escaped from custody; it means that the suspect is out in the community but is being actively sought. Being 'unlawfully **at large**' is a criminal offence, usually preceded by an escape from prison or police custody.

BANANAS

Bananas was the nickname for a notorious police squad also known as the SPG (Special Patrol Group), which had a reputation for violence, brutality and corruption in London from the 1960s up until the '90s. SPG officers were said to be yellow, bent and to hang around in bunches, hence the moniker. There is a strong suspicion that the SPG were responsible for the death of schoolteacher Blair Peach at a demonstration in Southall in 1979. Mr Peach died from head injuries received during an anti-racism protest against the National Front.

BATTLE TAXI

A **battle taxi** is any police vehicle used to transport riot-squad officers to an incident or protest; the name derives from the the fact that these officers will be hyped up and ready to face 'the enemy'. Some officers revel in the police force having a combative image and all the paraphernalia, and like nothing better than steaming into a load of protesting students or teachers; it gets their blood up, especially as they are kitted out with shields, batons and protective clothing and the 'enemy' is not. Quite a large minority of police officers join up specifically for this kind of action.

BATTY SQUAD

A **batty squad** is a police motorcycle squad that speeds through the streets on powerful motorbikes. To other police officers the motorcycle squads seem a bit batty (mad or stupid) for choosing the relative dangers of two wheels over the safer four-wheeled police vehicles.

THE BIZZIES

In Liverpool the police are commonly known as the **bizzies**, because they make themselves 'busy' around criminal activities.
See Dibble

BLACK BASTARDS

This is Northern Irish slang for the Royal Ulster Constabulary (now called the PSNI – Police Service of Northern Ireland) who wore black uniforms and were widely hated by the Catholic nationalist minority in Ulster for their suspected collusion with loyalist paramilitary organizations. The vast majority of RUC officers were Protestants, which did little to foster good relations between the two sides of the community.

BLACK RATS

Police officers call traffic police **black rats**, partly because of the black uniform they wear, partly because they're seen to be in a 'cushy number', away from any real danger, and partly because they don't give any leeway to fellow officers, on or off duty, who they stop for driving offences. It's become a point of pride for traffic cops not to discriminate in favour of their colleagues, and it is widely rumoured within police ranks that a traffic cop would nick their own crippled mother for having a broken rear light.

BLUES AND TWOS

Blues and twos are the lights and sirens used when a police vehicle is rushing to the scene of a crime or accident to warn pedestrians and other vehicles that the police vehicle is coming through at speed. 'Blues' are the flashing blue lights on top of the vehicle and 'twos' is the two-tone siren. Despite the use of blues and twos, there have been cases of pedestrians being hit by police vehicles. In the 1970s, the police called the siren and lights 'late for teas', as their use was fairly unregulated and coppers would employ them any time they were in a hurry – to get past traffic jams or when they were late for tea.

BOBBY

A **bobby** is a policeman, named after the founder of the police, Sir Robert Peel. It's a very middle-class, middle-England word and not much favoured by the modern criminal, who prefers **the filth** or **rozzers** or, in the case of some youngsters, 'the feds'.
See The Filth, Peelers, Rozzers

BOGEY

Bogey is an old-fashioned word for a police detective and was extensively used by villains in the 1940s and '50s. Some of the people I've spoken to say it's a reference to the Hollywood actor Humphrey Bogart, also known as Bogey, because British detectives at one point adopted his style of dress – the fedora hat and raincoat. But another definition of 'bogey' is something that worries or annoys, and it's certainly true that the police will worry or annoy criminals. It's a case of pay your money and take your choice.

BOTTLE SQUAD

The **bottle squad** is an undercover plainclothes squad dedicated to investigating and catching pickpockets. They mingle with crowds in city centres, railway stations and shopping centres and try to catch pickpockets in the act. They're known as the bottle squad because of the criminal slang for working pickpockets, 'on the bottle', meaning to follow someone closely. The London bottle squad, based at West End Central police station, had a less than savoury reputation in the late 1970s and early '80s for **fitting** people **up**, but they were certainly efficient at harassing the **dippers** and keeping them out of the West End.

See the Bull

BOY DEM

Some black youths call the police **boy dem**, implying that they are no more than boys. The West Indian patois 'dem' is a corruption of 'them', so a literal translation would be 'boys, them'.

CHIMPS

Chimps is how regular police officers refer to their less qualified brethren the Police Community Support Officers (PCSO); although they wear a uniform, they can't issue warrants or make arrests. It's an acronym for Completely Hopeless In Most Police Situations. Generally, the police do not have much respect for PCSOs, and think of them as 'plastic coppers'. Chimps are sometimes known as 'hobby bobbys', a reference to the fact that PCSOs only work part-time.

COCO

Coco is Scottish slang for the police, named after the popular children's cereal Coco Pops (rhyming slang: Coco Pops = cops). It's a pretty mild piece of slang on the face of it, but it's also a bit barbed, as there was a famous clown called Coco, and most Scottish villains will refer to the police as 'a bunch of clowns'.

COLLAR

In police slang, a **collar** is somebody who has been arrested, as in 'I done well with that burglary case, made two decent collars', from the days when a police officer had to physically grab suspects by the collar in order to make an arrest.

See Pinch

COPPER

There are several explanations as to how **copper** became slang for the police. I've heard that it comes from the copper badges the first police force wore, or from the fact that their wage was a (copper) penny a day. Some people say it's from the acronym for Constable On Patrol. I don't know which is the correct explanation, but it's still very common and one of the few less insulting slang words. It was very big in American gangster films of the 1930s and '40s, frequently used by James Cagney, Humphrey Bogart and George Raft, the big-screen gangster actors of the period. Think Jimmy Cagney in *White Heat* – 'A copper, a dirty, stinkin' copper . . .'

See Old Bill, Rozzer

COPSICLES

Copsicles is a slang term for the new breed of police officers who patrol on bicycles, particularly apt in the winter months, when they have to brave the bad weather. It's a play on the words 'cop', 'popsicle' and 'cycles'.

CROSSING TARGETS

A 'high-profile' criminal will almost inevitably become a target for various police squads. In my own experience with the Flying Squad, I was often a target. A squad will put a suspect under surveillance, follow them, tap their phone, put a tracking device or listening bug on their vehicle and note their every move and word to gather 'intelligence' that might be used as evidence in any attempted conviction. The squad will do the same to the suspect's family, friends and business acquaintances. Usually, each target (the people the police deem to be a part of a suspect's 'criminal network') is given a number, so the main target is known as **Target 1** and anyone else the police are interested in are Target 2, Target 3, and so on. **Crossing targets** is when a target being watched by one squad (say, the Flying Squad) makes contact with a target being watched by a different squad (say, the Anti-terrorist Squad). The two targets won't know (if the police are good at their job or very lucky) they are being watched, but it will be noted by both squads that there's a connection between the targets and they'll have to decide which squad takes precedence. A lot of professional criminals mix with a diverse group of acquaintances who usually have their fingers in more than one pie. For example, a quartermaster for an armed robbery team might get firearms from someone with a connection to terrorism, or a professional burglary team may fence goods through someone who has a connection to car ringing. The world of the professional criminal is a relatively small one.

See Ringers and Clones, Target 1

CRUSHERS

Crushers was a nickname for the police, popular in the nineteenth century, suggesting their brutality. It was originally a naval term for the Royal Navy Regulating Branch, who policed sailors and seamen and were classed as 'hard men' who would brook no nonsense and were quick to violence.

C***-STABLE

C***-stable is an insulting term that emphasizes the first syllable of 'constable'; it's usually used to wind up any police officers within hearing range, often by Saturday-night drunks and **100-yard heroes**.

DARBIES

Darbies are handcuffs. Nobody knows for sure where the word comes from. Some say it's because, when two prisoners were handcuffed together for transport they were known as Darby and Joan; others that the name probably comes from the phrase 'Darby's bonds', meaning a rigid bond and named after an infamous sixteenth-century usurer. It's very old-fashioned and is rarely used nowadays. *See Double-cuffed* (p. 190)

DESK JOCKEY

Desk jockey is a disparaging term for any officer who prefers paperwork to patrolling or 'real' police work. Some officers are confined to their desks due to illness or injury, but it's the permanent desk jockey who chooses this line of work who is held in contempt.

DIBBLE

In Manchester, the police are known as **Dibble**, as in 'I nearly had the door open, then Dibble shows up with the **blues and twos** screeching', after the police officer in the children's cartoon *Top Cat*, about a gangster-style cat who lives in a dustbin and his alley-cat gang. They are forever scheming to pull the wool over the local beat cop, Officer Dibble. Dibble is a stickler for the rules but also very stupid.

DONE UP LIKE A KIPPER

To be **done up like a kipper** means to be stitched up or treated very badly. The phrase comes from the fact that kippers are caught, gutted, boned and smoked before they're eaten. According to most professional criminals, the police are experts at doing people up like kippers.

DUCKS AND GEESE

Cockney rhyming slang: **ducks and geese** = police.

EKKY

Ekky is another word for the police and comes from the fact that, when seen in the rear-view mirror of a vehicle, the police sign is backwards – ECILOP ('ekkylop', which is shortened to ekky). Slang names for the police can be extremely localized and rarely heard beyond a specific manor or region. For example, in Streatham, South London, the police are known as 'the shrubs' because Streatham police station is situated on Shrubbery Road. But this name would mean nothing to people who do not live or steal in Streatham.

F&M

This is a police acronym for false and malicious information. Some people, for various reasons, will use the police and the law in order to satisfy their own agendas. **F&M** is particularly prevalent in rape and other sex-offence cases and there have been many well-publicized instances in recent years of both women and men making false and malicious allegations against people.

FIDO

FIDO is an acronym (Fuck It, Drive On) used by the police for any crime or offence they witness but deem unworthy of their attention. Some police officers only want 'big' nickings – the serious crimes such as burglary, robbery, serious assault – and can't be bothered with petty crimes such as littering, vandalism or loitering. Some police officers are very ambitious and they know that the way to gain promotion is by going for serious crimes and offenders. A good 'thief taker' will always be admired and revered in the police force, but a copper who nicks every offender, no matter how petty the offence, is classed as a nuisance who just creates paperwork. Of course, there are police officers for whom 'zero tolerance' is the only way to go.

THE FILTH

The filth is usually reserved for the non-uniformed branches of the police, or the CID, and is just another example of the absolute contempt most criminals have for the police. It was very commonly used in the 1960s and '70s, when there was widespread corruption in the British police force, in particular among the CID and plainclothes squads.

FIT-UP

A **fit-up** is when corrupt police officers falsify or fake evidence in order to get someone convicted of a crime. They will 'fit' the evidence to the suspect so it looks as though they are guilty. Some police officers will do this as a matter of course if they truly believe the suspect is guilty. A lot of small-scale police corruption is considered fair game, things such as 'verballing' (saying that suspects have admitted something when they haven't), planting evidence or priming witnesses by 'accidentally' giving them information about a suspect so that they will be predisposed to believe them guilty.

See Noble-cause corruption, Verbals

FLATFOOT

Flatfoot is an old-fashioned word for uniformed police, not much used nowadays as police officers rarely do foot patrols. It acknowledged the amount of walking done by a uniformed officer pounding the beat and the idea that this would lead to them having flat feet.

FOUR-UP

Four-up is four people in a vehicle, as in 'Yes, Sarge, it's a Ford Cortina with four-up.' It's used mostly by the police but sometimes also by criminals.

FRAME

To **frame** someone is to fix the evidence of a crime to fit the person you suspect, or would like to accuse, for it, and is a means of gaining a conviction when there is little or no chance of arresting the real offender. Framing can involve something as simple as planting a small piece of evidence that points to the suspect, or as complicated as a large-scale conspiracy in order to get people convicted. Think of the Birmingham Six, the Guildford Four, the Bridgewater Three, the Broadwater Farm Three, the Cardiff Newsagent Three, Judith Ward, Stefan Kiszko, Barry George, Colin Stagg . . . the list goes on. These are all victims of wrongful convictions, and all were cleared, eventually, by the courts. *See Noble cause corruption*

THE FUZZ

The fuzz is American in origin and was in popular usage among the hippies of the Haight-Ashbury area of San Francisco during the 'flower power' years of the 1960s and '70s to describe the police. Although some members of the public were then growing their hair long, the police and most figures of authority favoured very short hair, usually a buzz cut or flat-top, which left only a 'fuzz' of hair on the head. Any undercover plainclothes police officers could be recognized by their short fuzz of hair.

GAVVERS

Gavvers is a Romany term for the police, as in 'You don't wanna be going down there, mush, there's gavvers all over the place.' Any place where Gypsys encounter a large police presence is known as 'gavvers' town', and the name came about because whenever there was a police action to move Gypsies on, the police would 'gavver' (gather) them up and put them back on the road. 'Gavvers' has now entered the world of everyday criminal slang and is used not only by Gypsies and Travellers but by all sorts of criminals.

GROID

This is police slang for a black person, as in 'Yeah, I nicked a couple of **groids** last night, it was a good shift.' The reason police once used this offensive word is because on all their official forms they have to describe the ethnicity of those arrested, of the victims of crime and the witnesses, and the box they used to tick for Afro-Caribbeans in less enlightened times read 'Negroid'. Police officers shortened this to groid and felt they could use it and the general public wouldn't twig, so it was a secretive way to express racist views. *See Police IC codes*

HAVING A TRADE

To **have a trade** with **Old Bill** means that you are bribing the police, either with cash or stolen goods or by giving up other criminals. From the 1950s until the '70s, it was an accepted part of being a professional criminal. A lot of career criminals drank and socialized with CID officers, particularly the Flying Squad and the Vice Squad. The police justified this by saying they were gathering intelligence and making contacts in the criminal world, and criminals justified it by saying they were making contacts that might be able to help them out if they got their collar felt in the future. The divide between plainclothes police and professional criminals was wafer thin and some police officers often crossed it by selling their services – losing evidence, failing to question witnesses properly, and even giving information about possible targets for criminals to rob. Some police squads had a terrible reputation for corruption, and it all came to a head when a criminal, with the help of two newspaper reporters, secretly tape-recorded two members of the Flying Squad asking for a bribe in order to 'lose' evidence in a case. One of the officers taped talked of the CID being 'a firm within a firm' and this led to a major investigation into police corruption that centred on the Metropolitan Police.

IC8

This is an addition to police Identification Codes – the shorthand for a person's national or racial origin; **IC8** is code for a 'ginger male'.
See Police IC codes

JAM SANDWICH

A **jam sandwich** is a police patrol car, so called because of its white-and-red livery; the red stripe running around the middle of the car looks like a smear of jam between two slices of white bread. The term became popular in the early 1980s when the Metropolitan Police started using the 3.5 litre Rover SDi as their patrol car of choice. A patrol car is also sometimes called a 'bacon sandwich', a sly reference to the fact that, to a minority of people, the police are known as 'pigs'.

THE KREMLIN

The Kremlin is what many ordinary police officers call New Scotland Yard. It seems, from listening to conversations between police officers over the years, that most of the lower ranks in the police force have nothing but envy and disrespect for their upper-echelon superiors and equate them to a foreign (Soviet) government passing down diktats and edicts.

LOB

LOB is police acronym meaning Load of Bollocks, usually marked on forms and personal notebooks to indicate that the officer does not believe a word of what they are being told.

See NFI

MEAT WAGON

A **meat wagon** is a police or prison van used for transporting prisoners, after its cargo of living meat. The vehicle was also once known as the paddy wagon or Black Maria. 'Paddy wagon' is American slang, particular to New York, where a disproportionate number of Irish emigrants joined the police force, but the phrase was imported to the UK and ended up with another meaning, related to the large numbers of drunken Irishmen picked up by police vans in cities such as London and Birmingham on a Saturday night. In the 1950s and '60s a lot of Irish navvies came to England to help rebuild the cities after their destruction by the German Luftwaffe during the Second World War. They helped to construct the Tube network, the motorways and roads, as well as houses and other buildings. Being, on the whole, single young men far from home, the navvies would work all week and go out and get drunk at the weekend. Almost inevitably, some would end up fighting or being drunk and disorderly, so they would be picked up by the police and taken away in the paddy wagon. 'Black Maria' comes from the Victorian era when the horse-drawn police wagon was called a Maria, and the ones used by the police were painted black.

MING ON THE WING

Travellers call the police or anyone in authority the 'ming', from the Romany word *mingro*. So if you are driving about, or on your way to or from a bit of skulduggery, and somebody says, '**Ming on the wing**,' it means there's a police vehicle within sight of your vehicle. Some London criminals say that 'ming' is short for Emperor Ming the Merciless, who was the baddie alien in *Flash Gordon*, but then, some people also think there's such a thing as a 'kettle of scotch'!

See Gavvers

MOP

This is a police acronym for Member Of the Public, used as shorthand when filling in notebooks and reports. The police use many acronyms, and different forces in different parts of the county often use their own local versions. **MOP**, however, is standard for the majority of, if not all, police forces.

MUPPET (1)

MUPPET is an acronym, for Most Useless Police Person Ever Trained, used by the police for an incompetent idiot.

NFI

NFI is a police acronym meaning Not Fucking Interested, usually marked on notes or reports that also carry the acronym **LOB** (Load Of Bollocks) to indicate that the officer thinks there is little or no point in pursuing the reported crime or offence.

NOBLE CAUSE CORRUPTION

Noble cause corruption is a phrase used to describe the practice by some police officers of falsifying evidence against a suspect, or suspects, who they personally believe is guilty. It's said that a lot of the corruption involved in the major miscarriages of justice of the twentieth century was perpetrated through 'noble cause'.

The Guildford Four (four young people who were accused, convicted and jailed for over seventeen years for terrorism and bombings) were a prime example of this kind of police corruption. The police really believed, despite glaring evidence to the contrary, that the accused had planted bombs in two public houses in Guildford, Surrey, in 1974, and this absolute belief led the police to torture the suspects until they admitted the crime, 'lose' evidence that would have proved their innocence and falsify other evidence that could point to their guilt.

The sad thing is that noble cause corruption is still quite prevalent in the police force today; a lot of policemen believe that the uniform gives them the absolute right to decide who is guilty and who is not. It doesn't help that it is they themselves who investigate their own wrongdoings: despite so many cases of miscarriages of justice, institutional racism, casual brutality towards members of the public and the many deaths at the hands of the police it is still as rare as rocking-horse faeces to see a police officer in the dock for any of it.

See Fit-up, Verbals

NODDY BIKE

Noddy bike was a nickname for the old police motorscooters that were used for patrolling rural areas in the

1950s and '60s. Named after children's writer Enid Blyton's character.

NONDIE

The police have their own particular slang, and **nondie** is one of theirs. It's short for nondescript and is usually used as a name for undercover vehicles used on surveillance, as in 'If we are going on surveillance tonight then best we take the nondie in case we get spotted by any of the local heads'. Police forces will have at least a couple of nondies to use for surveillance work. Up until the early 1990s, the police, and the London Flying Squads in particular, would hire their nondies from a nationwide company called Budget Rent-a-Van (because it was cheap). As more and more people were being arrested and noticing these vans (they all carried the company's logo) being driven around or parked locally in the days leading up to the arrest, the secret got out. Once it became known that the police were using this company's vehicles for surveillance work, every Budget vehicle on the streets became suspect and it was pointless for police surveillance units to use them. It is well known that the Flying Squads have at least two black London cabs for use in surveillance and for surprise arrests.

See Ready-eye

OBBO POST

An **obbo post** is an observation post, a spot from where police officers can keep a target under surveillance, for example a building that overlooks a target's home or place of work, or a hiding place close to a spot where the police have intelligence that a crime may be committed. Criminals describe being under this form of police attention as being 'under obbo'.

See Ready-eye

OLD BILL

Old Bill is such a common term for the police that there was a long-running television series about the goings on at a fictional police station called *The Bill*. I've never really been able to find out for sure where this term originated, but I believe it started in the twentieth century with the introduction of the Flying Squad. The Flying Squad was the first to use motorized vehicles to combat crime. They were originally called the Mobile Patrol Experiment (very catchy!) but nicknamed the Flying Squad because they were the first police squad that had permission to cross geographical police boundaries and 'trespass' on the patch of any other force or district – fly in, fly out – without getting permission from anyone. All of their vehicles had the registration letters 'BYL', which I think led to them being known by criminals as 'the bill'. This eventually became 'Old Bill'.

See the Sweeney

OPERATION COUNTRYMAN

Unfortunately, almost since the beginning, UK police have had a bad reputation for corruption. In the 1970s an investigation was started into corruption, specifically, initially, in the City of London Police, but then spread out to the Metropolitan Police; the investigation was code-named **Operation Countryman**. Operation Countryman exposed widespread police corruption to the public via the media, the first time this was done on such a scale. The operation was conducted between 1978 and 1982 at a cost of over £3 million, and it led to eight police officers being arrested, though none was charged or convicted. The investigation was launched when a police informant claimed that some **coppers**, including several from the elite Flying Squad, were taking bribes from criminals in return for warning them of imminent police raids, as well as having charges dropped and fabricating evidence against innocent men. Operation Countryman got its name from using officers from rural police forces such as Hampshire and Dorset, as it wasn't clear who could be trusted in the City of London and the Met area. The operation was ordered by then Home Secretary Merlyn Rees and began by investigating police activity around three major robberies – an armed robbery at the *Daily Express* offices in 1976, which netted £175,000; a £225,000 armed robbery outside the HQ of Williams & Glyn bank in 1977; and a £200,000 payroll robbery at the offices of the *Daily Mirror* newspaper in 1978. During the *Daily Mirror* robbery a Security Express guard was shot and killed. The HQ for the investigation team was originally at Camberwell police station in South London, but there were attempts by some of the target officers and their friends to steal or destroy evidence and documents there, so the HQ was moved to Godalming police station in Surrey, out of the immediate reach of the Met. The results of the six-year investigation were presented to the Home Office and Police Commissioner with recommendations that officers should face criminal charges, but no officer was ever charged as a result of the investigation. The findings of the investigation have never been made public.

See the Sweeney

THE OTHER PEOPLE

This term may be London specific, as I've never heard anyone from outside the Smoke using it. It's a name for the police, as in 'I was just about to take the **joey**, when **the other people** turned up'. It's often used in connection with **having a trade**, as in 'Don't trust the geezer, I hear he's been having a trade with the other people'.

See Having a trade, Joey

PADDING

In police slang **padding** is adding bits to evidence or reports to make it look as if the police officers have put in more work than they have. Padding the crime figures means downgrading certain crimes and giving the perpetrator a caution rather than making an arrest so it looks as though there's been a drop in crime, thus making a station or district look as though they have reduced crime figures when, in reality, they have done nothing of the sort.

PANDA CAR

Panda car was a nickname for police cars of the 1960s, usually Morris Minors, which were painted with large panels of black and white or blue and white. The Morris Minor had a rounded panda bear shape, and in its black-and-white livery looked a bit like a sleeping panda.

PEELERS

An old-fashioned name for the police dating from the 1830s, when Home Secretary Sir Robert Peel pushed through a bill creating the modern police force. In England police officers were nicknamed **bobbies** after the shortened version of Peel's first name, but in Ireland, where Tory MPs were held in a bit more contempt, they took the nickname from his surname. **Peelers** did eventually catch on in England, through the Irish communities there, and became popular slang for the police.

PINCH

A **pinch** is police slang for an arrest, dating from the days when police officers had to pinch the collar of an individual. *See Collar*

PLAIN BROWN WRAPPER

In a **plain brown wrapper** describes police in an unmarked vehicle and originated with the CB radio craze of the early 1980s, when a lot of American trucker slang made its way into the language.

PLOD

Plod is an inoffensive nickname for uniformed police officers, after PC Plod in Enid Blyton's Noddy books, and still much used today. The female equivalent is PC Plonk.

POLICE IC CODES

IC (Identification Codes), which were introduced in the 1970s, are used by the police in radio communications and written reports in order to describe the ethnic origin of suspects and witnesses. Officially, there are seven IC codes, though there is also an unofficial eighth code. The ethnic codes of people are usually initially attributed to them by police officers on visual assessment. If someone is then arrested or stopped for a search, they may be asked their ethnicity and police are required to use this self-defined ethnicity over their own assessment. Police IC codes are as follows: IC1 is White, European; IC2 is Mediterranean, Hispanic; IC3 is African/Afro-Caribbean; IC4 is Indian, Pakistani or any other South Asian; IC5 is Chinese, Japanese or any other South-east Asian; IC6 is Middle Eastern; and IC7 (sometimes known as IC0) is 'origin unknown'.

See IC8

POV

POV is a police acronym for Personally Owned Vehicle, which means something other than a marked and liveried police vehicle or one of the nondescript vehicles used by plainclothes or undercover officers. A lot of police officers class themselves as never being off duty so, even in their leisure time, they will be on the lookout for crime and criminals and may arrest someone who is wanted or who commits a crime they happen to see. When filling in reports about these incidents, if they were driving their own car they will use the acronym POV.

READY-EYE

A **ready-eye** is an ambush, particularly when officers are hoping to apprehend armed robbers. If the police get information that a robbery, or other crime, will be going off at a certain place at a certain time, they will get to the target area long before the criminals and position themselves discreetly close by. They could be disguised as traffic wardens, builders, road workers or tramps. Once the crime is in progress, or very soon after, the police will reveal themselves and ambush the villains. For a serious armed robber, the ready-eye is a kick in the teeth, as not only will he usually be nicked, he will also know that someone close has informed on him, as that's the only way the police will have come by the information. Sometimes a ready-eye will be activated if the police have been following a suspect or suspects for some time and have a good idea of what the villains are after and when.

ROZZER

Rozzer, meaning a police officer, is a derivation of the slang word 'cozzer', which is itself a derivation of the slang word **copper**.

See Copper

RTA

RTA is an acronym for Road Traffic Accident. Any crash or ding involving vehicles is classed as an RTA, which is the shorthand police use when they fill in their contemporaneous notebooks or write official reports. The police do love an acronym.

RTFL

An acronym used between police officers, **RTFL** stands for Read The Fucking Log – an instruction for officers to familiarize themselves with the log recording what has been going on before they come on duty.

SFQ

SFQ is a police acronym for Stupid Fucking Question, usually in response to a query from a member of the public or a superior officer, both of whom the police seem to hold in equal contempt. As they are now under increased scrutiny in these times of mobile-phone cameras and CCTV, the police are mindful that using acronyms and slang is necessary in order to avoid embarrassment should they be recorded or overheard by the public.

SHOUT

If a police officer says he's had a **shout** it means he's had an urgent radio message about a crime in progress and he must go to the scene.

THE SQUAD

The Squad is a police nickname for the Flying Squad. A bit like Madonna or Beyoncé, this elite force of coppers is so well known that it can dispense with its full name.

STARBURST

A **starburst** is when police are chasing a stolen car containing more than one person, the car comes to a halt and everyone inside jumps out of different doors and heads in different directions. It's named after a firework called the starburst which shoots into the air at great speed before exploding sparks and colours.

THE SUITS

The suits is a term used by uniformed police officers for their plainclothes colleagues in the CID (obviously because they don't wear police uniform).

THE SWEEDY

The Sweedy is any plainclothes police squad from outside London. It's a play on **the Sweeney** and 'swede-bashers', which is what London police call anyone who isn't from London. The Met class all other police forces as 'farmers and yokels', less sophisticated than them, and hate having them doing any investigation on their patch. 'The Sweedy' was originally coined during **Operation Countryman**, an investigation into corruption in the Flying Squad led by the police forces of Hampshire and Dorset. Ever since, the Met have despised non-London forces and use this term pejoratively.
See Operation Countryman, the Squad, the Sweeney

THE SWEENEY

The Sweeney are the four London Flying Squads, which deal exclusively with armed robbery in the capital (rhyming slang: Sweeney Todd = Flying Squad). Sweeney Todd was the fictional demon barber of Fleet Street who killed his clients, chopped them up and sold the meat to a local pie shop. The term has fallen out of vogue with criminals ever since it came into common usage by the general public via the 1970s television drama series of the same name. *The Sweeney*, starring John Thaw and Dennis Waterman as DI Regan and DS Carter respectively, was very popular and did much to glamorize the real Flying Squad. Regan and

Carter were portrayed as hard-drinking, womanizing thief-takers who liked nothing better than a shoot-out or a punch-up with the villains they were hunting. Unfortunately, the real Sweeney began to believe their own hype. Since the 1960s the Flying Squad have been under investigation on many occasions for bribery and corruption, and many Flying Squad officers have taken 'early retirement' or been dismissed. The official name for the Sweeney is SO8 (Special Operations 8), but most armed robbers now refer to them as the **heavy** mob (because of their penchant for violence), **the Squad**, or Huns with guns. In 2011 Ray Winstone and Ben 'Plan B' Drew starred in a feature film directed by Nick Love based on the original television show. The film was a blatant glamorization of the Flying Squad and depicted the officers almost as superheroes who run around London firing off machine guns, cracking lame jokes and working in state-of-the-art offices. Needless to say, this was far from the truth, as the real Sweeney usually work out of pokey offices in the back of police stations and are as terrified of being shot by the armed robbers they hunt as the robbers are of being shot by them. The film also intimated that Sweeney officers are in the job for life, when, in fact, their tenure in the squad is usually for a maximum of four years. This rotation is so they cannot get too comfortable in the job and succumb to corruption.

See the Sweedy

TARGET 1

When the police put a professional criminal under surveillance they will give them a code name, usually **Target 1** if there are other targets involved. The importance of the target is in direct relation to his number, so the top man is

Target 1, the second most important in the organization is Target 2, and so on. It's handy for radio shorthand when the police are following or watching criminals. The terminology is pretty old hat now, though, as a lot of professional criminals use scanners to listen in to police radios and understand the slang and jargon used by the police.

See Crossing Targets

THREE NS

Three Ns is offensive police slang for any female who appears to be dressed in a ridiculous or outrageous manner. It stands for No mum, No mates, No mirror, meaning there is no one or nothing to tell them how terribly they're dressed and/or made up before they venture out on to the streets.

TINNED PORK

Tinned pork is a derogatory term used by villains for police officers in vehicles, as in 'Leave it, leave it, a tin of pork has just pulled in'.

TIT HEADS

Tit head is a derogatory term for a uniformed constable, based on the shape of the helmet they wear, and is used by non-uniformed staff to express their amusement and contempt at their 'inferior' colleagues. The phrase 'take the tit off your head' means to relax and stop being a copper for a minute.

TROJAN UNITS

Trojan units are police units, usually consisting of two or three officers, who patrol in high-speed cars containing a gun safe. The officers are all **AFOs** (Authorized Firearms Officers) and the safe contains weapons such as sub-machine pistols, automatic rifles, shotguns and gas grenades. The officers have a personal sidearm – usually the Glock 9mm semi-automatic pistol – and are on alert for any calls involving firearms, serious violence or terrorism. In London the Trojan units usually use Volvo estates, highly tuned performance models, so they can get to call-outs very quickly. En route they might receive radio confirmation from a chief inspector allowing them to open the gun safe and get the big guns out. They got their name from the Trojan Horse of Greek mythology, the huge wooden horse left outside the fortified gates of the city of Troy after the siege had, supposedly, ended. The Trojans pulled the horse inside the gates, not realizing that it was full of battle-hardened and heavily armed Greek warriors, who descended from the belly of the horse in the dead of night and opened the city gates to the rest of the Greek army. Let's face it, how many villains are going to think that a Volvo estate would hide a high-performance engine and more firearms than some South American dictatorships? These units were well named.

UNDIES (1)

Undies is youth slang for undercover police officers. There are many cases of police officers going undercover in order to infiltrate criminal or protest organizations, which involves a police officer adopting a completely new identity, sometimes that of a hardened criminal, in order to gain the acceptance and trust of their targets. Some undercover policemen immerse themselves in this murky world for years on end, and it has recently come out that some of them instigated, planned and committed crimes while undercover. Unfortunately, the laws of the UK do not include a defence of agent provocateur (as does the law in some countries), so if a police officer (undercover or in plain sight) incites a citizen to commit a crime there would be no defence for that citizen. Put simply, if a plain-clothes police officer inveigled his way into your life, worked hard at becoming your friend and then told you there was easy money to be had from stealing or robbing something and you, after much persuasion, succumbed to his cajoling and encouragement to commit a crime, you would be arrested and convicted, and stating the fact that you would never have done it without the intervention of an undercover copper would have no legal weight at all. Watch out for the undies!

VERBALS

This term was very common up until the PACE (Police And Criminal Evidence) Act was introduced in 1984, and is still used in some cases. **Verbals** or 'verballing' is when a police officer claims that a criminal has said something incriminating, either at the moment of arrest or in an interview. I, personally, have been verballed on many occasions. Verbals will be recorded in a police officer's notebook soon after arrest and usually take the form of an admission to a crime. The typical police notebook verbal will go something like this: 'The arrest was made at 12.47. I said to Mr Smith, "You know why we are arresting you, don't you?" Smith replied, "Yes, I knew it was coming, I'm just glad you've caught me before I ended up shooting someone."' Of course, Mr Smith may well be an experienced career criminal and would say nothing of the kind at the moment of arrest. The police officers see verballing as a way to bolster their case; their notebooks will be read out in front of a jury. If there are two or more police officers swearing that you spoke the incriminating words and presenting their notebooks of contemporaneous notes as evidence of this, some juries will be swayed. Since the PACE Act was introduced, it's very hard to verbal someone in an interview, as interviews are now recorded, but sometimes the police will claim that the accused made admissions on the way to the interview room or in a cell. A friend of mine, who got tired of being verballed by the police, decided to speak at the moment of his arrest for the robbery of a security van. When the Flying Squad officers told him he was nicked, he said, very loudly, 'Okay, it's a fair cop, guv.' The police officers recorded these words in their notebooks, very pleased that they didn't have to make anything up. But when my friend got in front of a jury and the comments were read out, he just smiled and told them, 'Come on, d'you honestly think I would say that? It sounds like something from an episode of *Z Cars*, or a line from some cheap black-and-white British gangster film!' It seems the jury agreed with him, as he was found not guilty. You could say he did a bit of reverse verballing. Nevertheless, despite the PACE Act, verballing by the police remains a problem.

See Fit-up, Noble Cause Corruption

WASPS

Wasps is modern slang for uniformed police officers in high-visibility vests, and is meant to denote that they can be a nuisance, dangerous and that, if there is trouble, they will swarm.

THE WHITE RABBIT

Back in the 1980s there was a strange tale going around about **the White Rabbit** in Wembley police station. Prisoners who had become a bit stroppy told of late-night visits to the cells by a big white rabbit that gave them a good kicking. Of course, when they complained to magistrates or their solicitors their claims sounded ridiculous. Imagine turning up at court, covered in bruises, and telling the magistrate that a big white rabbit entered your cell in the middle of the night and gave you a good kicking! Anyway, the white rabbit of Wembley became a sort of urban legend. Just recently, I was told by a serving police officer that when they were refurbishing the police station a locked cupboard on the top floor was forced open and, inside, they found a fancy-dress white rabbit suit complete with bloodstains.

WOODENTOPS

Woodentops is a now-dated derogatory term, taken from the children's television puppet show *The Woodentops*, for uniformed police, usually used by members of the CID.

ZOMBIE

A **zombie** is what the police call a police officer close to retirement and now merely going through the motions. It can also mean a lazy police officer who does the bare minimum, shuffling from one job to another with no enthusiasm. Most police officers hate zombies with a passion, as they tend to make everyone else's job harder as others have to pick up the slack.

Doing Bird

6. *The Language of the Greybar Hotel*

Let's face it, we're living in very troubled times. These days, you don't have to be a serious criminal in order to attract the attention of the police and find yourself on the wrong side of the law. In fact, you don't have to be any kind of criminal at all. In some cases, all you need is a brown face, a beard and an opinion and you can find yourself pacing an eight-by-ten cell inside a Special Security Unit before you can say 'God is good'. And even if you're a white-faced, beardless atheist, prison is still only an unpaid television licence away. Britain jails more men, women and children per capita than anywhere else in Europe. When it comes to dishing out the porridge, we're right up there with those other models of liberality and tolerance Russia, China and the USA. Heady company indeed. It is estimated that by 2017 the British prison population will hit the 100,000 mark, and this won't include people who are on parole or the large proportion of citizens who will have served a prison sentence but aren't in prison at that moment. In its first decade in power, the New Labour government introduced into British law twenty-four new Criminal Justice Bills – over 3,000 new offences and 115,000 pages of legislation. When you consider that before 1997 one Criminal Justice Bill was introduced, on average, every ten years, it's clear what an effect this statute frenzy has had in criminalizing large sections of the population and leaving them eligible for imprisonment. To put it simply, in the not-too-distant future a substantial chunk of the British population will have had some experience of imprisonment, if not personally, then through family or friends. And yet, to the vast majority of people, the reality of prison remains a mystery.

In this section I will talk about prisons: their slang names, a bit of their history and a smattering of the language used within their walls. There are a lot of stories to be told. For example, not a lot of people know that HMP Brixton in South London was once a female prison. It only started taking male prisoners when HMP Holloway, a mixed prison since it opened in 1852, was designated female-only in 1903. Or that HMP Belmarsh was built on marshland and is sinking into the marsh at the rate of an inch per year. The state-of-the-art underground 'security tunnel' there, built in order to deliver high-security prisoners to nearby Woolwich Crown Court without motorized transport, has been closed most of the time the prison has been in operation because leaks regularly cause floods in the tunnel. To paraphrase a former Home Secretary, it's all very well having innovative security ideas but they must at least be 'fit for purpose'.

Of course prisoners use slang, but so do prison officials. It's known as 'screw-speak' and often involves abbreviations and acronyms. The ordinary man on the street would be hard pressed to understand one word in every five spoken by a prisoner, but he might struggle to understand one word in every three uttered by prison officials. For example, screws in different prisons address their charges differently, so you might be called 'blue', 'bud', 'fella' or **scrote**, depending on which prison and which part of the country you are in. In London and southern prisons, 'fella' is the most common form, as in 'Get behind your door, fella' or 'What's your number, fella?'. 'Bud' is big in Welsh prisons and is short for 'buddy', which might seem a jolly, friendly way of addressing prisoners but only means that, on the whole, prison officers cannot be bothered learning the prisoner's name. 'Scrote' is the rudest and is mainly used by security and punishment-block screws, as well as a lot of landing screws. It's short for 'scrotum' and a term of abuse used heavily by the armed forces and the police as well, as in 'Get behind your door, you horrible little scrote!'. To a lot of people in uniform, the non-uniformed population are nothing more than scrotes. Let's face it, your outlook on life has to be tinged with more than a touch of bitterness when you resort to describing those around you as nothing more than flesh bags full of bollocks! Prison officers have a motto, 'Happiness is door-shaped', which means they are happy when every prisoner in the jail is locked behind their cell door. A typical exchange between a screw and a con in prison may sound something like this:

Con: Oi, guv, what's the apple with my peter? I'm feeling tom and need to get in my flowery but there's a gang of kangas giving me a **spin**. [Excuse me, officer, what's going on in my cell? I'm feeling quite ill and need to get in but there are several officers searching it.]
Screw: Wind yer neck in, fella. The **DST** are doing LBBs in there, so stop being a **numpty** or I'll stick the red pen on your page 16 and get you put on **Basic**. [Stop bothering me. The Dedicated Search Team are checking Locks, Bolts and Bars, so be patient or I'll write you up and have you put on the Basic regime.]

'Peter' in criminal and prison slang dates back to the Victorian era, when it was used as a word for anything that was bound by heavy locks, so, for example, a safe, as well as a prison cell. The reasoning was that in paintings and statues Saint Peter is depicted holding a large bunch of keys – to heaven – so anything that could be opened with a key was named after him. The con also uses 'spin' for a search by police, customs or prison officers. The word comes from the fact that they tend to move everything and never clean up the mess they make, so the place looks as though it has been spun around at top speed.

The most common word for a prison officer is 'screw', from the days of the 'separate system', when prisoners were forced to carry out hard labour in prisons, such as walking the treadmill or picking oakum from rope, and most of the labour was done behind the cell door or in specially built compartments so that prisoners couldn't see each other. One hard-labour punishment was known as 'the crank': a large wooden crank handle inside the cell was attached to a counter outside it. Prisoners were told to turn the crank a certain number of times each day (sometimes it could take fourteen hours to achieve this) and each turn would be registered on the counter. A screw on the outside of the door could be used to adjust the amount of effort needed to turn the crank. Some jailors, or turnkeys, would delight in turning the screw to make the work that much harder for the prisoner, and these turnkeys became known as screws.

'Screw' remains the slang template for prison officers, but endless variations have evolved over the years, most of them revolving around rhyming slang popular at the time. For example, in the 1970s *Scooby Doo* was a popular children's television cartoon, so screws became known as 'scoobies' (Scooby Doo = screw), as in 'Oi, Knuckles, call that scooby and get him to un-Chubb my peter, will you?' Other variations are 'fourbe' (four-by-two, a carpenter's measure of wood), 'penny' (penny chew) and the ubiquitous 'kanga' (kangaroo), which is very much in vogue at the moment. ('Fourbe' and 'penny' are also used as rhyming slang for 'Jew'.)

Different regions of the country have different slang terms for prison officers. In prisons in the north-east they're known as 'long-tails' (rats), in Liverpool as 'the Germans' (an allusion, of course, to the most hated enemy in two world wars and many international football matches), and in the south they are sometimes called 'roaches'. I think we can safely assume that there's no love lost between the prison guard and their charges. A lot of the general public have no experience of prisons other than what they read in the tabloids or see on the telly. *Porridge*, the 1970s sitcom, is usually their first port of call. There are often stories in the red tops about 'holiday camp' jails in which smug cons are served smoked salmon and quince by servile warders as they lie in luxury watching Sky TV . . . or something like that. Well, let's scotch that one right here: prisons, in reality, are brutal cesspits where the murder rate is seven times higher than it is 'outside'. Lots of people die in our prisons, and still more become insane and are quietly sectioned under the Mental Health Act. On the whole, the atmosphere is one of despair.

At the turn of the twenty-first century the prison system began to introduce **ICE** (in-cell electricity), which led to in-cell television being standard in most prisons. Prisoners can 'hire' a small-screen portable TV for between £1 and £1.50 per week and, considering the average prison wage is £7 per week, that's a sizable chunk of their income, when they must also purchase phone credits, toiletries, smoking requisites, stationery, stamps and tinned food in order to supplement the meagre prison diet. The televisions were bought in bulk by the prison system at around £25 each, so the money accrued from the rentals represents a very profitable return for the Ministry of Justice. In-cell television has been responsible for a decrease in violence in prisons, and the reason is simple: before this, prisoners could be locked in their cells for up to twenty-three hours a day. They could read (according to official statistics from the Bromley Briefings and the Howard League for Penal Reform, up to two-thirds of prisoners have the reading and writing skills of children under the age of ten) or listen to the radio, if they had one (although, for some unfathomable reason, only medium- or long-wave radios were allowed, not FM). If neither of these appealed – and, even if they did – prisoners spent a lot of their time shouting insults at each other through the cell windows. This would inevitably, in some cases, lead to violence as soon as the prisoners were let out of their cells and able to get at each other. In prison parlance, the prisoners who shout abuse and threats from their cell windows are known as **window warriors** and are mostly held in contempt by other prisoners. In my own experience, window warriors were responsible for around 30 per cent of violence in local prisons before the introduction of in-cell TV in the late 1990s. Nowadays, when cells are unlocked prisoners are eager to converse about programmes they may have seen on the telly during **bang-up** (any period spent locked in a cell). As a result, there's certainly less early-morning violence in prisons. Before televisions were introduced to the prison system there was a roaring trade in hand-held, battery-operated tellies which would sometimes be smuggled in by prison staff for a price. The slang word for a telly in those days was 'custard' (custard and jelly = telly), as in "Ere, any chance of a go on your custard during bang-up?'. Some people earned a lucrative penny by renting out their illegal custard. The going rate was either three joints (cannabis cigarettes) or half an ounce of tobacco to use someone's custard for a night.

You can get almost anything on the prison black market as long as you have the financial wherewithal. Some people – in some cases, prison staff – can earn a small fortune supplying things which prisoners would find hard to get their hands on otherwise. For example, a throwaway mobile phone that costs less than a 'cockle' (corrupted rhyming slang: cock and hen = ten) on **The Out** (the world outside prison) can fetch up to £300 once it's been smuggled on to the prison landings. Such a phone is often called a 'dog' (dog and bone = phone) or a 'moby' (short for 'mobile'), and smuggling them into prison is a growing business. Being in possession of a mobile phone inside has recently been made a criminal offence punishable by up to two years. I can understand some of the reasons behind HMP not wanting prisoners to have access to unregistered phones – i.e. intimidating witnesses, running a criminal business, etc. . . . – but these things can be achieved by any prisoner who has visits from friends and acquaintances. Banning things that allow the prisoner not to use the overpriced services offered by the prisons seem to be the Prison Service's default setting. Some prisoners, believe it or not, use illegal mobile phones to keep in touch with their families. Use of a prison phone can be charged at more than ten pence a minute. Also, there is a limit to how much a prisoner can spend on phone units per week, usually around £20 (which doesn't last long if you have to phone a mobile outside). The Ministry of Justice and the Prison Service pay great lip-service to their claim of wanting prisoners to maintain family ties, but at the same time you could say they're cashing in by overcharging. Plus – and it's a big plus – conversations held on prison phones are recorded and may be analysed by security officers and the prison's police liaison officer. Think about it: how would you feel knowing that every word you said to your loved ones – children, parents, friends – was potentially going to be scrutinized by uniformed officials? It's natural for prisoners to want to use a phone where they don't feel they have to watch every word.

So, what are the various prisons in this country really like? Well, as an ex-'guest' for over three decades, I wouldn't give you ten bob (that's fifty pence in today's money) for the lot of them. That said, some of them are interesting to read about, if not to live in, so let's take a look behind the high walls and razor-wired fences of HMP.

43OP

43OP is the prison rule by which a prisoner may request to be segregated from the rest of the prison population for their own safety. The initials 'OP' stand for 'Own Protection', which denotes that the prisoner has requested protection rather than the authorities segregating them against their will. In recent years, Rule 43 has been replaced by Rule 45, but most prisoners still refer to the old rule in conversation. Since the change, it's also known as being 'on the numbers'.

See Cab caller

86

86 is prison slang for a sex offender whose crimes are so horrific that he deserves to be 'on the numbers' twice. It comes from the old Prison Rule 43 which was used to segregate sex offenders from other prisoners: 2 x 43 = 86. Prisoners such as paedophiles and child killers will all be classed as 86s by the majority of the prison population. The Prison Rule 45OP ('OP' stands for 'Own Protection') has replaced the old Rule 43, so I suppose a modern-day 86 would now be upgraded to a 90.

See 43OP, Cucumbers, Home Office numbers, Nonce

A1

On reception into prison every prisoner will be examined by the prison doctor and classified according to what form of labour they're fit for. The standard fitness classification is **A1** (fit for all labour). The examination is cursory, to say the least, and unless you have any visible physical disability your file will be stamped 'A1'. The examination might be nothing more than the doctor looking in at you through the spyhole in a cell door and declaring you fit and healthy without having spoken a word to you. Sometimes the doctor will ask, 'Are you fit?'; an affirmative answer could have you working at anything from digging holes to putting washers on bolts for ten pence per thousand in the prison workshop.

See Quack

ABLUTIONS

Ablutions is one of those quaint Victorian words you hardly ever hear in the modern world – except in prisons. To be 'at your ablutions' means to wash, shave, use the toilet, etc. It's still in use because a large proportion of English prisons date from the Victorian era and still have the original signs on the doors, and ABLUTIONS is still the sign above communal bathrooms, or 'recesses', in various prisons. The rule book for the old juvenile **borstals** and **DCs** (detention centres) stressed that trainees, as young prisoners were euphemistically described, had to perform their ablutions each morning before the breakfast bell. Failure to do so was cause for disciplinary action, usually a swift kick in the arse and the loss of two days' remission.

See Borstal, DC

ADAS

ADAs, or Additional Days Added, is the new name for what used to be called loss of remission. The breach of any prison rule that results in **adjudication** before the governor or an independent adjudicator can be punished by ADAs. These days are added to an existing prison sentence and have to be served after the initial sentence is finished.
See Adjudication

ADJUDICATION

An **adjudication** is a disciplinary hearing chaired by a prison governor or independent adjudicator to deal with any breach of prison rules or regulations by a prisoner. The prisoner receives a charge sheet outlining the charge before being marched into the adjudication room. The evidence is then read out by the charging officer and the prisoner is asked to plead guilty or not guilty. The prisoner may then be found guilty and given an **award** by the presiding official. This award can be anything from a caution to loss of remission (now known as **ADAs**), loss of wages, a fine or a period in solitary confinement. Prisoners mostly refer to adjudications as **kangaroo courts**. At the time of writing, there are twenty-five offences for which a prisoner can face adjudication. There is an apocryphal tale amongst prisoners about an inmate at HMP Wandsworth accusing the charging officer of lying about his evidence on adjudication. The governor said, 'If my officers tell me you were riding a motorbike around the landings, the only thing I need to know is where you got the petrol from.' The governor will generally believe the charging officer over the prisoner in adjudications.
See Award, Block, Fit-up (p. 106), Frame (p. 106), Nicking

ADMIN

Admin is how almost everyone in prison refers to the administration block, which is invariably run by female civilians. An essential part of every prisoner's daily life, the admin block and its workers deal with all the paperwork, including the calculation of sentences, the issuing of parole and release dates, money and wages, and the booking and issuing of visiting orders, among many other things. Admin workers are never seen by the prisoners, and this has led to a long-standing rumour that there is actually no such thing as admin and that all paperwork issues from a massive super-computer kept in the bowels of the Home Office. This is obviously untrue because that which does not have a heart, a conscience or a soul will surely have no need of bowels.

ADVANCE

An **advance** is given on a prisoner's reception into prison. It's a credit note for the canteen and will enable new prisoners to purchase items such as tobacco, phone credits or toiletries. The advance is never more than £5 and is automatically deducted from a prisoner's pay at the rate of fifty pence a week.

AFCS

AFCs, or Accommodation Fabric Checks, must be carried out in every cell of every prison at least once a day. They involve at least one screw visiting the cells and physically checking that there are no holes or tunnels being dug or bars being sawn through. The screws also check that the lights and emergency cell bells are working properly.

Anything suspicious, such as contraband, or any suspicious behaviour will be reported to the Security Department immediately or be written up on an SIR (Security Information Report), depending on its urgency and seriousness. AFCs became the norm after a much-publicised escape from the Special Secure Unit (SSU) at HMP Brixton in 1980, when three Category A men, including IRA active-service-unit volunteer Gerard Tuite, broke through the walls of three cells over a period of days. Tuite escaped along with London robber and gangland hitman Jimmy Moody and armed robber Jimmy Thompson. Tuite (who was claimed to have been responsible for at least eighteen bombings), Moody and Thompson dropped into a yard and then used abandoned scaffold boards to scale the fifteen-foot perimeter wall. Tuite's escape led to the police issuing 16,500 'wanted' posters picturing him under the heading 'TERRORIST ALERT. THIS MAN MUST BE CAUGHT'. Tuite was arrested in the Irish Republic two years later and sentenced to ten years for possession of explosives. Jimmy Moody was never recaptured and was shot dead in a pub in North London eighteen years after the escape. Thompson, who had been on trial for security-van robberies, gave himself up after two weeks, as the jury at his trial (which had carried on in his absence) came back with verdicts of not guilty on all counts. He handed himself in to the authorities and was given three years for the escape.

ALLOCATION

Every time a prisoner is transferred between prisons he has to go through the **allocation** process. In theory, unless a prisoner is being **ghosted**, or 'shanghaied', the Observation, Classification and Allocation (OCA) Department has to take lots of factors into account, such as crime, length of sentence, special medical needs, distance from family, the category of the prisoner and anything else on their record that might make them unsuitable for the move. In my opinion, though, it's often only the prisoner's security classification that's considered, and the prisoner is sent wherever there's a prison space that needs filling. If you're a Londoner, I'd say you can almost guarantee you'll be allocated to a jail in Birmingham, Manchester or Cardiff. *See Ghosted*

ANKLE-BREAKERS

Ankle-breakers are the uneven, jagged pieces of masonry fitted to the base of the outside wall of a prison, a security precaution designed to make escape without injury difficult for any prisoner who manages to scale the wall and hopes to jump or drop down outside.

APP

The **app**, or written application to give it the full title, is one of the ways by which the British prison system contributes to the annihilation of the rainforests and the gradual destruction of the planet. Almost anything you might want to know in prison is handled by way of the app. There's even an appointed hour every morning in every prison in this country which is dedicated to the writing, submitting and distribution of apps. If, for example, you are in need of toilet roll, you must fill out an app form and submit it to the relevant member of staff. Depending on what it is that you want, your app will be passed to, say, the wing manager or a governor, who will approve your request, or not. If your app is approved, it will be passed

along the line to the relevant department. In the case of toilet roll, the app goes to the storeman, who will add his comments and then pass it on to the cleaning officer, who will pass it to one of the inmate cleaners, who will then issue (or not) your toilet roll. In some prisons this process takes so long you'd be better off wiping your arse with the app in the first place. (Incidentally, in prison, each prisoner's toilet-paper ration is six sheets a day.)
See John Wayne

ARAMARK

Aramark plc was one of the main companies that took over the running of prison canteens after the partial privatization of the prison system. It's an American company and is universally hated by prisoners for what they believe are its extortionate prices, lack of choice and charging for items they have not supplied.

ARSE BANDIT

An **arse bandit** is a predatory homosexual who will take what he wants, by force if necessary. In prison these men are usually housed on the protection wings with the sex offenders.

ARSE-LICKER

An **arse-licker** is any prisoner who hangs around the screws hoping to gain favourable treatment, such as getting a decent prison job, home leave, parole, etc. Detested by other prisoners and always suspected of **grassing**, these prisoners have no shame and more front than Brighton.
See Office cat

ARSONIST

There seems to be an abundance of **arsonists** behind the walls of our prisons and mental-health hospitals, and they come in many varieties. Arsonists may do it for money, i.e. torching a business for the insurance, or for revenge, which, although they should never be condoned, you can at least understand the reasons behind, but there are some arsonists who get 'turned on' by lighting fires, and these are harder to understand. If you're in prison, it goes without saying you should avoid having this kind of arsonist as a cell mate. Anyone who can only have a wank when the flames are dancing is going to be a serious liability in a cell the size of the average family bathroom.

ARYAN BROTHERHOOD

The **Aryan Brotherhood** is a white supremacist gang that is very big in American prisons. Its members deal drugs, murder, take on 'hits' (killing people for money) and, generally, engage in gang activities. Since the rise of the Muslim Brotherhood in UK prisons, the Aryan Brotherhood is making inroads into the British prison system. There are still only a handful of members, but it's catching on gradually as white prisoners find themselves increasingly isolated by Muslim gangs. The original Aryan Brotherhood was an Irish gang which formed for protection after the desegregation of the Californian prison system led to a spate of murders and stabbings. This is why all Aryan Brotherhood members have a tattoo of an Irish shamrock somewhere on their bodies.

ASPIRIN WATER

Aspirin water is simply aspirin dissolved in water: a cure-all, according to prison medics. Since the introduction of Mandatory Drug Testing in 1994 any painkiller or other drug that may show up in a urine test will only be issued with the approval of a doctor in consultation with the Security Department, so aspirin water is the main medication offered to sick or injured prisoners. The other choice is nothing.

See Quack

ASSISTED PRISON VISITS (APVS)

APVs is a national scheme whereby families of prisoners who are on low income or claiming benefits can receive financial help in order to visit a family member who is in prison.

ASSOCIATION

Association is another one of those quaint words used daily by the prison system and is any period of the day when prisoners are allowed to mix with each other. In most prisons the association area is on the ground floor of the wing, where there'll be a communal television set and tables on which prisoners can play cards, chess or backgammon. Some prisons also feature a small pool table, table-tennis table or table football. The duration of association time varies from prison to prison and, in the past, some prisons, such as HMP Wandsworth, took great pride in providing no association time for prisoners. (These were – and are – known as '**bang-up** nicks' because of the amount of time prisoners spend locked up in their cells.)

Up until the 1980s, in some prisons, association time had to be earned by good behaviour and there was a minimum six-month bang-up period before association was allowed. Since 1994 there have been payphones in every prison and the association period is when prisoners can use these phones to speak to family, friends and legal advisers.

AVs

AVs are Accumulated Visits. Prisoners who are being held in a prison far away from their home area and so find it difficult to receive visitors can save up, or accumulate, up to six months' worth of visiting orders, then request a temporary transfer to a prison closer to their home area in order to have visits. The transfer will be for a maximum period of twenty-eight days and whether this is granted depends on the behaviour and record of the prisoner and whether there is space in the **local prison**. During the AV period the prisoner may be allowed a visit every day, depending on how many VOs he has accumulated and whether space is available in the visiting hall. AV prisoners and their visitors are subject to the same security procedures as any other. During times of prison overcrowding the AV facility is usually the first thing to go. Despite the prison system's mealy-mouthed lip service to the importance of family contact, a prisoner's contact with their family is essential only as long as it coincides with the Ministry of Justice's financial and warehousing policies.

AWARD

For some archaic reason, prisoners are always given an **award** (punishment) on **adjudication**. Awards vary from a caution to loss of remission and solitary confinement.

'Award' seems to be another one of those words that has a strange context when used by prison officials.
See Adjudication

THE AWAYS

The aways are members of a criminal gang or family who have been jailed and are serving their sentence. Some might say that there is no honour among thieves, but whenever the gang or family outside nick a nice few quid, there will always be a share put aside for the aways. Sometimes benefit parties are held to raise money for the aways and the proceeds are sent to them in prison or handed to their families.

BACCY TINS

Baccy tins is the name given to prison-issue plastic shoes, because they are square-toed and resemble a pair of tobacco tins. Real tobacco tins (that is, tins for storing tobacco) are very popular in prison where, due to the cost of **tailor-made** cigarettes, most smokers tend to roll their own. There is a big market for decorated tins, either painted or covered in matchsticks or wood. If you wear baccy tins in prison, you must expect to be singled out for light-hearted abuse and insults.
See Adidas sex-case, Fila c***s, Jack the Rippers, Nigerian Nikes

BANANA SUIT

The **banana suit** is prison-issue high-visibility clothing worn by **E men** (those who have escaped or attempted to escape from custody). It usually consists of a two-piece blue denim uniform with a broad bright-yellow stripe running down it. The banana suit is also issued as a one-piece bib-and-brace overall with the same yellow stripe. The idea behind it is that E men can be easily picked out of the crowd and observed. Also, should the wearer of a banana suit escape, he'll be easier to spot outside – or at least until he changes clothes. In the early 1990s prison-issue banana suits could fetch up to £100 on the outside from the rave crowd, as the yellow stripe was luminous under strobe lights and, apparently, looked great when whoever was wearing the suit was dancing. This proved a nice little earner for the staff and cons who worked in the prison clothing stores. Cons would smuggle them out of jail packed inside stuffed toys and via the prison hobbies class. The banana suit was all but replaced in the late 1990s by a one-piece coverall made up of different-coloured panels. This is worn by E men and Category A men during transfer between prisons. Not as popular as the banana suit, possibly because of its unflattering cut, or maybe due to the decline in popularity of the acid-house rave scene, it was quickly nicknamed the 'Noddy suit' by prisoners (though most people who have seen it tend to agree that it bears more of a resemblance to the attire of 1950s children's puppet Andy Pandy than to the snazzy two-piece worn by Enid Blyton's racist pixie.)

See E men

BANG-UP

Bang-up is prison slang for any time spent 'behind your door' in a cell. It was originally shouted by screws at the end of association period – 'Bang up! Get behind your doors, bang-up time!' – and refers to cell doors banging shut. It's now a phrase used by cons and screws alike. Another meaning of this phrase, not so commonly used now, is to inject drugs, usually heroin. So if you're a junkie and new to prison, don't get too excited when you hear that seven-thirty is bang-up time. The term is also used by ex-prisoners, as in 'Yeah, just got out of bang-up'.

See Window warriors

BAR L

Bar L is the nickname of Scotland's most famous/infamous (delete as appropriate) prison, HMP Barlinnie. Scottish prisoners sometimes also call it 'the Ranch', apparently because it's full of cowboys!

BARMY WING

Every prison will have a **barmy wing**, where mentally ill prisoners are kept. Once upon a time, barmy wings were officially known as prison hospital wings, but then came the rebranding of prisons in the mid-1990s, after the Strangeways riots, and the hospital wing became known as the healthcare centre in the push to gentrify and sanitize the public's perception of jails. The government, fully aware of the bad publicity surrounding the Woolf Report into the riots, which spoke of a run-down, dilapidated and brutal prison system, made a few cosmetic changes, such as renaming the punishment block the 'segregation unit', solitary confinement 'segregation', and so on. But prisoners are not great lovers of change for its own sake so they still call the healthcare centre the barmy wing.

BARON

Baron is a bit of an old-fashioned term for the prisoner who would run the black market on each prison wing. It dates back to before the 1970s, when tobacco was the only currency in prison and whoever had access to large amounts of 'snout' could virtually control their wing. Each 'snout baron' would run their little fiefdom as they saw fit, setting credit terms, punishments for late payers and **knockers**, and exchange rates for snout and money. A prime fictional example of an old-school prison snout baron is the character Harry Grout from the BBC television comedy series *Porridge*. Incidentally, in modern prison parlance 'Harry Grout' has become rhyming slang for 'snout', a case of life imitating art if ever there was one. Barons usually earned enough from their dealings to do their bit of 'sparrow' in comfort and were left alone by the screws because they were seen as a necessary evil. In some cases, the authorities might ask the baron to use their influence to intervene when there was unrest brewing. Barons were universally envied and hated by other prisoners because of the control they exercised, and had to keep a constant eye out for coups by the serfs and takeover bids by would-be barons. As Billy Shakespeare once said, 'Uneasy lies the head that wears the crown.'

See Knockers (p. 292)

BARRICADES

Putting up **barricades** is one of the traditional tools of the recalcitrant and subversive prisoner. The most common place for a barricade is in the cell: various items of cell furniture stacked in front of the door make it difficult for a C&R (Control and Restraint – the staff heavy mob) **extraction team** to get in. Prisoners will barricade for various reasons – to delay or postpone transfer to a worse prison, as a protest against a real or perceived problem, as a 'cry for help', out of insanity or just for the fun of it. The prison authorities take barricading very seriously, as the whole prison has to be locked down in order to deal with the incident. There are specially trained negotiators at most prisons, who will take control of the situation almost immediately and try to talk the prisoner out. Michael Peterson, aka Charles Bronson, 'Britain's Most Dangerous Prisoner' (according to the tabloid media), has been involved in many barricades and hostage-takings.

See Extraction team

BASIC

To be put on **basic** is a punishment for having the wrong attitude rather than for any specific breach of prison rules. It is the lowest rung on the three-tier Incentive & Earned Privilege scheme (IEP), introduced by the Home Secretary Michael Howard in 1993 as part of his 'austere but fair' prison policy. Every prisoner starts out on the middle rung – standard level – and can be promoted to **enhanced** level or demoted to basic level. Prisoners on basic have to wear prison uniforms and have fewer privileges than other prisoners, including fewer family visits and a lot more **bang-up** time. Each prison practises its own refinements on the three-tier system, and some are more draconian and spiteful than others in the way they treat basic prisoners. This 'punishment' (though the prison system claims it isn't one) is frequently used by prison staff to 'adjust the attitude' of prisoners who they consider to have a bit too much spirit. In effect, the three-tier system has created a class system amongst prisoners, with basic being the underclass.

See Enhanced

BATTER SQUAD

The **batter squad** is any bunch or gang of screws who will attack a prisoner mob-handed. There will be a batter squad in most punishment blocks or segregation units, and they believe it's their job to teach cheeky or subversive prisoners a lesson by beating them into submission. Some of them are psychopaths, some are sadists and some are just plain thugs – HMP is an equal opportunities employer. In 1997, after complaints by many prisoners, backed up by statements from the Board of Visitors (**BOV**), police started an investigation into the behaviour and actions of a large group of prison officers at HMP Wormwood Scrubs, West London. Twenty-seven prison officers at the prison were suspended during the investigation, and six were convicted of torturing and abusing prisoners in the segregation unit at the jail. Three prison officers were sent to prison and a number of prisoners and ex-prisoners were compensated for torture and sexual abuse. There have been many other incidents of abuse by prison officers in prisons up and down the country.

See Extraction team, MUFTI

BEAST

A **beast** is any prisoner in for a sexual offence, especially one involving children. These prisoners are treated like scum and are subject to constant vilification, threats and severe violence from other prisoners, and sometimes from prison staff.

See 86, Bacon (p. 267), Biff/Biffa, Nonce

BED AND BREAKFAST

A night in the punishment block before appearing in front of the governor for **adjudication** is known as **bed and breakfast**, as is an overnight stay in any prison while en route to another one. For example, getting from HMP Parkhurst, on the Isle of Wight, to HMP Dartmoor, in Devon, can take up to three days and involves bed and breakfast at HMP Winchester and HMP Exeter. This was before the prison transport system was privatized and the prison officers' union secured very generous payments and expenses for members who volunteered for escort duties and overnight stays. (Now it can take weeks!) The typical journey from the Isle of Wight prisons (there are three: HMP Albany, HMP Parkhurst and HMP Camp Hill) would hit HMP Winchester, HMP Highpoint (known as 'HMP Knifepoint' because of the number of stabbings there) in Suffolk, HMYOI Onley in Warwickshire, HMP Bristol, HMP Channings Wood in Devon, HMP Exeter and, finally, HMP Dartmoor. For the prisoners on transfer it was three days of rattling up and down A roads in an extremely uncomfortable prison transport, being heavily chained and having overnight stays in grim local jails – but for the screws it was the chance of a 'foreign piss-up' and plenty of overtime.

BEGGAR'S LAGGING

Beggar's lagging is two months' imprisonment under the Vagrancy Act.

BEHAVIOURAL WARNING

A **behavioural warning** is one given by the prison authorities to any prisoner whose behaviour they consider unacceptable. If a prisoner receives two written behavioural warnings, he will automatically be placed on **basic** level. A prisoner doesn't have to actually breach any prison rule or regulation to receive a behavioural warning, just their 'attitude' is enough.

See Basic

BEIRUT

In a lot of prisons there are 'problem' wings, or landings, which are akin to war zones. The worst place in a prison, apart from the punishment block (brutal) and the prison hospital (mad), is usually the induction wing, invariably known as **Beirut**, or 'the Bronx', because of the noise and the violence. These parts of the prison are normally run down and lack amenities because of the high turnover of prisoners; the population housed in them is transient. They also house loud, violent and, in some cases, mentally ill prisoners and only the most brutal and ignorant staff seem to be chosen to meet the challenge of running them.

See Induction

BENDING UP

Bending up is practised by C&R and **extraction teams** and involves incapacitating a prisoner by using a series of painful martial-arts pressure holds. Many prisoners have suffered broken bones and more permanent damage from being bent up. The holds themselves, when administered by two or three screws, cause the prisoner's body to bend out of its normal shape, hence 'bending up'. Bending up is mostly used on prisoners who refuse to cooperate.

See Extraction team

BIB

A **bib** is a brightly coloured nylon vest issued to prisoners in some jails to wear on social visits. The bib is to make prisoners stand out and be easily identifiable amongst their visitors in a crowded hall and is worn for security reasons. The wearing of bibs started to be seriously enforced in high-security prisons (Category A and B jails) after some high-profile 'walk out' escapes from prison visiting rooms. In 1994 a prisoner nicknamed Houdini (for obvious reasons) walked off a visit in HMP Swaleside on the Isle of Sheppey (a Category B prison) and was let out through eight locked gates and doors by staff. Once outside the prison, he walked to a local pub and phoned a taxi. He got clean away and was out for nearly a year. He had been serving ten years for serious armed robberies. The staff laid the blame for their poor security procedures on the fact that prisoners were allowed to wear their own clothes on visits and could not easily be distinguished from the civilian visitors, which led to enforcement of the bib rule. When the escaped prisoner was recaptured he was put into Category B HMP Maidstone. He immediately scaled the twenty-foot wall and escaped again.

BIBLE PAGES

The average wage paid to UK prisoners is £7 per week, so prisoners who smoke have had to learn to be resourceful. There is an abundance of Holy Bibles in prison, due to the propensity of religious zealots to see any atmosphere of misery and desperation as an opportunity for a conversion, and the thin pages of these religious manuals are perfect for roll-ups. Some prisoners who cannot afford to buy rolling papers will roll their tobacco in **bible pages** and smoke the printed word of God along with their cheap shag. The traditional cry of those who smell the burning pages is 'Holy smoke!'

See Burn

BIFF/BIFFA

Biff or **Biffa** is an offensive name for sex offenders. It comes from a character in *Viz*, Biffa Bacon. Biffa Bacon is not a sex offender, but sex offenders have traditionally been known as **bacons**. 'Biff' can also be used to describe a complete idiot, particularly in Scouse slang.

See 86, Bacon (p. 267), Beast, Nonce

BIRD

Serving a prison sentence is known as 'doing your **bird**' (bird lime = time). It dates back to the Victorian era and came about because most prisons had high walls and towers that were invariably covered in bird lime (avian excrement). A short sentence is known as a bit of 'sparrow' (a small bird). 'Do yer bird' is an encouragement to get your head down and do your time without making a fuss, often heard being shouted from cell windows to people who are making too much noise, or to newly arrived prisoners as a dig that they are just starting their sentences.

BIRDMAN

A **birdman** is a prisoner who has served a very long prison sentence or many prison sentences with short breaks of freedom in between, after the 1962 film *Birdman of*

Alcatraz, starring Burt Lancaster as real-life birdman Robert Stroud, a convicted killer who became an avian expert while in prison.
See Bird

BIT

To do a **bit** is to serve a prison sentence, normally quite a short one, as in 'Yeah, just got out of **The Ville**, done a twelve-week bit for **hoisting**'. This is an Americanism that has made its way into British usage through film and television.
See Carpet

BLADE

A **blade** can be any sharpened implement with a cutting edge or a point used for inflicting injury, or sometimes death, in prison. Inside, almost anything can be made into a blade. Favourites are tin lids (usually from cans of tuna, which can be bought in the prison canteen), scissors (broken in half to make two blades) and even a piece of hard plastic or perspex. Plastic, sharpened by being rubbed against brickwork or concrete, is a particular favourite in top-security prisons, as it does not show up on the metal detectors, and the screws in such prisons carry **wands** (hand-held metal detectors) in order to check prisoners for weapons without actually searching them.

BLANKET JOB

A **blanket job** is one of the ways prisoners deal with any 'undesirables' that end up in their midst – sex offenders, informers, granny bashers, etc. It involves creeping up on the victim and throwing a prison blanket over their head before dishing out a stabbing or severe beating. The blanket serves three purposes: it stops the victim being able to identify his attackers; it prevents the attackers getting blood or other forensic evidence on their clothing; and it increases the fear and disorientation of the victim.

See Mattress Job (p. 260), *Sheeting* (p. 261)

BLOCK

The **block** is the common name for the punishment block, where prisoners are held in solitary confinement for any infraction of prison rules. Most blocks are cold and dirty with no redeeming features or comforts. The prisoner will spend twenty-three hours a day locked in a small cell with nothing except a plastic **pisspot**. Some block staff have a bad reputation for brutality. If a screw is deemed 'a bit too quick with his stick' while working in his normal location – if he is involved in one too many 'incidents' – he will normally be sent to the block to work off his frustrations. In 1997 twenty-seven screws at HMP Wormwood Scrubs, most of them working in the punishment block, were suspended from duty for violently and sexually abusing prisoners. Six of them were convicted of criminal offences and sentenced to prison terms. Witnesses spoke of a 'torture room' with padded rubber walls in the block where they would be taken to be assaulted. Many blocks in prisons around the country have similar or worse reputations than the block at HMP Wormwood Scrubs. In recent, years the prison system has attempted to sanitize the public perception of the punishment block by rebranding it as the 'segregation unit', but prisoners still call it the

block and it's still the place they are taken to be punished.
See Chokey

BLUE BOXES

Since the introduction of 'volumetric control' in prisons in 1995, prisoners have to be able to fit all their possessions into two **blue boxes** supplied by the prison. This includes bedding, clothing, canteen goods, books, magazines, legal paperwork and toiletries. Any item that does not fit into the boxes is confiscated. The boxes used by all prisons are of standard size and issue.

BLUES

Blues was the common name for the uniform worn by all convicted prisoners up until the mid-1990s. It consisted of a blue denim jacket and jeans. The colour blue was used to distinguish them from those on remand and yet to be convicted, who wore either **browns** or their own clothes. Both uniforms were replaced by 'Spider-Man suits' for those who could not, or would not, wear their own clothes.
See Banana suit, Browns

BLUE STRIPES

The prison-issue shirt with **blue stripes** was part of the standard prison uniform before the rules were relaxed to allow even convicted prisoners to wear their own clothes. The reason the British Government changed their policy on this was because IRA prisoners had refused to wear prison uniform from the start (they classed themselves as political prisoners rather than criminals). IRA prisoners wearing only prison-issue blankets was an embarrassment to the government, so they came up with the rather devious solution of letting all prisoners wear their own clothes so as not to be seen to be giving in to the IRA. Problem solved. British prisoners, therefore, can thank the Irish Republican Army for the fact that they no longer have to wear uniform. Blue-striped shirts – made of 100 per cent cotton and with thin light-blue stripes on a white background – were the only popular part of the original prison uniform and were a favourite both in and out of prison. Up until the turn of the twenty-first century, prison-issue blue-striped shirts could command prices of up to £50 outside (as long as the shirt had the official HMP stamp on the inside front panel). Many prisoners made extra money by smuggling them out of prison, usually stuffed inside soft toys they had made in the hobbies class, and selling them to market traders, particularly in places like Camden Market and Petticoat Lane, for resale to the public. A typical prison-made teddy bear could contain up to ten blue-striped shirts. It was a nice little earner for the newly released prisoner. Inside, there was also a huge black market for altered and tailored blue-stripes – with short sleeves, breast pockets and granddad collars being the favourites. Every prison tailor shop had at least two prisoners who could modify blue-stripes, and they earned more from this than from their official job, even though any prisoner caught altering or modifying prison property could be **nicked** and lose up to fourteen days' remission. Any prisoner caught in possession of altered clothing would get the same. That said, most staff would turn a blind eye. Eventually, the prison system, seeing an opportunity for an earner and knowing it would be almost impossible to stop prisoners smuggling the shirts out, decided to cash in and sell the shirts themselves through their own outlets. Unfortunately, whether they flooded the market or people no longer wanted blue stripes because there was no longer a frisson of illegality about them, the price of a blue-striped shirt dropped to £12. There are still plenty of blue stripes around in the prison system today, but they are all old stock and no longer in demand. This piece of prison-issue clothing has become a design classic.

BODY BELT

A **body belt** is a form of restraint used in prisons in order to control and incapacitate violent prisoners. It consists of a broad leather belt that locks around a prisoner's waist, with a handcuff on each side of the belt in which the prisoner's wrists are secured. Once a prisoner is locked into a body belt they cannot lift their hands above waist height. This is a very vulnerable position to be in, and many prisoners, including Charles Bronson, have complained of being attacked by screws while they were helpless in the body belt. The body-belt guidelines say that this type of restraint should not be used on a prisoner for longer than twelve hours, but this time limit is often abused with the excuse of 'exceptional circumstances', the favourite get-out clause of most rules and regulations enforced by prisons.

BOILER

Almost every prison wing or landing has a **boiler**, a machine which dispenses boiling water so that prisoners can make hot drinks (since the prison system no longer supplies **diesel**). Sometimes, the boiling water from these machines is used to scald or **jug** other prisoners. The prison system considers these activities and the horrific injuries that result from them a lot cheaper and far less work than having to bring hot water or tea around to each cell at intervals during the day, which is how it used to be done before communal boilers were fitted in the mid-1990s. 'Boiler' can also be used as a slang word for an old and ugly woman who is still sexually active, as in 'I ended up lagging drunk and rumped some old boiler out of the club'.

See Diesel, Jugging (p. 259)

BOLTED BEDS

In most modern prisons the beds are bolted to the floor. The reason for these **bolted beds** is to prevent prisoners using them to **barricade** themselves into their cell. However, this would be almost impossible in most modern jails, because the cells are built with 'reversible cell doors', that is, doors that can also be opened outwards by removing a restraining pin.

See Barricades

BOMB SQUAD

In 1997 the British Government announced to the world that slopping out, the practice of prisoners having to use a pot or bucket as a toilet and then empty it communally every morning, had ended. Before this, a lot of prisoners had to resort to defecating in newspapers laid out on the floor of their cell and then making it into a 'parcel' and throwing it out of the cell window. These parcels were known as 'bombs' or 'shit parcels'. So every prison had its **bomb squad** – a group of prisoners whose job it was to clean the yard and remove the bombs that would inevitably litter the ground around each prison wing. Escorted by an unlucky screw and armed with gloves, shovels, stiff brooms and a bin on a trolley, the bomb squad would deal with a daily labour on a par with Hercules' cleaning of the Augean Stables. Some of the shit bombs would be well wrapped, but the contents of others, which had come from the higher windows, would be splattered all over the concrete yards. Being on the bomb squad was a much-hated job, and no one but **divs**, **hobbits** and 'grovellers' would do it. Since 1997, most prison cells have had toilets fitted, though to this day there are ten prisons that are still slopping out and still have a bomb squad.

See Div (p. 279)

BOOB

Boob is another word for prison, as in 'I've just spent three **moon** in the boob', indicated that being in prison was a temporary mistake or boob.

BOOSTERS

Boosters are a means by which prison psychologists can keep on milking the cash cow of the prison system long after their 'work' with the prisoner is done. If a prisoner completes one of the many Offending Behaviour Programmes (OBPs) – for example, Enhanced Thinking Skills, Cognitive Thinking, CALM or the Sex Offenders Treatment Programme, etc. – early in his sentence, he may be ordered to take a booster course before being released, or even afterwards, as a condition of parole or licence.

BOOT ROOM

A **boot room** is a good beating, generally administered by a group of prisoners. It comes from the old juvenile Detention Centres and **borstal** institutions, which usually had a windowless room at the end of each wing where prisoners had to store their work boots on racks so as not to trail dirt on to the highly polished floors of the wings. The screws rarely entered the boot rooms, and this was where prisoners would be attacked, or scores settled, away from the prying eyes of the authorities. The term is now taken to mean any blind spot on a prison wing where attacks take place.

See Stabbers' Alley (p. 261)

BOO YAKKA!

Boo yakka! is an exclamation of excitement, meant to resemble the sound of a gunshot, often heard shouted from cell windows by prisoners of West Indian origin and **jafakens**. You hear it quite a lot when music or live sport is broadcast on television or the radio. It's a verbal throwback to the Jamaican custom of firing guns into the air at sound-system music gigs.

See Brixton Gunshots, Jafaken

BORSTAL

The **borstal** system originated in 1902 and was named after the first juvenile prison of this kind, which was situated next to the village of Borstal in Kent. This prison became His Majesty's Borstal Institution Rochester. By the 1920s there were borstal institutions in many parts of the country. Borstals took boys between the ages of fourteen and twenty-one and subjected them to military-style training – lots of physical work, exercise and kit polishing. The original borstal sentence was called a 'nine to three', meaning you could serve as little as nine months or as much as three years, and borstal trainees were able to earn maximum remission for good behaviour and compliance with the regime. This changed at the end of the 1960s, when the sentence became a minimum of six months and a maximum of two years – a 'six to two'. Closed borstals (as opposed to open borstals, which were for non-violent, low-risk petty offenders) were no more than **gladiator schools** for young offenders and universities of crime for up-and-coming young criminals, and many graduates of the borstal system went on to become worse criminals in adult life. The most realistic, and perhaps only, depiction of the borstal system on film was the 1979 movie *Scum* starring Ray Winstone, among many other young British actors who went on to become familiar faces on the Brit Flick scene in the 1980s and '90s. It was Ray Winstone's first film. Originally commissioned as a television drama, the resulting film was deemed too brutal and violent to show without an X certificate and so went into cinemas. There was also a borstal system which took violent and recalcitrant girls between the ages of sixteen and twenty-one, and a film was made about this too, *Scrubbers* (1982). The borstal system was abolished in 1983.

See DC, HMDC, HMYOI

BORSTAL DOT

A **borstal dot** is a spot tattooed in blue ink, usually on the face, that indicates that the person sporting it has been to **borstal**. It was very popular amongst young tearaways in the 1970s. The borstal dot can also be tattooed on the hand, between the index finger and thumb. Another version tattooed on the hand is four dots in a square with one in the middle, which is meant to indicate the four walls of prison and the prisoner inside.

See ACAB (p. 92), Borstal

BOSS

Boss is an informal and indiscriminate form of address used by prisoners to prison officers, mainly in prisons in the Midlands and the North. (Southern prisoners tend to use 'guv'.) Some northerners also use 'boss' as an exclamation of admiration and surprise, as in 'That phone is fucking boss!'.

BOV

The **BOV** (Board Of Visitors) was a supposedly independent body which regularly visited prisons in order to make sure no liberties were being taken with prisoners. Widely detested by the prisoners themselves, however, the BOV mainly consisted of middle-class 'worthies' with plenty of time on their otherwise idle hands, and had a lot more in common with the governor than it did with the wretches whose interests they were supposed to be safeguarding. The independence of the BOV was questionable, as those on it were 'vetted' by the Home Office and directly appointed by the Home Secretary. Until the 1990s the BOV also chaired **adjudications** against prisoners for breaches of prison rules that were considered too serious for the prison governor to deal with. For certain charges – Gross Personal Violence to a Prison Officer, Mutiny and Incitement to Riot – the BOV could take unlimited remission from a prisoner's sentence. This endeared them even less to the prison population they were supposed to be looking after. It has to be said that some BOV members took their hobby seriously, and did on occasion highlight faults within the prison service. In 2001 the name Board Of Visitors was changed to Independent Monitoring Board (IMB), but it will take a lot more than a change of letters before most prisoners will ever fully trust it.

See Batter squad

BREAKFAST PACK

A **breakfast pack** will contain a small box of cereal, a carton containing one-third of a pint of milk, a bread roll, a pat of margarine and a sachet of 'sweet spread'. These packs are distributed every evening in most prisons for the following morning's breakfast, but the food rations are so meagre in most prisons that the breakfast pack is eaten as soon as it's handed out.

BRICKO

HMP Brixton, in South London, has long been known as **Bricko** by its inhabitants. Built in 1820 and originally called the Surrey House of Correction, HMP Brixton was intended to house 175 prisoners. It had a reputation as 'the worst prison in London' in the 1840s (some feat, when you consider that there were seventeen prisons in London at that time), and this reputation became even worse when HMP Brixton became one of the first prisons to introduce the treadwheel. The treadwheel was hard labour, but at least it wasn't pointless 'make-work', as the wheel was used to mill corn.

HMP Brixton was expanded and was housing over 800 prisoners by the 1850s. In 1853 the decsision was made to convert it into a female prison. Later in the mid-nineteenth century a nursery was opened inside for children up to the age of four, and by 1860 the prisoners were allowed to keep their children under sixteen years of age with them in the prison until the end of their sentence.

Between 1882 and 1898 HMP Brixton became a military prison for men and, to this day, it remains a male prison and remand centre. HMP Brixton has provided accommodation for many famous prisoners over the years, including Rolling Stone Mick Jagger (convicted of drug possession), philosopher and activist Bertrand Russell (jailed for pacifism under the Defence of the Realm Act in 1918), disc jockey and presenter Simon Dee (jailed for vandalizing a toilet seat with singer Petula Clark's face painted on it) and James Earl Ray, the man who assassinated Martin Luther King. James Earl Ray escaped to England after the assassination and was arrested in London and remanded to HMP Brixton to await extradition.

Bricko also has a long history of escapes and other scandals. In 1980 three Category A prisoners tunnelled through the walls of their cells on the segregation unit and got clean away. In the early 1970s there was an attempt at mass escape from the prison's C wing, when members of the notorious bank-robbing Wembley Mob hijacked a bin lorry and tried to crash it through the gates. The lorry got jammed and the escape was foiled. Then, in 1974, several prisoners tied up members of staff and escaped from B wing on a Sunday evening when staff numbers were low. They got to the perimeter wall and prison staff released several German Shepherds on them; however, the prisoners had taken fire extinguishers from the wing and fired them at the guard dogs. The powder from them frightened the dogs and drove them back, allowing the prisoners to scale the wall. Once outside the prison, several prisoners hijacked passing vehicles and managed to escape.

See AFCs

BRIDGE

The **bridge** is the connecting walkway between prison landings, and is often used by the screws as a vantage point from which they can survey the wing.

BRIXTON GUNSHOTS

Brixton gunshots is what white prisoners call the often heard noisy exclamations of excitement issued by a minority of young black and wannabe-black prisoners. *See Boo yakka!*

BUCKETING

Bucketing was quite common in UK prisons during the 1980s and '90s. It was (and, in some cases, still is) another weapon in the arsenal of the rebellious and violent prisoners of the top-security-prison estate. Bucketing is normally reserved for a screw or governor who is particularly despised and hated by the prisoner population. It involves several prisoners defecating and urinating into a plastic bucket which is then thrown over a particular member of staff. Sometimes prisoners cut cards or draw straws to choose who does the actual throwing of the bucket, as the authorities class bucketing as a serious assault on staff and will punish accordingly. If you bucket staff in most nicks, you can expect a serious beating by the screws and loss of remission and privileges.

BUG HATCH

On every prison wing there is a **bug hatch** of some description. It's usually a window in the 'medical room' through which medication is dispensed to prisoners. It has been estimated that over 70 per cent of UK prisoners are suffering from two or more mental conditions; add to this the fact that over 80 per cent of the prison population are addicted to drugs or alcohol (according to HMP's own statistics on the introduction of Mandatory Drug Testing in prisons) and also the increasing number of elderly prisoners, and you begin to get an idea of just how much medication is passed out daily in prison. The bug hatch is where the prisoners queue to get their meds and takes its name from the behaviour of mentally ill, the 'bugs' (old American slang for somebody who is not quite right, acting as though they have bugs in their heads; a few American gangsters of the Prohibition era had 'Bugs' as their nickname because of their crazy behaviour – Bugs Moran, Bugsy Siegel, etc.) in the queues.

See Fraggle (p. 282)

BURGLARS

In prison the **burglars** are not, as you might expect, inmates who are in for burglary. In prison slang, burglars are Security or the **DST** (Designated Search Team). They are known as burglars because they can descend on a prisoner's cell any time, day or night, and take anything they want from the cell, anything they consider to be contraband or against prison rules.

See DST, Spin

CAB CALLER

A **cab caller** is someone who needs to get off a wing or out of a prison very quickly as their life or wellbeing is in danger – either because of debt or because they've been 'sussed' as a 'wrong un'. The means of 'calling a cab' differs from person to person. Some prisoners will simply pack their property and go to the safety of the wing office and ask to be placed on protection in the segregation unit. Others, those with a shred of pride left (usually those in debt), will 'kick off', either smashing their cell up or going 'on one' in order to make the screws drag them to the **block**. Once in relative privacy there they will either request protection or simply refuse to go back on to normal location. Refusing to return to a wing will result in a **nicking** under prison rules for disobeying a lawful order, but this does at least give the cab caller the sparse comfort of a nicking to cover their embarrassment at having to run. It's also known as 'gangster's numbers', as the recipient will be housed in the safety of the block yet still be able to keep their pride intact by putting their situation down to the authorities.

See 43OP, Nicking, Home Office numbers

CARPET

A **carpet** is a three-month sentence. Up until the 1960s short-term prisoners generally worked in their cells, and one of the jobs they were given was weaving carpets or mats. It took three months to produce one carpet and so a prison sentence of that duration became known as a carpet.

See Bit

CAT/PUSSY

Up until the 1960s prisoners could still be sentenced to corporal punishment in prison by a visiting magistrate. Serious breaches of prison rules, such as rioting or assaulting prison staff, were punishable by official beatings. If you were sentenced to the **cat**, or **pussy**, you would be beaten on the bare back with a cat o' nine tails, a leather whip with nine separate strands, sometimes weighted. The pussy could draw blood and was a very painful experience. Prisoners were also given strokes with the birch.

CHINA

This term was in widespread use up until the abolition of the **borstal** system in 1983. Your **china** is your best mate (rhyming slang: china plate = mate). It was the done thing in juvenile borstals for kids from the same manor (geographical area) to 'go chinas'. This meant that they would watch each other's back and share whatever they had for the duration of their sentences. The word suddenly went out of vogue when the borstal system was abolished, although it is still used by some London villains of a certain age.

CHIP NET

The **chip net** is the metal mesh safety net strung between each prison landing; it's also known as the suicide net. A lot of the older prisons are up to five levels high and there is always the danger of prisoners falling, being thrown or jumping over the landings. The high-tension metal net is there to make sure that, if this happens, then at least the person will not be killed outright.That said, landing on a metal net from five floors up will still do a lot of damage.

CHOKEY

Chokey usually refers to the punishment block of a prison where prisoners are held in isolation, as in 'Freddie just

got fourteen days' chokey for chinning a screw'. It comes from the Hindi *cauki*, a lock-up.
See Block

CIVVY

In prison parlance a **civvy** can be a **tailor-made** (real, manufactured cigarette), as opposed to a hand-rolled smoke, but it can also describe anyone in the prison who is not part of the staff or prison population – a civilian worker, for example.

CLAIRE RAYNERS

If someone in prison says that your **Claires** are rank, it is not a compliment. It's rhyming slang (Claire Rayners = trainers), after the celebrity agony aunt. In prison and, particularly, in young offender prisons, you can be judged by the make and state of your trainers. A report from the Crown Prosecution Service (CPS) in the 1990s revealed that the trainers worn most commonly by criminals, and especially burglars, are Reebok Classics. This was discovered by analysing footprints left at crime scenes. Reebok Classics are cheap and stylish and, like most trainers, leave a recognizable print.

CLINK

Clink is a somewhat dated term for a prison, in use until the 1970s, after a prison in Southwark which started taking prisoners from the twelfth century and closed only in 1780. The prison was owned by the Bishop of Winchester and stood next to Winchester Palace. It housed both men and women and was one of the first prisons in England. It is said that the name derives from the sounds made by the wrist and leg chains the prisoners had to wear. In 1450 rioters protesting against the Statute of Labourers released all the prisoners and burnt the Clink to the ground. The prison was rebuilt but was then used mainly to imprison heretics; in later years it became a debtors' prison.

These days, The Clink is a prison museum, and in 2008 HMP Highdown in Surrey started up an in-prison restaurant called The Clink, in which serving prisoners can train to become chefs and waiters. The restaurant is open to sections of the public by application and has a great reputation for serving up gourmet food – and for getting ex-prisoners into work in the catering trade. Of course, the food in HMP Highdown has always been a contentious issue – before the opening of the restaurant the prison had a terrible reputation for **jank** grub.

See HMP Pie-down

CO DE

Your **co de** is the person or persons who have been charged alongside you with any sort of criminal enterprise. In serious cases, the prison authorities will usually split co des up and keep them well away from each other before the trial to prevent collusion. In some cases, particularly serious fraud, conspiracy and drug dealing, there can be several co des, some of whom you may never have met before the trial.

CON

In **local prisons** there is a mix of prisoners, including those on remand and not yet convicted of any offence: JRs, or Judge's Remands, who have been convicted but not yet sentenced; civils, who are serving sentences for civil-law crimes such as contempt of court, failure to pay maintenance or compensation; and convicts – prisoners who have been convicted and sentenced. A lot of older prisoners refuse to be labelled as inmates and prefer to be called **cons**.

COOPER'S TROOPERS

In the 1970s and '80s there was a psychiatrist named Dr Cooper who ran the special unit for the criminally insane at HMP Parkhurst. This unit contained some of the most violent men in the British prison system, and Dr Cooper treated them with a mixture of medication and one-to-one therapy. The prisoners in this unit were widely known as **Cooper's Troopers**.

COWBOY HAT

A **cowboy hat** is the cardboard waste pot supplied in the strip cell or 'strongbox' of the segregation unit, so-called because it very much resembles a cardboard Stetson when turned upside down. (And because they are sometimes worn on the head by mentally disturbed prisoners.) If someone in prison tells you they've just had two weeks 'wearing the cowboy hat', it means they have been held in a strip cell.

CRACK UP

In prison, it's quite common for people to **crack up** – have a mental breakdown – and it's not always those who are serving a long sentence. The most common form is when a prisoner literally cracks and starts smashing up his cell.

This usually happens late at night when time and claustrophobia hang heavily on the mind. In most cases, the screws will just leave the distressed and ranting con locked in until morning and then **nick** him for damaging prison property when he has calmed down.

Do say: Call a doctor.

Don't say: Stop whinging, this is a holiday camp according to the *Sun*!

See Bang-up

CRANK

The **crank** was a device from the days of hard labour in prisons and consisted of a wheel and counter on the outside of the cell, directly connected to a crank handle inside the cell. The prisoner, held in solitary, had to turn the crank handle for a set number of revolutions per day, often for up to fourteen hours. If the prisoner didn't meet the target, or was deemed to be slacking by the warders, a small screw could be tightened on the wheel, making it harder to turn and making the 'work' take even longer. Prison warders were awarded the title of 'screws' directly because of this.

There is also another prison use for 'crank' and in this sense it is someone who is not quite right, a little bit mad, or constantly angry. This usage of the word persists into the modern prison system but comes from the days of hard labour on the crank handle when prisoners who had been held in solitary and forced to turn the handle, sometimes for months on end, would emerge from the sentence understandably insane.

See Bread, Radio Rental

CUCUMBERS

Sex offenders and other 'protection-heads' (debtors, grasses, cell thieves, etc.) are usually segregated for their own safety under Prison Rule 45 (formerly 43); this is also known as going 'on the numbers'. They should not be confused with prisoners held in the **block** (the segregation unit) under Prison Rule 45 GOAD (Good Order and Discipline). **Cucumbers** is rhyming slang for 'the numbers', which is itself prison slang for seeking the protection wings. It is called 'the numbers' because you will be moved to the segregation unit under Rule 45, paragraph 2 before you are moved on to a protection or **VP** (Vulnerable Prisoner) wing.

See 43OP, 86, Cab caller, Home Office numbers, Nonce, On the bingo

CUT UP

Cut up is slang for self-harm with a sharp implement. Cutting up is very common amongst prisoners, particularly among the young, and among female prisoners and the mentally ill. Almost anything with an edge can be used to cut up, including toothpaste tubes and fingernails.

DADDIES

The **daddies** were the **chaps** of the old **borstal** system, leaders who had clawed their way to the top of the borstal food chain by showing gameness and the ability and willingness to inflict serious violence on their fellow detainees. Each wing had a daddy, who would rule, usually with an iron fist, and accept tribute (by way of canteen items and favours done) from other prisoners. Some of the old borstal daddies went on to become chaps in the adult prison system.

See Borstal

DC

DC, or Detention Centre to give it the official name, was also known as 'the short sharp shock'. In the 1970s it was believed that the way to rehabilitate juvenile offenders was to treat them as harshly as possible, make them do plenty of physical exercise and hard labour and subject them to brutal beatings. This was the torture and ill treatment of children sanctioned by the state. The Detention Centre system took kids from the age of fourteen to seventeen, for sentences of between three and six months. Some of the most discipline-obsessed screws in the prison system staffed these juvenile prisons and did their best to make things as uncomfortable as possible for their young charges. As an encouragement not to reoffend, it didn't work, as the harsh treatment tended to make the young detainees bitter and resentful and fostered an anti-authoritarian streak in a lot of kids. After bad publicity surrounding the deaths of some inmates the system was quietly phased out in the early 1980s. The most notorious junior DC in the south was Her Majesty's Detention Centre Send, in Surrey, which later became an adult male Category C prison, before changing again, in the late 1990s, to become an adult female prison.

See Borstal, DC, HMDC, HMYOI

DEAR JANE

The **Dear Jane** letter is the female equivalent of the **Dear John**. It sometimes escapes the public's notice that there are a lot of women in prison in this country, the majority for non-violent crime, and they, too, can suffer the breakdown of their relationships.

See Dear John

DEAR JOHN

A **Dear John** is something men serving prison sentences, or sometimes even on remand, dread. It is the letter from your wife or girlfriend telling you that the relationship is over. It is hard enough when you are in the outside world and your relationship ends, but to be locked up, helpless, and unable to see your partner and hear it from them face to face is a nightmare for a lot of men. Getting a Dear John is part and parcel of being given a long sentence, as relationships rarely stand the trials and tribulations of two people being apart for so long. Imagine if you were in prison for ten years and the only contact you had with your wife or partner was a couple of thirty-minute visits per month, during which you're under the scrutiny of CCTV, gimlet-eyed wardens and in a room full of other people. The only other ways to keep in touch are letters (which are opened and read by a prison censor) or by prison telephone (which is overpriced, and recorded and listened to by the authorities). Keeping a relationship alive whilst serving a prison sentence is almost impossible, despite the guff about helping prisoners to maintain family relationships which you read in the HMP mission statement. Many men who receive a Dear John feel as though they have nothing left to live for, and their behaviour in prison deteriorates.

See Dear Jane

DEATH CELL

Almost every local prison has a **death cell**, where, before the death penalty was partly abolished in 1968, prisoners condemned to death were held awaiting execution. Most of these cells are now used as storerooms or offices, though a few remain as cells and still house prisoners. Prisoners, being a superstitious lot on the whole, try to avoid being housed in them, and there are many stories of bad atmospheres, sightings and ghostly sighing emanating from these cells. Cynics might of course say these things are par for the course in prisons and have more to do with drug use and prison overcrowding than with the paranormal.

DEP

In the prison system **Dep** (singular) is an abbreviation for Deputy Governor – the right-hand man or woman of the **Number-one governor**. It is the Dep's job to deal with all other governor grades and to take any flak that is meant for his boss. In reality, the Dep can set the running of the prison regime and instruct the attitudes of the rest of the staff towards prisoners. How draconian or easy the prison regime is will usually be dictated by the personality and attitude of the Dep.

See Number-one governor

DEPS

A prisoner's **deps** are his court depositions, the bundle of written statements, photographic evidence and index of exhibits that make up the prosecution case against them. Every defendant in a Crown Court case must be issued with the evidence against them in advance of the trial. A prisoner's deps are his 'passport' in some of the more dangerous prisons in the UK, particularly if the prisoner is unknown and there is no one to vouch for their status as an 'ODC' (Ordinary Decent Criminal). Many undercover informers and sex offenders will try to mix with other prisoners on normal location to gather information for the authorities about breaches of prison rules or law-breaking, so they can trade it for perks or, in some cases, early release. If you are suspected of being any sort of 'wrong un', then you will be ordered to show your deps as proof of who you are and what you are in prison for. If you refuse to show them, you're immediately a 'suspect' and violence will inevitably follow. It has long been rumoured that sex offenders and paedophiles on protection wings trade each other's deps as pornography, as they contain evidence photos of victims and detailed statements given by the victims. It is also strongly rumoured that some undercover police informers are issued with false deps by the police or the prison system in order to allay the suspicions of other prisoners. These are jokingly known as **laminated pages** and are supposedly handed over when the suspect leaves prison and used by the next informer.

See Paperwork

DESPERATE DAN

Clan is a foul-smelling pipe tobacco that is sold in every prison canteen; the rhyming slang for it is **Desperate Dan**. It is one of the cheapest tobaccos on sale in prison and is only bought by those who are really desperate and short of funds. It's always smoked in roll-up rather than in a pipe. Smoking Desperate Dan is viewed as a sign that you have pretty much hit rock-bottom as a smoker, as it's a terrible smoke; the alternative is to become a **swooper**.

DETERMINATES

Convicted, sentenced prisoners are divided into two main categories: **determinates** and **indeterminates**. Determinates are those prisoners with a fixed sentence and a final release date. They have both an **EDR** (Earliest Date of Release) and an LDR (Last Date of Release), and they cannot be held in prison longer than this.

See Indeterminates, IPP

DIESEL

Diesel is slang for prison tea. Made with one huge netting teabag in a copper boiler the size of the average family bath, weaker than a knock-kneed sparrow with emphysema and more bitter than a miser who has lost a penny down a bottomless well, prison tea is not for the faint-hearted. Sans sugar and served by surly-faced warders and their brown-nosed convict serfs from dirty steel buckets, it's called diesel because it invariably has a rainbow-hued film of scum on the top, much like spilt diesel in a rain puddle. Fortunately, the word, and the form of tea it described, are not so widespread these days, since the advent of tea packs in most prisons.

DIGGER

Digger is yet another word for a prison punishment block, and is particularly popular in the nicks of the South-west, such as HMP Exeter, HMP Dorchester and HMP Dartmoor. It's said to date from a time when prisoners had to work while they were in solitary confinement, usually 'make-work' like digging holes, then filling them back in again.

See Block, Chokey

DIP TEST

A **dip test** is a form of drug testing carried out in prisons. Unlike MDT (Mandatory Drug Testing), which is expensive and requires laboratory testing outside the prison, the dip test can be carried out on the spot and is relatively cheap. Compliance tests and VDTs (Voluntary Drug Tests) are both forms of dip test. The prisoner provides a sample of urine in a disposable beaker, then the drug-testing staff dip a pre-prepared plastic wand into the sample and wait for a reaction (a bit like a home pregnancy test). If the indicator shows two unbroken lines, then the sample is clear of drugs. One line, or any break in the lines, indicates that drugs are present. A 'reasonable suspicion MDT' will then be called for, before the prisoner can be charged with breaching prison rules. Dip tests can be used to test for specific types of drug, such as opiates, amphetamines or cannabinoids, but there is also a multi-test which can test for the presence of any drug (although this is expensive compared to the standard dip test). If a prisoner proves positive for drugs, he will be charged and adjudicated upon, possibly having days added on to his sentence.
See Adjudication, Nicking

DIRTY PROTEST

The **dirty protest**, made popular by IRA prisoners, is hated by the prison authorities and therefore a legitimate weapon in the arsenal of any unruly or disruptive prisoner who can stand to do it. It involves smearing your own waste (shit, piss, vomit) on every part of your cell and on yourself and then refusing to leave the cell. The smell alone can shut down an entire cell block and force the screws to evacuate prisoners from the cells on either side of the prisoner protesting. The screws have to kit themselves out in biohazard suits and tape off every crack around the door of the dirty cell. They'll still, however, have to open the door of the dirty cell several times a day in order to deliver meals, etc. Although the screws get a special bonus for doing this work, they still hate and fear it. Some prisoners go on a dirty protest in order to draw attention to a specific complaint or the general conditions they are held in. Other prisoners will smear themselves with shit and other waste out of fear of being assaulted by the screws: they know that the screws are loathe to mix it with a prisoner when there's a danger they'll come into contact with bodily waste. Some dirty protests last for months. Ronnie Easterbrook, a South Londoner convicted of armed robbery, holds the record for the longest dirty protest – eighteen months, in the punishment block at HMP Whitemoor.

See Hang One Up

DISCHARGE BOARD

Every convicted prisoner who is in the last couple of weeks of a custodial sentence is supposed to appear before a **discharge board**. The board, which should include senior prison staff, probation staff and a doctor, assesses the prisoner's fitness for release and deals with any queries or problems they might have around their imminent release. In reality, the prison system has neither the time nor the manpower to convene a discharge board for every prisoner being released, particularly with prisons as overcrowded as they are. Prisoners these days think themselves lucky if they get to see a doctor before release.

See Discharge Grant

DISCHARGE GRANT

A **discharge grant** (at the time of writing) is the one-off payment of £46 (apparently representing one week's benefits) given to prisoners when leaving prison. It's only paid to prisoners who have been convicted and completed a custodial sentence. Remand prisoners (those in custody but yet to be convicted), though they may sometimes spend up to three years in prison awaiting trial, are not entitled to a discharge grant, and neither are civil prisoners or recalls. The meagreness of the discharge grant is in great part responsible for the massive reconviction rates in this country, as has been revealed by the Howard League for Penal Reform and the Prison Reform Trust in many of their reports. The grant is supposed to cover the expenses – rent, food and transport – of the newly released prisoner for their first seven days, until they find a job or finalize a claim with the DSS (Department of Social Security). In reality, it can take six weeks or longer to sort out a claim with the DSS and, if a newly released prisoner is lucky enough to get a job on release from prison, they will more than likely have to work a week or month in hand. This £46 may be the only money they have, and a lot of prisoners lose their homes as a consequence of being in prison and so have nowhere to live on their release. If the authorities were to sort out a realistic plan to help newly released prisoners into housing and work, instead of turfing them out of the gates of prison with a measly £46 and their belongings in a plastic bag, then maybe we would have much lower reconviction rates in this country.

DISPERSAL

Dispersal prisons were one of the measures implemented after Lord Mountbatten's 1966 inquiry into prison security. A small number of top-security prisons were designated as dispersal prisons, into which high-risk, subversive or 'problem' prisoners could be dispersed at short notice. It was a means of having the most violent and dangerous prisoners in the system in a few prisons rather than spread throughout the system. If a designated top-security prison suffers an escape, serious unrest or fails its security audit, it's immediately removed from the dispersal system. In recent memory, both HMP Parkhurst and HMP Gartree have been removed from the dispersal system following high-profile escapes: three prisoners scaled the wall at HMP Parkhurst and two were lifted off the yard at HMP Gartree by helicopter. The only dispersal prison not to lose its status after an escape is HMP Whitemoor in Cambridgeshire. Five IRA men and a London robber (in fact he was serving time for hijacking the helicopter that lifted the two prisoners from HMP Gartree) broke out of the SSU (Special Security Unit; basically, a prison within a prison), scaled fences and walls and shot two prison officers. At the time of writing, the dispersal prisons of England are HMP Frankland (North-east), HMP Full Sutton (Yorkshire), HMP Long Lartin (Worcester), HMP Whitemoor (Cambridgeshire) and HMP Wakefield (Yorkshire). HMP Belmarsh (London) is a provisional dispersal prison, due to the fact that it has an SSU.

DLP

A **DLP** (Discretionary Lifer Panel) is the board set up to deal with sentence progression for prisoners who have been sentenced to life imprisonment at the judge's discretion. This means that their crime or crimes would not normally attract a life sentence but the trial or sentencing judge feels that one would be appropriate, given the circumstances of the case.

DO A RUNNER

To **do a runner** is to escape, usually from prison, as in 'I hear John managed to do a runner from the unit at HMP Durham'.

DOG BOX

A **dog box** is a tiny cell, about the size of a dog kennel, normally found in prison reception areas, for holding vulnerable or dangerous prisoners. In most prison reception areas there will be at least three dog boxes so that prisoners who may be attacked by other prisoners (for being informers or sex offenders or because they owe money to other prisoners, and so on) or prisoners who are volatile and violent can be segregated while they go through the reception routine.

See Cucumbers, Nonce

DOG SCREW

A **dog screw** is a prison officer who hates all prisoners and uses every bit of his power to make life as hard as possible for them. Every prison in the UK has its share of dog screws, though some prisons have more than others. Some pretty damaged people are attracted to the job of prison officer, which requires no qualifications and has no real vetting process. Like any other job, the prison service attracts a mix of characters – some good, some bad – but, unlike most other jobs, the twisted, spiteful and damaged in the prison service have control over the daily lives of a disenfranchised and sometimes vulnerable minority.

See Batter squad Block, Care bear, DST, Extraction team, MUFTI

DORMS

Some prisons, usually those with the lower security category of C or D, house prisoners in dormitories. In some prisons the **dorms** hold only six or eight prisoners, but many of the lower-security-category prisons have huge dorms holding up to eighty. In recent years these huge dorms have been partitioned off and each prisoner now has their own cubicle of private space. Dorms are generally hated by prisoners because of the lack of privacy. They were the standard form of accommodation for most of the old **DC** and **borstal** institutions.

See Borstal, DC

DOUBLE A MAN

A **double A man** is a Category A prisoner who is deemed so high risk that he is afforded even more scrutiny and security precautions than a standard Category A prisoner. They are usually kept in one of a handful of **dispersal prisons** or **SSUs**. Every transfer or court appearance involves armed police escorts and a helicopter guard.

DOUBLE BUBBLE

If you borrow anything in prison, you will usually have to pay **double bubble**. This means that whatever you borrow

you have to return with 100 per cent interest, so, for
example, a loan of one ounce of tobacco means a return
payment of two ounces. Some prisoners make a living in
prison by loan-sharking at these extortionate rates.
See Baron

DOUBLE-CUFFED

To be **double-cuffed** is to be secured for transport in two
pairs of prison-issue handcuffs. First, your wrists are cuffed
together in the conventional way, then one cuff from the
second pair of handcuffs is fastened around your wrist above
the first shackle and the second cuff is attached securely to
the wrist of another prisoner, who is double-cuffed to a
prison officer. This is very uncomfortable, as prison-issue
handcuffs are heavy, weighing in at about two pounds a set.
Sometimes prisoners travel for hours trussed up in this way.
When crossing the Solent – to any of the three prisons on
the Isle of Wight – prisoners are kept handcuffed and chained
to the floor of the prison transport in the hold. If the ferry
happens to sink, then the shackled prisoners will be going
with it. Prison staff on these escorts will usually be found
upstairs in the bar enjoying a quick drink.
See Body Belt, The Island

DRY BATH

A **dry bath** is a strip search, usually carried out by police or
prison officers searching for contraband. It's called a dry
bath because you have to take all your clothes off and then
put them back on again when the search is finished. Police
officers have the power to take you under arrest to the
nearest police station, or sometimes just into the back of a
police van on the side of the street, and demand that you

strip if they suspect you may be concealing drugs or weapons.

DRY CELL

A **dry cell** is a punishment-block cell in which there's a drainage hole in the middle of the floor and the floor slopes gently towards it. These cells are used to house prisoners who are on long-term **dirty protests**, as the sloping floor and drain make it easier to hose the cell down.
See Dirty Protest, Hang One Up

DSPDU

The **DSPDU**, or Dangerous and Severe Personality Disorder Unit, operates as a separate unit within a couple of **dispersal** prisons, at the time of writing HMP Whitemoor and HMP Frankland. It attempts to treat violent, high-risk prisoners by means of therapy and one-on-one work. So far, the DSPDU is in its infancy, so there are few figures on whether this approach works with the mad, bad and dangerous, but it is the only therapeutic treatment available for Category A prisoners outside the special secure hospitals such as Broadmoor, Rampton and Ashworth.
See Bread (pp. 271, 302), Radio Rental

DST

The **DST**, or Designated Search Team, is a unit of prison officers who have been specifically trained in the 'art' of searching prisons and cells for contraband. Most prisons have a DST, and the officers on it are almost universally hated and despised by prisoners for their intrusive and heavy-handed tactics – like stripping prisoners and forcing them to squat over mirrors, and leaving cells in a terrible state. The DST wear a black, paramilitary uniform with their trousers tucked into their boots – it's as if they're on jungle exercises with the SAS – and carry aluminium briefcases that contain tools to help them dismantle prison furniture in their search for contraband. It's a common rumour amongst prisoners that all the officers on the DST are military fantasists who read Andy McNab books and like to feel that they are a special elite, rather than just a bunch of prison officers who have been trained to search. Prisoners contemptuously call the DST **burglars**.

See Spin

DUBBED UP

To be **dubbed up**, a phrase of Scottish origin, is to be locked in a prison cell, as in 'Aye, I was dubbed up for three days in the **Bar L**'.

See Bar L, Jockney

DUFF

Duff is a military word for any dessert, but usually it's a steamed pudding. It's become a common word in prisons to describe dessert, as in 'I'll give you five roll-ups if you give me your duff for the next week'. Real duff – that is, steamed pudding with treacle or raisins – is highly prized in prison, as it is one of the few things most prisoners like to eat. 'Duff' can also mean to beat up, as in 'I duffed him right up'.

EARWIG

An **earwig** is someone who listens to other people's conversations, which, in the paranoid and secretive world of crime and prison, can be dangerous for all concerned. Unlike in the world of the straight-goer, where you might suffer a dirty look for earwigging on people, in jail this behaviour can quickly develop into violence.

Do say: 'I'm not interested in your conversation.'

Don't say: 'Can you speak up? I'm trying to record you.'
See Busy, Sweetgrass

EDR

Within the first month of your sentence, you will be given a slip of paper with your **EDR** marked on it. EDR stands for Earliest Date of Release, and this is the date on which you will leave prison, barring any unforeseen circumstances, such as being granted early parole or losing remission.

E MEN

E **men** are prisoners who have escaped from custody, or attempted to escape or have conspired to escape from police, court or prison custody. To make these prisoners highly visible to the authorities they have to wear **banana suits**, brightly coloured overalls with thick yellow luminous stripes on them. They also have extra security, such as staff escorts during their movements around the prison, and special escape-resistant cells. Their every move is recorded in a book. At night, the E man must hand over all clothing and possessions from his cell, and these are sealed in a box and kept in the wing office. E men also have to keep a red light on in their cell throughout the night and are on a thirty-minute watch (they must be checked every half-hour throughout the night). E men, like Category A men, have to change cells every twenty-eight days so that any attempt to tunnel out of the cell or work on bars or locks is thwarted.

See Banana suit, Night clockey, Night light, On the book

THE ENCHANTED

The enchanted is a sarcastic term for prisoners who are on the **Enhanced** Privilege Level of IEP (Incentives & Earned Privileges scheme) introduced by Michael 'Something of the Night' Howard when he was Home Secretary in the early 1990s. It's a three-tier system for prisoner's privileges in which the top band, which all prisoners should aspire to, is 'enhanced level' – this entitles them to one extra visiting order and the right to spend more of their own money in return for good behaviour.

See Enhanced

ENHANCED

Enhanced is the highest level a prisoner can reach on the three-tier tier class system introduced into prisons in 1995 by then Home Secretary Michael Howard as part of his 'austere' prison regime. To be an enhanced prisoner, a prisoner must demonstrate model behaviour, including undertaking voluntary drug tests (which of course must test clear).

See Basic, The Enchanted

ETS

ETS (Enhanced Thinking Skills) is one of the main psychology-based Offending Behaviour Courses (OBCs)that has been introduced into the British prison system (despite failing and being scrapped in every other country in Europe) since 1990. Its aim is to teach prisoners a new way of thinking which will be less destructive than the thinking that led them into prison in the first place. Though officially a 'voluntary' course, prisoners who do not complete the course, and/or other similar courses, are at a distinct disadvantage when it comes to progressing through the system to parole and release. At two points in the history of this course – in the mid-1990s and again in 2002 – it was deemed unsuitable for prisoners convicted of armed robbery, as research showed it would make them better able to plan and thus able to carry out their crimes more efficiently. On both occasions, however, the prison system and psychologists backtracked and allowed armed robbers to take the course, having realized that few short-term prisoners were interested in doing it.

EXERCISE YARD

Every prison or jail has an **exercise yard**, usually a large square of bare concrete around which prisoners are allowed to walk for a minimum of thirty minutes per day, weather permitting. The exercise yard is a bit of a misnomer, as no actual exercise is allowed on the yard, other than walking. In most prisons you're not allowed to run or jog on the yard, or play football or any other sport, so whoever came up with the idea of calling it an exercise yard can never have read a copy of the prison rules. The yard is where a lot of deals are done for drugs and other illicit items, and it can also be the arena in which disputes are settled. Every prisoner is given a rub-down search before being allowed on the yard – some jails even use a **wand** (metal detector) – but it's quite easy to smuggle a weapon on to the yard. The yard is also where prisoners pass on information about crime to each other. (There's little else to talk about while you're walking around in circles – flapping your tongue is the only real exercise you get.) Officially, exercise on the yard should be cancelled only in case of 'inclement weather', the definition of which is that the weather should be so bad as to obscure the view of the perimeter wall or fence, but in reality prison staff will cancel exercise if they feel one stiff breeze or one small raindrop. Standing in twos in the rain or cold watching a bunch of cons walking around is not their idea of fun. The old nursery rhyme 'Here We Go round the Mulberry Bush' was written about the exercise yard at HMP Wakefield, which had a mulberry bush at its centre.These days HMP Wakefield holds more child-killers and paedophiles than any other prison in the country.

EXTRACTION TEAM

All top-security prisons have at least one **extraction team,** a bunch of screws who have been trained in removing recalcitrant prisoners from cells using surprise, speed and force. A proportion of the screws who volunteer for this job – where they can practise legally sanctioned violent techniques on prisoners while outnumbering them vastly – have the gung-ho bully-boy mentality of gang members. It's a simple fact of life that the job of prison officer (for which you need no educational qualifications or people skills) will attract some very dubious characters. Not all prison officers are psychotic bullies,

sadists and psychopaths – there are some very decent
staff working in prisons – but the reality is there are still
quite a few.

See Batter squad, Care bear, Dog screw, MUFTI

FILA C***S

Fila c*s** is a prison expression for any footwear supplied
to prisoners by the prison system and is usually used in
connection with prison-issue plimsolls that have thick
rubber soles and blue canvas uppers. It refers to the fact
that the Fila brand is held in low esteem by most criminals
and prisoners (they are classed as cheap and unstylish),
and it's a play on words (Fila c***s = feel a c*** (for wearing
them)). Only the poorest prisoners and foreign national
prisoners would be seen dead in them. The majority wear
their own shoes or trainers.

*See Adidas sex-case, Baccy tins, Jack the Rippers, Nigerian
Nikes*

FTS

FTS, or Fuck The System, is the common cry of the
prisoner, and a common way of signing off **jail mail** to
others in the same position. To British prisoners, 'the
system' is everything from straight society and the police
to the courts and prison – one big mass which they believe
is permanently against them, so they are constantly
looking for ways to fuck them right back.

FUCKWIT

Fuckwit is a big favourite with screws and prison manage-
ment to describe prisoners who don't meet certain

educational standards, such as prisoners taking remedial education classes.

GATE ARREST

A **gate arrest** is when a serving prisoner has outstanding crimes which are discovered after his current conviction and imprisonment. The police, often without giving any prior warning, will wait at the gate of the prison on the day of a prisoner's release and immediately arrest them. This was very common in the 1970s. The idea was to encourage criminals to 'cough the lot' on their initial arrest and get all their crimes taken into consideration, thus clearing the books and making the police look good. Sometimes the police would 'discover' a crime, or allegation of a crime, after the criminal had refused to clear their books, gate arrest them and ask for a remand into custody right away. This was to encourage criminals to admit everything or risk further imprisonment. The psychological effect of a gate arrest cannot be overestimated as, naturally, prisoners count off each day and make plans for their release. At least nowadays the law expects police officers to behave in a reasonable manner and visit the prisoner beforehand to lay the charges and get a response before setting up a gate arrest.

GATE FEVER

Gate fever is a disease some prisoners are prone to when they reach the end of a prison sentence. They become so intoxicated by the thought of freedom that they start to behave recklessly. Sometimes prisoners with gate fever will piss off prisoners who still have a while left to serve, which is never a good thing and can lead to trouble. It's considered bad form to rub your good fortune in the face of a largely violent and emotionally unstable community.

GHOSTED

Being **ghosted** means being transferred to another prison suddenly and without notice. This can happen to any prisoner at any time and for a variety of reasons. For example, if the prison authorities suspect that a prisoner might be planning something – an escape, a protest, a riot, etc. – then they will be ghosted. Even being a 'bit of a nuisance' is enough to do it. It's called being ghosted because the prisoner will just disappear: one minute they can be walking down a prison landing and the next they have been bundled on to a prison transport and are heading for a prison unknown. The idea behind it is to disorient the prisoner and keep them away from any contacts, inside or out of prison, who might be able to help by launching a legal challenge. The prisoner quite often will end up on the 'ghost train', being endlessly transferred from prison to prison.

GLADIATOR SCHOOL

Gladiator school is the name given to juvenile jails, where violence is an everyday occurrence. The **borstal** system was particularly violent, as young criminals fought to prove themselves and build a reputation.

THE GREYBAR HOTEL

The Greybar Hotel is an American term for prison which is sometimes used in the UK, somewhat tongue-in-cheek. A lot of British cons call their prisons hotels, in a sarcastic way, of course. If you compared British prisons to hotels you would be looking at the Bates Motel from *Psycho* or *Fawlty Towers*. Check into the Greybar Hotel and you will definitely need a holiday to get over it!

GUV'NOR'S SHUFFLE

The **guv'nor's shuffle** is the walk from a cell in the punishment block to the **adjudication** room, where the prisoner will be tried for any breach of prison rules or regulations. It's called the shuffle because the prisoner has to wear prison-issue slippers which are usually two or three sizes too big for them, and they will have a screw holding on to each elbow. This is to make sure no harm comes to the governor: the slippers and screws will hamper your movements, should you try to attack him.

HAIRY

If someone tells you they are in for **hairy**, you can safely assume that person has been convicted of rape (rhyming slang: hairy ape = rape). In prison, those convicted, or even charged and awaiting trial, for a bit of hairy will be in danger of being seriously assaulted by their fellow prisoners, who will not tolerate sex offenders of any kind living among them. Those in prison for hairy often have to seek protection on **VP** (Vulnerable Prisoner) wings.

HANDFUL

A **handful** is a five-year prison sentence, for reasons that should be clear enough. It can also mean a fearsome fighter or troublemaker, someone so big or violent you would have to use a weapon to subdue him. For example, Charlie Bronson is definitely a handful: as would any man be who can get to the roof of Broadmoor once, let alone three times.

HANG ONE UP

To **hang one up** is the first step in starting a **dirty protest**: it is smearing the walls of your cell with your own shit. A small percentage of prisoners will be willing enough, or frightened enough, to hang one up. Some prisoners do it as a way of protesting against the prison system, or in order to try to blackmail the system into giving them something they want, but some also do it because it can protect them from a beating from the screws. Once a prisoner is covered in shit, it would take a screw with a stomach of iron to grab hold of him and give him some stick.

THE HATE FACTORY

The Hate Factory is what prisoners call HMP Wandsworth, which at one time was considered the most brutal jail in the British prison system. Wandsworth screws seemed to take some sort of twisted pride in their reputation for giving prisoners the bare minimum in terms of everything from rations to clean clothing, and for brutalizing prisoners daily. HMP Wandsworth is also sometimes called 'Wanno' by prisoners. It was the prison from which in 1965 Great Train Robber Ronnie Biggs made his escape from a thirty-year sentence by scaling the wall of an **exercise yard** and dropping into a roofless furniture van. Even throughout the 1990s HMP Wandsworth had an unparalleled reputation for having brutal and violent prison staff. It was one of the last Category B prisons to allow prisoners to wear their own clothes.

See HMP Wandsworth

HAVING IT

To **have it** with someone means to be friends or crime partners with them and to spend time together for a common purpose. When you enter a prison, other prisoners will partly base their judgement of your character on who you have it with, or were having it with on **The Out** or in your previous prison.

HERMIT

A **hermit** is a prisoner who rarely ventures out of his cell, either through fear or mental illness. There will be at least one hermit on every prison wing.

HMCIP

Her Majesty's Chief Inspector of Prisons (**HMCIP**) is a post created and established by the Criminal Justice Act 1982. Appointed by the Justice Secretary, from outside of the prison service, the Chief Inspector provides independent scrutiny of detention in England and Wales by carrying out announced and unannounced inspections of detention facilities. They cover prisons, young offender institutions, police cells and immigration detention centres. Both the prison system and the Ministry of Justice have been heavily criticized in HMCIP reports in recent years by successive inspectors. The inspectorate is invaluable at pointing out the flaws, mistakes and deliberate negligence that are rife in prisons.

HMDC

HMDC is an abbreviation of Her Majesty's Detention Centre. Detention centres (**DCs**) were places of incarceration for juvenile and young offenders where the emphasis was on what politicians and tabloid editors used to call the 'short sharp shock'. They were designed to brutalize youngsters into giving up crime. Detention centres ran very harsh regimes, with plenty of physical exercise and back-breaking work, such as digging holes and filling them back in, and running around in circles for hours on end. It was believed that if you took a load of young offenders, locked them up together and treated them badly, they would soon see the error of their ways and give up their lives of crime. Unfortunately, all it did was to show them they were not alone in their criminality and give them a common enemy – society – to fight and rebel against. In HMDC a juvenile's head would be shaved on reception, he would be beaten and verbally abused by the screws and forced to run everywhere at the double. Some youngsters died in detention centres because of the harsh regimes, and by the 1990s they had been closed down and replaced with **HMYOI** (Her Majesty's Young Offender Institution).

HMP (1)

HMP stands for Her Majesty's Prison. This is the prefix to the name of every prison, and even applies to the privatized prisons that in fact belong to huge European and American conglomerates. Every item of uniform or equipment found in prisons will be stamped with the crown and the letters 'HMP'. As Oscar Wilde once said, 'If this is the way Her Majesty treats her prisoners, then she doesn't deserve to have any.'

HMP (2)

HMP, or to be detained at Her Majesty's Pleasure, is the official name for the life sentence given to juveniles on conviction for murder. It's an open-ended sentence with no fixed release date and can only end when the Parole Board, acting on behalf of Her Majesty, decides to release the prisoner. HMPs start their sentence in the **HMYOI** (Her Majesty's Young Offender Institute) system and are then transferred to an adult prison at the age of twenty-one. Quite often, HMPs will spend decades in prison before release.

HMP PIE-DOWN

This was the name given to HMP High Down in Surrey by prisoners incarcerated there. The name refers to the dire quality of the food that was served up. The 'cooks' believed they could get away with serving any old **jank** as long as they put a pastry crust on it. Pie was on the menu almost every day, and it wasn't advisable to look too closely at the contents while you were attempting to eat it. The food was supplied by an outside catering company, as opposed to being sourced by HMP, and this led to claims by prisoners that they were being given the cheapest and most rotten, out-of-date food so the private caterers could pocket a profit. HMP Highdown was opened in 1992 (officially 1993) and was built on the site of the old Banstead Lunatic Asylum, which had been there since 1877. Within its first three months as an operational prison, two prisoners managed to force their way into the healthcare centre and launch a six-hour siege. They helped themselves to various drugs from the 'secure' cabinets and one of them later died in mysterious circumstances – supposedly while being shipped out on a sweatbox on its way to HMP Wandsworth. HMP Highdown is one of the new-build prisons, based on a Canadian design, and is supposedly riot-proof and escape-proof, although at different times in its short history the prison has been downgraded from holding Category A prisoners (due to poor security) and then upgraded again as security improves. At the time of writing, HMP Highdown is designated as a Category B adult male jail. In 2008 a new chef took over the kitchens and pretty soon HMP High Down was serving up some of the best food in the British prison system. The prison now has its own working restaurant within the grounds.

See Clink

HMP WANDSWORTH

From the 1940s right up until the turn of the twenty-first century the prison most hated by prisoners in the southern part of England was HMP Wandsworth, also known as the **Hate Factory** or Wanno. Most regions had a harsh **local prison** with a terrible reputation for the treatment of prisoners – HMP Durham in the North-east, HMP Winson Green in the Midlands, HM Remand Centre Risley in Cheshire, HMP Walton in Liverpool, HMP Armley in Leeds and HMP Dartmoor in the extreme southwest – but none was more feared and hated than HMP Wandsworth.

Built in 1851, it was known as the Surrey House of Correction (back in the days when the area of Wandsworth was still in Surrey) and was designed according to the 'separate system', in which a number of corridors radiate from a central hub in what was called a 'panopticon'. This meant that staff could stand in the centre of the prison and see every cell from that one spot. Each prisoner had toilet facilities in their single-cell accommodation. The toilets were later removed in order to pack more prisoners into the cells and the single cells now house up to three prisoners each. The practice of slopping out was ended at HMP Wandsworth only in 1996.

The punishments at HMP Wandsworth were varied, cruel and given out for the slightest infractions of the rules, from being given only bread and water in solitary confinement to floggings with the birch and cat o' nine tails. In 1930 a prisoner called James Spiers, who was serving a ten-year sentence for armed robbery, committed suicide in front of a group of Justices of the Peace who were there to witness him receiving fifteen lashes of the **cat**. In 1951 HMP Wandsworth was chosen as the site for keeping a national stock of two implements used for serious corporal punishment inflicted in prison under magistrates' orders. The birch and the cat were used on prisoners either as part of their original sentence or as a disciplinary punishment under prison rules.

The most famous escape from HMP Wandsworth was by Ronnie Biggs, one of the Great Train Robbers. In 1963 the Glasgow to London mail train was robbed of £2.6 million in used banknotes by a South London gang. Most of the robbers were captured and jailed for up to thirty years apiece. Ronnie Biggs was held at HMP Wandsworth while awaiting **allocation** to HMP Parkhurst on the Isle of Wight. While there, he devised a plan to escape. On 8 July 1965, having served just under nineteen months, Ronnie Biggs and three other prisoners used rope ladders that had been thrown over by outside accomplices to scale the wall. Outside the prison was a high-topped roofless Luton van, and the escapees dropped into this before jumping into a Ford Zephyr MKII and leaving the prison in a trail of exhaust fumes. Biggs was on the run for 13,068 days before giving himself up in 2001, when he became seriously ill. In the reception of Wandsworth Prison the screws put on display the mailbag Ronnie Biggs had been sewing on the day of his escape, with a note to other prisoners that, no matter where he went in the world, one day Ronnie Biggs would be back to finish his mailbag and the rest of his sentence. Ronnie Biggs never went back to HMP Wandsworth, his mailbag remained unfinished and he was released on compassionate grounds in August 2009.

Almost twenty-five years to the day of the Biggs escape, I and several of my confederates were involved in an escape attempt that made the national newspapers. In July 1990, during the one-hour exercise period on D-wing yard at HMP Wandsworth, seven of us (all long-term prisoners) assaulted several prison officers and tried to hijack a JCB that was being used by civilian contractors to repair the concrete path in the 'sterile area' (the gap between the inner fence and the outer wall which prisoners are not allowed to approach). The plan was to use the JCB to smash down the wall and fence, allowing up to 150 long-term prisoners to escape, but things went wrong when the prisoner charged with driving the JCB couldn't get it off its hydraulic stands. The alarms were raised and scores of prison officers rushed to the sterile area and fought with the prisoners, eventually using the broken rubble from the path as missiles to pelt those taking refuge on the JCB. As punishment, we were all severely beaten by prison staff and thrown into the punishment block.

HMYOI

HMYOI stands for Her Majesty's Young Offender Institution – prisons for those under the age of twenty-one.

These prisons are, on the whole, more volatile and violent than most adult prisons.

See Borstal, DC, Gladiator school, HMDC, HMP (2)

HOBBIT HOLE

A **hobbit hole** is any place that any prisoner classed as a **hobbit** lives or spends the majority of their time. This could be their cell, the wing office or even the communal television rooms, where hobbits gather in numbers to watch soap operas.

See Vegetable Patch (p. 311)

HOBBIT SHOP

Almost every prison has a **hobbit shop** – a workshop where mind-numbing, repetitive work, such as putting washers on bolts or making prison brooms, can be undertaken, for a wage of around ten pence a day. Any prisoner with an ounce of self-respect will try to avoid being allocated to the hobbit shop; only **hobbits** are happy to work there.

See Noddy shop

HOME OFFICE NUMBERS

Very serious sex offenders and child killers who have been imprisoned in a blaze of publicity are usually put on to **Home Office numbers**, which means they don't have to make the usual request for protection from other prisoners under Rule 45 (formerly Rule 43); the Home Office automatically orders the prison governor to put them on protection. Even if the prisoner wants to go on to normal location, they will not be permitted to do so.

See 43OP, 86, Cab caller, Cucumber, Nonce

HOOCH

Hooch is prison-brewed alcohol, usually made from anything that can be stolen from the central prison kitchen – fruit, potatoes, rice. Bread can be used as the fermenting agent, as it contains small amounts of unfermented yeast. The prisoner will usually use plastic juice bottles or gallon floor-polish containers to make the brew. Here's how to do it. First, chop up the fruit then put it in the container with two kilos of sugar, several slices of bread (or just yeast if you have it), pour in a large amount of boiling water and mix thoroughly. Seal the container and put it somewhere warm, near the heating pipe in your cell, for example. About every six hours, make sure to undo the lid, because the fermentation process makes the ingredients swell with gases. This is the most dangerous part of making hooch because it will release a very strong smell of alcohol, and prison staff are always on the sniff for that. Making hooch is against prison rules and can be punishable by up to twenty-eight days' loss of remission or fourteen days' solitary confinement. Once the mixture has been 'down' for at least three days it can be drunk and will produce a mild alcoholic effect. The longer you leave it, the more potent it will be. Once the hooch is ready to be decanted, open the container and strain the liquid through a prison-issue vest or T-shirt. Then a good time can be had by all. Of course, if you leave it too long, the risk of it being found by prison staff is greater, and all your effort will have been for nothing. In some top-security prisons making hooch is something of a challenge and the determination of the staff to find it turns the situation into a war of attrition. Most prisons will have a master brewer, someone who makes quantities of good hooch and sells it to other prisoners for tobacco or drugs.

See Hooch Monster

HOOCH MONSTER

A **hooch monster** is a prisoner who, after partaking of an illicit brew, will go temporarily insane and behave completely out of character – shouting, singing, dancing, fighting or abusing everyone in sight. Hooch monsters draw the screws' attention to the fact that prisoners are drinking so are a bit of a nuisance. In top-security prisons the staff tend to turn a blind eye to the drinking of **hooch** on the wings – until a hooch monster appears to create havoc: then there will be a crackdown and the cells and wing will be searched and any 'fermenting liquid' confiscated and its owner punished.

Do say: 'I think you've had enough!'

Don't say: 'What about one for the road?'

HOOKING (1)

Hooking is a way of throwing a line between wings. Most prison wings face each other but have a sterile area between them, usually around fifteen feet across. If you want to pass something, or collect something, from someone on the opposite wing, you hook it. First, create a long-enough line by stripping threads from a prison-issue blanket and tying the lengths together. Then tie a weight, usually a pencil battery or a bar of White Windsor soap, on to the end of the line, along with a piece of prison-issue plastic cutlery (normally the fork). While you are doing this, your opposite number on the other wing is doing the same. Once the line is ready, reach out between the bars of your window and throw the weighted end of your line out as far as you can on to the ground of the sterile area. Your opposite number then has a target to aim for and will throw their line in an attempt to 'cross' yours.

This can take hours, sometimes days, but time is one thing prisoners are never short of. Once the lines have crossed, both parties reel in their lines until the weighted ends and cutlery hook together. Then the line is pulled back through both windows and the two wings are connected and items can be slid across. The line is so thin it can't be seen by screws passing below it.

See Sliding the mirror, Swinging a line

HOTPLATE

Prison meals are usually prepared and cooked in a central kitchen and taken to the wings in a heated trolley to be served by prisoners from the **hotplate** under the supervision of the screws. A lot of fights occur at the hotplate as, in some prisons, it's one of the few times in the day when prisoners congregate in any number and, also, food is a very emotive issue in prison, as there is a distinct lack of anything that looks attractive or nutritious. In the 1980s at HMP Parkhurst the best meal of the week was the Sunday roast, usually a sliver of roast beef so thin it looked as though it had been sliced with a laser beam. That was the only complaint. Anyway, one Sunday, as the men were queuing for the meal, a hit squad of prisoners, wearing home-made masks and carrying **chivs**, leapt on their victim, who was near the front of the queue and **teabagged** him. The attackers dispersed, leaving their victim unconscious and with twenty-eight stab wounds. The prisoner who had been behind the victim in the queue stepped over his prostrate body and said, 'Gi's his roast beef, he ain't gonna be up for eating it now'. Hard men – hard attitudes.

See Hotplate Hamster, Hotplate worker, Teabagging (p. 262)

HOTPLATE HAMSTER

A **hotplate hamster** is a screw who wangles duty on the **hotplate** in order to eat prisoners' rations rather than pay the price of a meal in the subsidized staff canteen. The food is served by **hotplate workers**, prisoners who wear white two-piece overalls and sometimes have a certificate in food hygiene, though this is far from common. The hotplate is usually overseen by at least one screw (in top-security prisons the food is served by prison staff only), who makes sure every prisoner gets their ration. It is a serious breach of regulations for a member of staff to eat inmates' rations, but hotplate hamsters will risk it and, if reported, will deny all knowledge.

HOTPLATE WORKER

A **hotplate worker** is a prisoner who serves meals from the **hotplate** and washes the pots, containers and ladles, etc. after every meal. Some prisoners like to work on the hotplate as they get a few perks, such as extra food and access to yeast (for brewing **hooch**) through contact with the kitchen workers. But, overall, it's a pretty thankless task because you have to bear the brunt of the prisoners' complaints about the state of the food and the size of the portions. Hotplate workers are often threatened with violence by other inmates if they don't hand over extra portions, or even if they look at someone 'funny'. On top of this, and the worst part of the job for a lot of prisoners, is having to make small talk with the screw who supervises the hotplate.

HUMP

Hump is used widely in prison and means to be severely annoyed with someone, as in 'Turn it in, mate, you're giving me the right fucking hump!' or 'I've got the hump with this gaff'.

ICE

ICE or in-cell electricity is a relatively new phenomenon in UK prisons. Up until the 1980s prisoners weren't even trusted to have access to their own cell light switch and the light was turned on and off by a prison officer from outside. In most prisons it was lights out at 10 p.m. Since the 1990s there has been a programme of supplying prison cells with electrical points so the prisoners can use a television, radio and kettle. The average prison cell now has a light switch and two power points.

ID CARD

An **ID card** is issued in the majority of prisons. It usually consists of a small plastic card containing the prisoner's name, number and photo. When a prisoner leaves the wing for any reason, this card must be carried or displayed, and it is also used as identification when collecting canteen goods and medication. Being off your wing without your ID card can lead to a **behavioural warning** or, in some cases, a **nicking**.

See Home Office numbers, Nicking

IN DENIAL

According to the Appeal Court's own figures, in the ten years from 1991 80,000 convictions were overturned on appeal, and it has been estimated that as many as 14 per cent of British prisoners may be innocent and have been wrongly convicted of the crimes they have been imprisoned for. The unofficial prison service term for these prisoners is that they are **in denial** or 'deniers'.
See PMI

INDETERMINATES

An **indeterminate** is someone who is serving a prison sentence with no actual release date. The indeterminate prisoner must rely on the Parole Board to decide when they are safe enough to be released. There are many indeterminates languishing in the prison system, unable to progress to release because the budget to convene Parole Boards to hear their case is limited. There is also a lack of funding for Offending Behaviour Programmes (OBPs), which indeterminate prisoners need to take in order to prove they no longer present a risk of reoffending and are ready for release. Successive governments, since the 1990s, have created more and more legislation allowing people to be jailed indeterminately. In effect, all indeterminate prisoners are serving ninety-nine years, even if their crime warrants a sentence of only nine months on conviction; in some cases, the judge's hands are tied by legislation and he must give out an indeterminate sentence.

INDEX OFFENCE

A prisoner's **index offence** will be the main and most serious charge on the indictment on which he has been convicted. If a person is convicted of several criminal charges, the charge that carries the highest prison sentence will be the index offence.

INDUCTION

Since 1997 most prisoners who enter prison for the first time are given an **induction**. They are kept separate from the main prison for a period of anything from two days to six weeks, depending on the prison and the length of time they are serving, and given time to acclimatize to the prison experience. During this induction period prisoners will be told what they'll need to know during their stay in prison – the **app** process, how to report sick, prison rules, information about the gym, the chapel, etc. When this process is taken seriously by prison staff it can be invaluable in helping prisoners to settle in. But most prisons – particularly **local** jails, which have a high turnover and transient population – only pay lip service to the induction process.

See Beirut, Induction Pack, Induction Wing

INDUCTION PACK

An **induction pack** is a folder containing relevant information, such as prison rules and regulations, which is handed to each prisoner when he arrives in prison.

See Induction

INDUCTION WING

An **induction wing** is a wing or unit of a prison where new arrivals are held for a period of time before being allocated. Because of the transient nature of the induction population, most of these wings and units are filthy and lack anything but the most basic amenities. In addition, they can sometimes be very noisy and violent, as mentally ill prisoners will also be housed there as an overflow from the prison hospital or to be assessed.

See Beirut, Induction

INSIDE

To be **inside** is to spend time in prison, as in 'Harry's gone back inside, so we won't be seeing him for at least a three-stretch'. A lot of ex-prisoners refer to prison as 'inside', just as they refer to the outside world as **The Out**.

IP

IP is an acronym for In Possession. Anything a prisoner has signed for as property (the items allowed to be kept by a prisoner, for example, a wristwatch, a wedding ring, a radio, etc.) is considered IP, if the prisoner does not request that it be stored in reception.

IPP

IPP (Imprisonment for Public Protection) is an **indeterminate** prison sentence that can be given by a judge if they feel that the specified offence or the record of the offender is such that the public should be protected. It was brought in to replace the two-strikes life sentence, by which anyone committing a second violent or sexual offence could be held in prison indefinitely. The two-strike life sentence was abolished after challenges were made to the European Court of Human Rights that it was unfair.

IPTC

If you are in prison and have a partner or family member serving a sentence in another prison at the same time then you can apply for an **IPTC** (Inter-Prison Telephone Call). Inter-prison phone calls are at the discretion of the governor and both prisoners involved must complete various **apps** in order to speak to each other.

See IPV

IPV

An **IPV** is an inter-prison visit. This can be granted on application if you are in prison and have a close member of your family in a different prison and wish to see them. Since the privatization of the prison transport system, it's almost impossible to get an IPV, as providing the security is very expensive. Nowadays they have mostly been replaced by **IPTCs** (Inter-Prison Telehone Calls) by which arrangements will be made to allow family members to talk to each other by telephone from their respective prisons.

See IPTC

THE ISLAND

The Island refers to the Isle of Wight, which contains three prisons, HMP Albany, HMP Camp Hill and HMP Parkhurst. Being sent to The Island is never a good thing. Apart from the fact that all three have terrible reputations for violence, they are also expensive and difficult for family and friends to visit. In order to get to The Island visitors have to travel by ferry or catamaran, and then drive or get a cab to the centre of the island, where the prisons are located. It's rumoured that some of the cab drivers on the island are, or were, screws and charge visitors to the prisons over the normal tariff simply because they can. In the modern British prison system, islands are very popular as a site for a prison. Whereas the Isle of Wight was once the only island in the UK with three prisons, nowadays the Isle of Sheppey also has three (HMP Swaleside, HMP Eastchurch and HMP Elmley), while Portland Bill has two (HMP The Verne and HMYOI Portland), and every island from the Isle of Man to Jersey contains at least one prison.

JACKET

Jacket is Yank slang that has made its way into British criminal usage. Your jacket is your police or prison record. Both the police and prison officials keep extensive records on those arrested and imprisoned, and these are usually in buff-coloured folders – the jacket – which will have the prisoner's basic details on the front. The initial page of this record will usually contain warnings about the prisoner's previous behaviour – whether they are violent, aggressive or an escape risk. If someone is an informer, this will be marked on his record. In American prisons, this is known as a 'snitch jacket'.

JACK STRAW'S

During the late 1990s and early 2000s **Jack Straw's** was any piece of prison property, particularly prison-issue clothing or food. Under the first New Labour Home

Secretary, Jack Straw, prisoners really believed the prison system would improve and become something better than it was under Straw's much-hated predecessor, Michael 'Something of the Night' Howard. Unfortunately, under Jack Straw things only became worse (even though most prisoners wouldn't have thought that possible), so his name became synonymous with anything that was crap or feeble in the prison system. For example, a prisoner might say to somebody who was wearing the prison uniform of acrylic tracksuit ('Spider-Man suit') and a pair of prison-issue plimsolls ('paedo pumps'), 'I see you have your Jack Straw's on.' Or, if a meal is particularly unappetizing, a prisoner might say that it was 'a load of old Jack Straw's!'. The term has fallen out of use in recent years but is still used in northern nicks, where people seem to have long memories.

JACK THE RIPPERS

This is rhyming slang (Jack the Rippers = slippers), and is used particularly for prison-issue slippers. Anyone who wears **Jack the Rippers** in prison is considered to be institutionalized and no longer aware of the dangers that may be lurking. If something kicks off, such prisoners will be at a severe disadvantage. Veteran cons will always be wearing footwear they can run or fight in at a moment's notice, and these do not include slippers or flip-flops. The atmosphere in prison can change from one moment to the next, and riots, fights and unrest can come apparently out of nowhere. Jack the Ripper was a notorious serial killer in 1888 who killed at least five women in the East End of London. His identity has never been discovered.
See Adidas sex-case, Baccy tins, Fila c***s, Nigerian Nikes

JAILHOUSE BRIEF

A **jailhouse brief** is much the same as a barrack-room lawyer – a prisoner or soldier with knowledge of the law and of rules and regulations who will dispense advice on these matters to his fellows. Some jailhouse briefs make a good career for themselves behind bars by charging a fee to other prisoners who may wish to sue the authorities. For this fee the jailhouse brief will handle all the paperwork, fill in the court forms and negotiate settlements with the Treasury Solicitors. The most common cases handled are for lost or damaged property or personal injury, in which cases the brief will usually settle for a small percentage of any compensation won by the claimant in payment for their services. There are also jailhouse briefs who will put their legal knowledge to use in order to effect change in prison rules and law. For these, the reward is in the satisfaction of effecting change.

JAIL MAIL

Jail mail is mail received from other people in prison. Many prisoners write to each other when they have been transferred between jails. Also, many prisoners of the opposite sex correspond with each other from their respective jails.

JAM ROLL

Jam roll is rhyming slang for parole. In UK prisons parole is given to long-term prisoners and those sentenced to life after they have served the bulk of their sentence or tariff period. In the case of lifers, parole is not an automatic right and they must be vigorously risk-assessed and passed for parole by a Parole Board, which includes a judge, and then be passed by the Home Secretary. Prisoners serving life sentences are on Parole for the rest of their natural lives and can be recalled to prison at any time for breaching the conditions of their licence. Those prisoners with determinate sentences receive parole automatically at the halfway point of their sentence and remain on licence until their sentence expires. They, too, can be recalled to prison for any breach of their licence.

JOEY

A **joey** is a parcel, usually of drugs, and is so called because it is secreted on the prisoner's body, rather like a joey (baby kangaroo) in its mother's pouch. Prisoners are expert at hiding things, especially drugs or weapons, about their person. One prison legend involves a particularly violent lifer who had a penchant for cutting screws and even governors by producing concealed razor blades at opportune moments, despite having been thoroughly searched every time. Rumour had it that he would make cuts in his flesh, and them cover them with salt until the flesh took on the consistency of a flesh 'pocket', into which he would slip the razor blade. The screws took to stripping him naked and searching all his clothes on a regular basis, yet still he was able to pop up with a blade whenever he felt like it.

JAM ROLL/PAROLE

JOHN WAYNE

John Wayne is prison-issue toilet paper, because it is so very tough, just like the cowboys played by the actor. Up until the first few years of the twenty-first century, prison-issue toilet paper was like tracing paper, all shiny and not fit for purpose. The daily issue for each prisoner is six sheets (not rolls, sheets!) and, in some prisons, that is all you'll get. In recent years HMP have switched to recycled paper, which, while not as rough as the original toilet paper, is barely fit for purpose either. If it's cheap, HMP will buy it, no matter how useless.

KAMIKAZE MISSION

A **kamikaze mission** is exactly what it sounds like. Named after the Japanese kamikaze pilots of the Second World War, who would fly their planes into targets knowing they would die in the process, criminal and prison kamikaze missions can sometimes be as fatal, but not often. In criminal parlance, it's a piece of work or action that will involve plenty of front and bottle but has a good chance of crashing and getting whoever does it hurt. It means going up against heavy odds, with at least a fifty-fifty chance of failure. In prison, a typical kamikaze mission might involve a prisoner 'rushing' the screws, even though the prisoner will be greatly outnumbered, or fronting up to a drug gang to whom they already owe a bundle of wonga and conning more drugs out of them when the prisoner has no means or intention of paying for them. Some prison escape attempts are kamikaze missions, with little hope of success.

KANGA

This is yet another (rhyming) slang word for a prison officer (kangaroo = screw). **Kanga** is of course the shortened version of the word and is widely used in every prison in the country by **cons**.

KANGAROO COURT

A **kangaroo court** is an unofficial, generally farcical, hearing held to determine the guilt (or, rarely, otherwise) of an offender. Most prisoners refer to governors' **adjudications** as kangaroo courts because, no matter what they say or what evidence they produce, the governor will inevitably find them guilty on the word of the staff alone. Some prisoners set up their own kangaroo courts in order to deal with fellow prisoners who they believe have offended against the prisoners' code, by, for example, stealing from another prisoner's cell, or **grassing**. The punishments meted out by prisoners are usually violent.

See Pad Thief

KIDDY FIDDLER

A **kiddy fiddler** is anyone who is in prison for sexual crimes against children. They are normally housed on the protection wings, away from the violent wrath of any ODCs (Ordinary Decent Criminals), who will severely serve them up if they get their hands on them. Kiddy fiddlers are hated and despised even by other prisoners on the protection wings.

KIDDY KILLER

Kiddy killer describes anyone who has killed a child. These prisoners are held in contempt by the rest of the prison population and in severe danger of being violently assaulted for their crimes.

KIT

Kit is any item issued to a prisoner by the prison authorities. Blankets and sheets are bed kit; shorts, singlet and plimsolls are PE kit; and all other prison clothing is general kit. Every prison has a weekly kit change, when prisoners can exchange items for clean or undamaged ones. In the days of **borstal** and **DC**, kit inspections, in which each trainee had to lay out every item of kit in a specified manner, were common for young offenders, and there was also a punishment called kit change, in which screws would order young prisoners to put on each item of a set of kit, rapidly, and then another. So a screw would stand at the top of a dorm or wing and shout, 'PE kit, *go!*' and every trainee had to quickly don their PE kit. Once they were all in the PE kit, the screw would shout, 'Best dress, *go!*' and it would be all change again. These punishments could go on for hours and were often given out for trivial infractions of the rules, such as talking after lights out.

KIT BAG

Kit bags are still issued in some prisons and in all **HMYOIs**. They are usually cloth or net bags in which prisoners carry their **kit** when moving cells, or when replacing it weekly with clean kit.

KIT NUMBER

A **kit number** is the numerical code issued to prisoners and YOs and is stamped on every piece of kit issued to that prisoner. This number means that all pieces of kit can be traced to each individual so that they can be held liable under prison rules for any loss or damage.

KNOCKBACK

The word **knockback** is well known and well used by life-sentenced and indeterminately sentenced prisoners. In order to be released, every lifer and indeterminate must appear before the Parole Board and prove they are no longer a risk to the public. Being refused parole is known as a knockback or KB. The knockback can be a big blow for any prisoner who has spent years in the system. It means they will have to reapply for parole further down the line. The average knockback a lifer may receive is two years, though it's not unknown for lifers to receive a seven-year knockback. It's almost impossible for a prisoner to prove that they no longer constitute a risk to the public, so they see parole hearings as something of a lottery. As soon as a paroled lifer hits the headlines for committing a further offence, those lifers left in prison know that they'll have to suffer a few more years of knockbacks as the Parole Board get spooked and stop releasing lifers for fear of being targeted by the tabloids. Welcome to 'justice' in the UK!

LAGGING

A prison sentence of two years is known as a **lagging**. I was once told that it was because two years and over turned

you into an old **lag**, an experienced convict who knows all the dodges.
See Lag boat (p. 293)

LAMINATED PAGES

If someone suggests that your **deps** may have **laminated pages**, then you are facing a serious accusation that you are a 'wrong un'. It's widely believed in prison that police informers and sex offenders who refuse to go on the **cucumbers** are given a fake set of depositions which claim that they are in for some 'honourable' crime like GBH or assaulting the police. Using the phrase is an insinuation that the authorities have supplied a prisoner with a fake passport to **the mains** that has been used so many times they've had to laminate the pages to save on wear and tear.
See Cucumbers, Deps, The Mains, Paperwork

LARGACTIL SHUFFLE

The use of anti-psychotic medication in British prisons has long been widespread and Largactil, or Thorazine, as it is known in the US, is a favourite. Also known as 'the liquid cosh', it is sometimes injected into prisoners who refuse to conform and, certainly up until the 1980s, was used as a tranquillizer. I was injected with it against my will when I was a juvenile prisoner in the 1970s. Once it gets into your system, it slows down your movements, walking in particular. The drug causes you to shuffle along like a zombie, taking very short steps, as there is a dull ache in your limbs that is only relieved if you keep moving. In the 1970s and '80s it was common to see **exercise yards** full of prisoners doing the **Largactil shuffle**.

LITTLE FELLAS

A slang phrase for cigarette ends, the term **little fellas** is widely used in northern prisons, as in 'Blimey, I'm dying for a smoke, you got any little fellas?'.
See Mud Huts, Swooper

LOCAL PRISONS/LOCALS

In the straight world your **local** is probably the nearest pub, but in the criminal world it usually refers to the **local prison**. When first arrested and remanded to custody, or on first conviction, a prisoner is sent to the prison nearest the court where they have been tried, and this prison is known as a local. Most big cities will have more than one local prison. For example, if you were remanded from a court in Liverpool you might be sent to HMP Walton or HMP Altcourse (also known as Fazakerley). If you are arrested in South London, you may be sent to HMP Brixton, HMP Belmarsh or HMP Wandsworth. All local prisons are Category B, though some can also hold Category A prisoners on special secure wings.

L PLATES

In prison, getting your **L plates** means getting a life sentence.

MAGICAL MYSTERY TOUR

The **Magical Mystery Tour** is what a prisoner is sent on if they cause serious trouble in prison. Whether they have incited a riot, assaulted a screw or are suspected of plotting subversive activities, they will be beaten, **double-cuffed**

and thrown into a prison transport with an escort of screws and sent around the country. The prisoner will spend some time in a number of prison punishment blocks and be moved at a moment's notice, day or night. Like the 'ghost train', this punishment is designed to disorientate disruptive prisoners, as they aren't left in any prison long enough to settle. It also makes it very difficult for them to keep in touch with family or any legal representative who may be able to make representations to stop the tour.
See Ghosted

THE MAINS

The mains is what prison staff and 'vulnerable prisoners' call the part of the prison that is outside the safe environs of the protection wings. The majority of **VPs** are terrified of being sent on to the mains, as they know they will become serious targets for the prisoners there, who love nothing better than catching a sex offender or informer in their midst. Serious violence often follows.

MAKE ONE

To **make one** is to escape, as in 'I hear Ronnie Biggs has made one out of Wanno!'. Outside prison, to 'make one' is to kick something off, i.e. to have a fight with someone. It's particularly common among football hooligans , as in 'We'll be making one at Man U on Saturday'.

MOGGY

Moggy has two meanings. In the outside world it's a slang word for a domestic cat and inside its meanings are also cat-related. A moggy was a stolen fur coat, in the days when stealing fur coats (either individually or in bulk) was in vogue. These days, there's very little call for real fur coats, so criminals have all but abandoned this crime. The word is also used in the phrase 'get the moggy' instead of **cat**, or **pussy**, to mean corporal punishment as administered with a cat o' nine tails.

See Cat/Pussy

MOON

In prison, **moon** is taken to mean 'month', as in 'I see Jerry got three moon for that bit of work'.

MUD HUTS

In prison, wages are very low and tobacco is very expensive, so a lot of prisoners who smoke tend to smoke roll-ups and re-roll their dog ends. **Mud huts** is rhyming slang for cigarette butts, as in, 'I'm dying for a smoke, got any mud huts in your ashtray?'.

See Desperate Dan, Little Fellas, Swooper

MUFTI

MUFTI, in prison, is an acronym for Minimum Use of Force and Tactical Intervention. The MUFTI was a squad of prison officers who were specially trained in riot control and taking prisoners down quickly, violently and effectively. They were the predecessors of the C&R **extraction teams** which are now on call within the prison system to deal with disturbances or violent prisoners who may be 'control problems'. In 1979 the MUFTI at HMP Wormwood Scrubs stormed a peaceful sit-down protest on D Wing (the lifer and long-term wing) and left sixty prisoners with

serious head injuries which had been inflicted by batons wielded by the MUFTI. To this day, the report into the 'riot' (which was how it was officially described) has yet to be published. The MUFTI was quietly replaced by Tornado squads and the modern C&R teams.
See Batter squad, Extraction team

NFA

NFA is an acronym for No Fixed Abode and describes a prisoner who has nowhere to live, no definite address. When being discharged from prison as NFA, the prisoner will be entitled to a higher rate of **discharge grant**, £90 rather than the usual £46, which is supposed to account for one week's benefits payment. Some short-term prisoners pretend they are NFA in order to get extra money to spend on drink or drugs on their first night out, though in recent years more and more prisoners are leaving custody as genuine NFAs.
See Discharge grant

NICK

A **nick** is a prison or police station to which a criminal will be taken once they are 'nicked'.

NICKING

A **nicking** is being informed that you have breached prison rules and must appear before the governor for **adjudication**. It's the prison version of an arrest. The prisoner will normally be informed verbally by a screw, as in 'You're nicked!', and then issued a charge sheet outlining the charge and telling them what rule has been breached.

Previous nickings are always taken into account by the governor in sentencing. It is very rare for a prisoner to be found not guilty of any charge brought against them. Previous nickings are also an issue when it comes to parole or any other prison privilege.

See Adjudication, Block

NIGERIAN NIKES

Nigerian Nikes are any prison footwear, but plimsolls in particular, and are so called because they are a big favourite among foreign national prisoners and, in particular, Nigerian prisoners (of which there are many in British jails). It's a prejudicial term indicating that the wearer is so poor and unstylish that they will wear anything on their feet and think they've had a result.

See Adidas sex-case, Baccy Tins, Fila c***s, Jack the Rippers

NIGHT CLOCKEY

The **night clockey** is the prison officer on duty overnight on each individual prison wing. The name comes from the fact that they have to patrol the landings at regular intervals throughout the night and turn a security key in a clocking device at the end of each landing in order to prove that all is well and that they have not fallen asleep.

NIGHT LIGHT

The **night light** is the red strip-light that is kept on during the hours of darkness in the cells of Category A and **E men**. It is kept burning so that the **night clockey** can check at a glance at regular intervals during the night that the prisoner is still in the cell. So it's a security precaution, as well as sometimes being used to monitor prisoners who are suicide risks or have been placed on a 2052SH (a constant or regular cell-watch for prisoners who are vulnerable to suicide or self-harm; the number is that of the official prison form that covers this, and 'SH' stands for 'self-harm').

NIGHT PATROL

The **night patrol** is a skeleton staff of prison officers who rove the prison they work in at night checking that all is well. They're on call throughout the night in the event of an escape or a prisoner falling ill.

NIGHT SAN

Night san, or the computerized night sanitation system, is installed in several prisons in the UK and is used where the cell is too small to have a toilet and sink fitted into it. The night san consists of a keypad fixed to the wall by the door in each cell that is connected to a central computer which, when the right sequence of buttons is pressed by the prisoner, will electronically unlock the cell door and allow the prisoner access to the communal toilet. Only one prisoner at a time is allowed out and, on returning to the cell and closing the door, he must punch in a four-digit number that is randomly displayed on a small screen on the keypad. This enables the central computer to lock the door and let the next prisoner out.

NODDY SHOP

Almost every prison in Britain will have a **Noddy shop** – a workshop where mind-numbing work is carried out by

prisoners. Here are some examples of the work that goes on there: putting strip-lightbulbs into boxes, screwing nuts on to bolts, counting washers, breaking cassette tapes with a toffee hammer, folding plastic bags – general stuff that requires no skill and no degree of interest. The Noddy shop is where those prisoners with no ambition or influence end up and is called the Noddy shop because most people would just 'nod off' if they were forced to do this work.
See Hobbit Shop

NONCE

A **nonce** is a sex offender, usually, though not exclusively, one who has committed crimes against children. Some people hold to the view that this term is due to the 'nonsense' nature of these crimes, i.e. that they do not make sense to normal people. But the true origin of this word dates from the days (pre-1960s) before each prison had a whole wing (or more than one) dedicated to the protection of these type of offenders and they were kept locked up on normal location amongst other prisoners. In order to make sure that the cells of the sex offenders were not unlocked at the same time as those of the general prison population, because they would be immediately attacked, the screws would mark the acronym NONCE on their cell doors. This stood for 'Not On Normal Courtyard Exercise' (as all the other prisoners would exercise together in the courtyard). In this way, the sex offenders were never let out on exercise at the same time as other prisoners. And the name stuck.

NON-STIMULANT PACK

A **non-stimulant pack** is issued to Mormons in the British prison system instead of the normal brew pack which is given to those of all other religious denominations. It contains hot-chocolate powder and Ovaltine instead of teabags and coffee sachets. Some prisoners will pretend to be Mormons just so they can get a non-stimulant pack. The packs, like normal brew packs, are issued weekly in prison.

NOTE IN THE BOX

Note in the box is reference to undercover grassing. Every prison wing has a locked box, usually fixed to a wall situated close to the wing office, into which prisoners put their outgoing mail for collection by the censor. If a prisoner wishes to pass on information to the authorities without being seen to do so, they will write a note and drop it into the box as though depositing an ordinary letter. Everything that comes out of the box when it is unlocked daily will be read by the censor, and any notes will be passed on to Security for investigation or action. Some prisoners will use the note-in-the-box tactic to try to have their enemies removed from the wing by claiming they are plotting an escape or dealing drugs. Some desperate prisoners, usually those who are heavily in debt, will drop a note in the box about themselves, saying that they are about to escape or assault a member of staff, in the hope that the screws will place them on GOAD (Rule 45: Good Order and Discipline) in the **block** and save them the embarrassment of asking for protection.

NUMBER-ONE GOVERNOR

The **number-one governor** of a prison is the governor who has been given overall control of the establishment. The number one will delegate the day-to-day running of his establishment to the **Dep** and other lower governor grades, but it is the number-one who will have to take the flak and responsibility if anything goes wrong. Most number-one governors will stay in charge of a prison for a minimum of four years or so before being moved on. The regime and reputation of a prison is informed by the attitude of its number-one governor. If they are a hard-line security freak, or an open-minded liberal, then the staff beneath them will usually fall into line with their views or request a transfer. If they are considered weak, the staff will ignore them and run the prison in the way they feel it should be run. Many weak governors have been responsible, albeit indirectly, for terrible regimes of brutality and intimidation instigated by their staff.

OFFICE CAT

Someone who hangs around in the screws' office on the wing is known as an **office cat** and is viewed with contempt and suspicion by other prisoners. The screws are the enemy, and anyone consorting with them is considered to be a traitor. Office cats sometimes come to grief and have bad 'accidents' when the screws aren't watching.
See Arse-licker, Cat's arse

OLD H

Old Holborn, or **Old H**, was once the most popular hand-rolling tobacco in prisons. In recent years it has fallen out of favour, due to its strong flavour and the fact that it is expensive compared to the cheap tobacco now on sale in prison canteens.

OLD VIRGIN

Old Virgin is the nickname given to Golden Virginia, a hand-rolling tobacco which is slightly milder than Old Holborn, its nearest rival. In the days when prisoners were allowed a tin to keep their tobacco in, Golden Virginia ones were very popular. Prisoners would customize them by covering them in matchsticks and painting them. Some would sandpaper the green-and-gold livery from the tins and just leave the words 'Old Virgin' from the full name G(old)en (Virgin)ia.

ONE OFF!

One off! is the traditional cry of the escort screw when removing a prisoner from any part of the prison where the prisoner has been marked on the roll. The cry is directed at whichever officer is in command of the area from which the prisoner is being removed. It is also the epitaph for any prisoner who dies in prison and whose name must be officially removed from the prison roll. It's used by prisoners, in a goading way, to antagonize staff whenever there is a successful prison escape. Cries of 'One off!' will echo around the prison as prisoners shout long into the night through their window bars.
See One On!

ONE ON!

One on! is the counterpart of the cry **One off!** and is shouted by any screw who escorts a prisoner into any part of a prison where a roll needs to be amended to take them into account. For security purposes, the staff in 'the centre' or 'control' (those who run the workings or mechanics of the prison) need to be kept informed of the whereabouts of every prisoner who is moving anywhere in the prison. Not adding a prisoner to a roll board, or forgetting to take one off, can seriously mess up the count and lead to a lock-down or stand-fast roll check that will disrupt the prison routine. *See One Off!*

THE ONES

The ground-floor landing is known as **the ones**. The upper levels are known as 'the twos', 'the threes' and 'the fours' respectively. Each level will contain a landing with cells on each side for housing prisoners.

ONE-UP

In prison parlance, a **one-up** is a cell for single occupancy. In police slang, it's a single person in a car and is used mainly by surveillance squads, as in 'Yeah, I've got a Jag coupé with one-up heading down the A3.'

ON THE BINGO

To go **on the bingo** is to ask the prison authorities for protection from other prisoners. It's called this because the prisoner has to request protection under Rule 45 (formerly Rule 43). It's also called going 'on the numbers'. (What not to say: Two fat rapists, clicketty click.)
See Home Office numbers, 430P, Cab caller

ON THE BOOK

Being **on the book** is to be a special-watch prisoner whose every movement and word must be marked down in a small, blue, passport-sized book kept by the screws. Category A and Category **E men** are all on the book and are watched and escorted everywhere by at least three screws, one of whom will be in physical possession of the book. These prisoners are considered to be dangerous and escape risks and must wear high-visibility clothing at all times. They can't leave a prison wing, or sometimes their cell, without being **double cuffed** and escorted by at least one prison dog and three screws. All their clothing and possessions are removed from their cell at night and a red light is left on throughout to make it easier for the **night clockey** to see them during his thirty-minute spyhole checks.

See Banana suit, E men, Night clockey, Night light

ON THE EARHOLE

To be **on the earhole** is to be looking for something for nothing. Somebody who is always on the cadge or looking to borrow things is on the earhole. It comes from the time when there was a strict **rule of silence** in UK prisons, and prisoners weren't allowed to speak to each other. They developed a sign language in order to communicate and touching your ear meant that you wanted to borrow something, so to this day someone who is on the ponce is said to be on the earhole.

See Rule of silence

THE OUT

The Out is how prisoners refer to the big world outside of the prison walls and fences, as in 'I knew him on The Out'. The Out is where all prisoners long to be. And, yes, it should always have capital letters.

PAD

In northern prisons a cell is known as a **pad**, from the swinging 60s word for a flat.
See Pad Spin

PAD SPIN

A **pad spin** is a cell search, usually carried out by the prison's Designated Search Team (**DST**).
See DST, Spin

PAD THIEF

A **pad thief** is a prisoner who will steal personal items from fellow prisoners' cells or **pads**. They are held in great contempt by most prisoners (with no sense of irony whatsoever). A typical punishment for pad thieving is to hold the fingers of the culprit in the cell door and slam the heavy door on them, breaking the fingers.

PAPERWORK

If you are unknown in prison, particularly in the top-security system, you will be asked to provide **paperwork** as proof that you are not a 'wrong un'. Your paperwork is your charge sheet (the document outlining the details of the charges laid against you, a copy of which will be handed to you at the police station) and your deposition bundle (the statements of all witnesses against you, including any photographs that are used in evidence, and your own statement; by law, these have to be supplied to all defendants before trial). If you can't produce this paperwork and have no other prisoner to vouch for you,

you must either brazen it out on the wing or seek protection. Top-security prisons are violent and paranoid places where dangerous men spend years, sometimes decades, in relative isolation and with little to do other than to try to smash the sameness of every day. 'Witch hunts' against sex offenders or informers are to long-term prisoners as bread and circuses were to the ancient Romans. Someone with no paperwork will be a prime target for organized violence, as there's no good reason for a prisoner not to have it – unless, that is, they have committed a crime they don't want people to know about, i.e. a sex offence, or have grassed on others.

See Deps, Laminated Pages

PATCHES

Patches is a prison uniform with prominent yellow panels worn by prisoners who have been captured after an escape or attempted escape.

See Banana suit, E men

PHONE CARDS

Prison **phone cards** were sold in prison canteens when inmate phones were introduced into the British prison system in 1992. The minimum cost of a card was £2, the maximum was £4, and a maximum purchase of £20 worth of cards was allowed to convicted prisoners. The cards were issued by British Telecom but were stamped with 'HMP' and were green and white in colour. The cards became handy as prison currency and it became an offence against prison rules punishable by up to fourteen days' loss of remission to be caught in possession of more than the maximum allowance. Five £2 prison phone cards became the going rate for a £10 bag of heroin. Some prisoners found ways to cheat the phone-card system, for example by smuggling in a 200- or 400-unit public card and then chopping the cards in half and matching them up. The first part of the prison-issue code on the card would activate the phone but the credits would be clocked up on the public-card half.

Another useful way of cheating the system and making the cards last longer was 'shaving'. Prisoners would rub the edge of the card against concrete until it had worn the edges and affected the chip. A shaved empty card would sometimes fool the phone computer into thinking there was still credit left on it. Some people would also shave cards in order to use them as a sharp-edged weapon that could pass through a metal detector. Several prisoners and a few prison staff ended up being seriously slashed with prison-issue phone cards.

Some enterprising prisoners collected empty cards and smuggled them out. Each card had a small strip on the back on which the prisoner's name and number was written, but most of the canteen staff who sold them wouldn't bother filling them in so it would be left blank for the prisoner to put in their own details. Once the used cards had been smuggled out, the ex-prisoner would fill in the strip on the back with the names and numbers of infamous prisoners – Reggie Kray being the most sought after – and then sell the cards as genuinely having belonged to that prisoner. At £2 per card, some people were on to a nice little earner.

Another lucrative scam was to shrink the cards in an oven, drill a hole through one corner of the card and sell them as a novelty key-ring at £1.50 a go. A nice few quid was earned by selling these at car-boot fairs, market stalls and on eBay. However, by 2004, most prisons had phased out the prison-issue phone card in favour of the **PIN** system, whereby a prisoner will pay for phone units at the canteen and have them transferred electronically on to their personal PIN. Prison-issue phone cards are now a thing of the past.

See PIN Number

PIE AND LIQUOR

Pie and liquor is rhyming slang for vicar. The only time you will see a vicar or any kind of priest on prison landings is when there is bad news to be given to a prisoner. News of family deaths and serious illness outside is always delivered by the chaplaincy team, so whenever a religious representative appears prisoners get nervous that he may be coming to see them.

PIN NUMBER

A **PIN number** (Prisoner Identification Number) is the unique code a prisoner is given so that they can access prison phones that are covered by the PIN system. The PIN system has been phased in to cover all prison pay phones so that conversations can be automatically recorded by a computer system at a central point rather than by staff inside each individual prison. Plus, prisoners have to sign a form when purchasing their phone time, in order to discourage misuse. (Prisoners had started to use **phone cards** as currency.) Prisoners are allowed a maximum of twenty phone numbers on their 'approved' list and the people they belong to have to be security vetted and give their permission to receive phone calls from the prisoner. PIN phones are charged at a higher rate than any other payphone, and prisoners pay ten pence a minute for their phone calls. The profits are split between BT and the prison system.

See Phone Cards

PISS BUCKET

The **piss bucket** is very similar to the **pisspot** but takes the form of a brown plastic bucket. They were issued from the late 1970s in an effort to encourage prisoners to defecate in them rather than throw 'shit parcels' out of the windows. The majority of prisoners would not defecate in the original pisspots because they were see-through plastic and the contents would be on show when they walked along the landings to slop out. The authorities failed to take into account that another reason for throwing shit parcels out of the cell window was because nobody wanted to spend up to twenty-three hours a day in a tiny cell with a loose-lidded container of excrement very close by! Not to mention the fact that you'd have to take the lid off the pot every time you wished to urinate during that time.

See Bomb Squad, Pisspot

PISSPOT

A **pisspot** is a see-through plastic chamber pot issued in prison before the partial introduction of in-cell sanitation. Prisoners had to use them as toilets during the hours of **bang-up** and empty them into a communal sluice at 'slop out' every morning. If you were in a single cell, you would have your own pisspot, but those prisoners who were crammed two or three to a one-man cell had to share one between them. These pots are still in use in over twenty British prisons today.

See Bang-up, Piss bucket

PMI

A **PMI** is a Prisoner Maintaining Innocence. According to the figures for overturned convictions reported by the Appeal Court since 1991, up to 14 per cent of people in British prisons are innocent of the crimes for which they have been convicted and imprisoned. Prisoners who refuse to accept their guilt are sometimes known as 'deniers' but the official term is PMIs. The catch-22 for PMIs is that in order to progress and be released from prison every prisoner must do at least one OBC (Offending Behaviour Course), and this means admitting and officially acknowledging their guilt and contrition for their **index offence**. If they are maintaining their innocence, they cannot do the OBCs and therefore (in the case of a life or determinate sentence) cannot be considered for release.

See In denial

QUACK

A **quack**, probably from the Afrikaans *kwaksalwer*, meaning a 'hawker of salve', or somebody who sells medicines, is a prison doctor. Prison doctors are usually not the sort of people you'd want to find in a doctor's surgery or health-care centre in the outside world. They *are* doctors, but not as you know them. Though it doesn't apply to every prison doctor, in my own personal experience of over three decades of imprisonment, the majority of prison doctors don't really prioritize their bedside manner and are more interested in pleasing the governor and the authorities than in easing pain or healing the sick in prison. Two paracetamol seems to be the standard cure-all. In British prisons Mandatory Drug Testing is in force, which has led to a national policy of refusing opiates or strong painkillers to prisoners in case they interfere with the results of this drug testing and lead to prisoners being able to disguise the fact they are taking illegal opiates. Most prison 'doctors' are prison officers who have taken a first-aid course which entitles them to wear a white coat and work in the prison hospital dispensing **aspirin water** and plasters. They are not to be confused with real doctors.

RAT

A **rat** is a prisoner or criminal who has informed or **grassed** on his fellows in order to save his own skin or gain a more comfortable existence, and is so called because rats will do anything in order to preserve their own lives and safety, even turn on other rats.

RICKET

To make a **ricket** is to make a serious mistake or error of judgement, as in 'I think I've made a serious ricket by not paying Charlie what I owe him; he's put a contract out on me'.

RULE OF SILENCE

In the early twentieth century there was a **rule of silence** operating in British prisons, i.e. prisoners were not permitted to communicate with each other verbally. It was thought the silence would stop the spread of criminal influence and knowledge within prisons and bring the inmates closer to God. But prisoners quickly devised a system that would allow them to communicate without words, a form of sign language. Touching your left ear meant that you wanted something, so, for example, doing this and then touching your nose meant you wanted some tobacco (your nose being your 'snout'). Only a few of these 'sign words' have lasted into modern prison usage, 'earhole' being one of them.

See On the Earhole

SHIT AND A SHAVE/SHIT AND A SHOWER

If someone tells you they've been in jail for a **shit and a shave** or a **shit and a shower**, it means they have served a very short prison sentence. It refers to the amount of time you would need to perform these **ablutions**.

SHIT WATCH

Whenever a prisoner starts a **dirty protest** there are certain official procedures that have to be adhered to. The door of the prisoner's cell is sealed with masking tape, all staff who go near the cell wear protective suits and masks, and meals are pushed into the cell with a stick so the staff do not have to enter. The staff designated to do all this are called the **shit watch**; they are responsible for the dirty cell and the prisoner.

SLIDING THE MIRROR

Sliding the mirror is a way in which prisoners can pass messages and small items of contraband to each other when their cell doors are locked. Every prison cell is equipped with a small, flat plastic mirror for prisoners to use while shaving – they are standard issue and have a small hole punched through each corner so they can be screwed to the wall. Prisoners usually unscrew the mirror from the wall and thread a line through one of the corners. They then tie their message, or item, to the mirror and place it flat on the floor of the cell, slide the mirror back and forth a few times in order to build up momentum, then slide it under the gap in the door with some force. (All prison cell doors have at least a half-inch gap at the bottom, for ventilation.) The aim is for the mirror to shoot across the corridor and under the door of the cell opposite. A prisoner can do this not only with the cell directly opposite but with any on the other side of the corridor they can see by lying on the floor and looking through the gap. Of course, you have to keep hold of the end of the line . . .

See Hooking, Swinging a Line

SPIN

A **spin** is a cell search, so called because once the **DST** (Designated Search Team) have searched your cell the place will look as though a tornado has been through it. The DST will rip a cell apart in their search for contraband, but the cleaning up after the search is left to the prisoner.

See DST, Pad spin

STARRED UP

A prisoner under the age of eighteen can be **starred up** – that is, have a star placed on their prison file – if they are considered too dangerous for the juvenile system. Once this has been done, they can be transferred to an adult prison.

STIFF

A **stiff** is a letter that has been smuggled out of prison in order to avoid the contents being read by the prison censor. It's called a stiff because, in the old days (up until the 1960s), prisoners weren't allowed to have writing paper so would have to write on bits of cardboard they had managed to rip from boxes in the workshop. A stiff might contain information that the sender does not want the authorities to know about, or it might just be a chance to write to a loved one without having their words read by a prison officer. If a prisoner, gets caught trying to smuggle a stiff out of prison, they will be charged with a breach of prison discipline and can receive up to fourteen days' loss of remission.

SWINGING A LINE

Swinging a line is how prisoners pass items from cell to cell, and sometimes from wing to wing, when they are banged up. There is a certain amount of skill involved. Firstly, you make your line, usually by unpicking lengths of thread or material from a prison blanket and tying them together, and put a weight on one end of it – a plastic prison cup, plastic spoon, a bar of prison soap, a sock with a battery in it, or whatever else you may have in the cell that has a bit of weight to it. Then you alert the person you'll be swinging the line to by calling to their cell window. The person catching the line will hold a rolled-up newspaper or magazine out between the bars of his window and patiently try to catch the weighted end. Both prisoners now have one end of the line and can pass packages – usually drugs, tobacco, a weapon or a note – back and forth along it.
See Hooking, Sliding the mirror

SWOOPER

A prisoner never has enough tobacco, simply because prison wages are so meagre and tobacco is so expensive.

Therefore there are prisoners – heavy smokers – who are always on the hunt for it. When a smoking prisoner runs out of tobacco and has exhausted his credit with other prisoners through constant borrowing, there are only two courses of action open to him – either kick the habit or start **swooping**. Swooping is picking up discarded cigarette butts from the exercise yard and anywhere else they can be found. The butts are either smoked as they are or broken open for the tobacco, which will then be rolled into a cigarette. Some enterprising non-smokers who have access to the screws' offices as cleaners will gather up discarded cigarette butts from the ashtrays, break them open, put them into a pouch and sell or trade them to smokers; the resulting tobacco is commonly known as 'Roadside Virginia'. Swoopers get their moniker from the fact that they will swoop down on any discarded cigarette butt, sometimes snatching it before it hits the ground.

Most swoopers have long abandoned any pride or self-respect in their pursuit of nicotine, but there are 'undercover swoopers', also desperate for their nicotine hit but unwilling to suffer the ridicule of their fellow prisoners. One undercover swooper I observed in HMP Wormwood Scrubs back in the 1980s would attach a piece of sticky tape to the toe of one of his shoes, and if he saw a particularly big cigarette butt he would press his toe on to it, it would stick and he would 'walk' it into his cell. Nicotine is a very addictive drug and probably the most sought after in prisons, where the percentage of smokers is much higher than in the outside world. Withdrawal from nicotine can cause already volatile men to become violent and disruptive. In fact, the government tacitly acknowledged this by exempting prison cells from the 2007 smoking ban. A recent blanket ban in HMP Jurby, the Isle of Man prison, has led to reports of prisoners smoking teabags, hair and cloth in order to try to satisfy their cravings. Assaults in this prison have increased by 48 per cent since the ban was implemented. It's a widely held belief among prisoners that were the authorities to try to implement a prison-wide ban on smoking there would be riots and unrest on a massive scale. We should also remember that even the most hard-line screws and governors acknowledge that British prisons can only be run with the consent and cooperation of the prisoners.

TAILOR-MADE

A **tailor-made** is a manufactured cigarette. The majority of prisoners who smoke will buy cheap tobacco and roll their own. The wages in prison are very low – £7 a week on average – so tailor-made cigarettes, at over £8 a pack, are a great luxury.

See Civvy

TWO BOB

If something or someone is described as **two bob** it means it is cheap and useless. In the days before decimalization, one shilling was known as a bob and little of any value could be purchased with it. The old two-bob piece is the equivalent of ten pence.

See Two-bob rocket

TWO-BOB ROCKET

If someone is described as 'going off like a **two-bob rocket**,' it means that they are not very convincing, a bit of a damp squib, as in 'Yeah, I thought Jimmy was going to smash the wing office up when that screw told him to fuck off, but he went off like a two-bob rocket and just kicked the door'.

UNDESIRABLES

Undesirables is the name given by some prison staff to sex offenders and other prisoners on the protection wings. On the whole, the staff who work with these kind of prisoners volunteer, because the prisoners are less violent and don't cause the same kind of problems as those on the main wings. However, this isn't always the case. Sometimes staffing levels mean that prison officers who don't want to be there are sent to work on protection wings.
See The Mains

UNDIES (2)

Undies are anyone on a prison wing who prisoners think may be undercover, for example, a prisoner in for a sex offence or another undesirable crime who is pretending to be in for something else rather than seek protection. The term can also be used for any prisoner who is suspected of being a grass or an informer, as in 'That ginger geezer on B wing is a bit sussy; I think he might be an undie'.
See Grass (p. 283), *Nonce*

THE VILLE

HMP Pentonville, in Caledonian Road, North London, has long been known as **The Ville** by anyone who has had the misfortune to cross its threshold. Opened in 1816, it was the first of the 'modern' prisons in London. The Ville originally had separate cells, with room for 860 prisoners sentenced to imprisonment or awaiting transportation to the colonies.

These days, it holds around 1,300 prisoners and is an adult male Category B and C jail. The cost of keeping a prisoner there in the 1840s was 15 shillings (75 pence) a week; today, it's £38,000 a year. Prisoners in The Ville tend to come from North London and round about and have their own slang and way of talking. For example, in other parts of the country a £50 note is called a 'nifty' (rhyming) or a 'bullseye' (the centre of a dartboard, worth fifty points), but in North London it's known as a 'McGarrett' (after Steve McGarrett, a detective from 1970s television show *Hawaii Five-0*). A bit like Scousers (the name comes from the name of a traditional Liverpool stew), the North London contingent have a pretty convoluted take on rhyming slang. Not to stereotype or generalize (which is exactly what I'm doing!), but I've found criminals and prisoners from North London tend to specialize in **hoisting**, 'the snatch' or 'blagging' (armed robbery) as their chosen method of crime. There is a large contingent of criminals based in the **Cali** (in and around the estates of Caledonian Road) who are prolific thieves and are always in and out of The Ville. It's as if some of them have their names on the cells.

VP

VP (Vulnerable Prisoner) is the official acronym for any prisoner who seeks protection from other prisoners. Prison protection wings are known as VP wings or VP units, and some non-vulnerable prisoners call them 'VIPs', as they believe those on them are treated better by the prison system than 'ordinary' prisoners.

WAND

In all top-security prisons any prisoner wishing to leave a wing or spur for any reason – to go out on the yard for exercise, or to go to the hospital wing, for example – will have at least a rub-down search by prison staff and probably will also be 'wanded'. The **wand** is a hand-held metal detector which the screws pass over the prisoner's body in order to scan for hidden **blades** or weapons.

WAREHOUSE

This is another term for a prison. A **warehouse** is a huge building used for storage, and a prison, on the whole, is a huge warehouse that stores humans. A warehouse prison is usually a **local** jail, where there is very little in the way of facilities for prisoners, very little training, education or rehabilitation. In them, prisoners may spend up to twenty-three hours a day locked in their cells. The warehouse analogy fits perfectly – think of row upon row of concrete boxes each containing one or more 'body' just waiting for their sentence to end.

See The Hate Factory

THE LANGUAGE OF THE GREYBAR HOTEL

255

7. *Prison Violence*

Prisons are brutal and violent places. Violence is committed by prison staff on inmates, by inmates on prison staff and inmates on their fellow inmates – in prison, violence is commonplace. The violence committed by prison staff on inmates is done so for a variety of reasons: power, anger, revenge, boredom and mental illness (believe it or not, there is no psychological evaluation of prison staff or anyone applying for the job). There are also many reasons for the violence committed by prisoners on staff (psychological evaluations *are* done on prisoners, and a recent report by the Social Exclusion Unit, on 'Psychiatric Morbidity among Prisoners in England and Wales' concluded that 70 per cent of offenders in prison have at least two or more recognizable mental illnesses).

Prisoners manage to make weapons in what is, ostensibly, a sterile, safe environment specifically designed to prevent weapons being used or made. It was recently estimated that the murder rate in UK prisons is seven times higher than in society as a whole. This can partly be explained by the fact that prison is where murderous and violent people are sent for their crimes and, if they behave in a murderous or violent way while they're outside, at large, then what's to stop them at least having the inclination to carry on once they're in jail? They no longer have the threat of prison to keep them in order, and that threat obviously didn't work in the first place, as they're in prison now! It can't be any surprise to anyone that the institution to which society sends its harshest, most violent and chaotic offenders is itself going to be a harsh, violent and chaotic place.

Prison violence is usually swift, merciless and carried

out on the spur of the moment. The creed of prison violence is: do it fast, do it good and do it first.

BED-LEG

Bed-leg is the common name for a **cosh**. The word comes from the small section of steel pipe used to separate prison bunks, which is put in a sock to make a weapon. Bed-legs are formidable weapons: heavy, and capable of caving a man's skull in with one blow. Prisoners will only use a bed-leg cosh when they mean to do serious damage to their victim.

CHIV

A **chiv** is any prison-made cutting or stabbing implement, of any shape or size, made from any material that can have an edge or a point fashioned on it. Due to the large number of metal-detecting machines in high-security prisons, chivs are no longer likely to be made from metal. In fact, most are now made from plastic, crudely sharpened by having been rubbed briskly against brick or concrete. The traditional chiv is a toothbrush handle which has had two razor blades melted into it. Other chivs favoured by purveyors of violence in prison are the six-inch nail, usually fitted into a piece of wood, or a pair of scissors snapped in half to make two separate blades.
See Blade, Shank, Stripe, Tram Lines

CORP THE FEEN

Corp the feen is a Romany term exhorting a companion to knock out, or 'kill', someone who has insulted them or issued threats. On the whole, true Gypsies are known for sorting their problems out via fisticuffs rather than by using weapons or going to the authorities.

COSH

A **cosh**, from the Romany word *koshter*, meaning stick, is any makeshift weapon used for hitting people. In prison, before the introduction of in-cell electricity, prisoners were allowed a battery-powered radio (MW and LW only), and a good one, such as a Roberts Rambler or a Hacker, would be powered by a PP9 battery: square, nine volts and weighing in at around a pound. Drop one of these batteries into a prison-issue sock and you have a very dangerous cosh. Drop two or three of them into a pillowcase and you have a devastating weapon. Some prisoners favour six or eight RS20 batteries (the large round ones) laid end to end, then tightly wrapped in newspaper and taped together for maximum strength, though this does take a little more time. In prison, almost anything can be turned into a weapon, even several bars of prison-issue soap wrapped in a T-shirt or vest – surprisingly effective for such a crude weapon.
See Bed-leg, Millwall Brick

FATTING UP

Perhaps the worst of prison violence involves the action of **fatting** someone **up**. This is normally reserved for the worst sex offenders – those who commit crimes against children – but is also sometimes used against prison staff. The method is to buy a couple of pounds of beef dripping from the prison canteen (top-security prisons allow long-term inmates to cook their own meals), then melt it on a hot ring of the communal cooker. Once the fat has liquefied and is bubbling hot, it is thrown over the victim. Burning fat causes terrible damage and immense pain. It's a truly horrific 'punishment', no matter what the crime. In HMP Whitemoor in 1995 a life-sentenced prisoner retired two prison officers by throwing a pot full of boiling fat over them. The governor of the prison decreed that, from then on, prisoners could no longer purchase oil or dripping from the canteen. Ever resourceful, they then began to use margarine to cook, and in fatting up. There is only one thing more painful and damaging than having hot fat thrown in your face, and that is having melted, boiling margarine thrown over you. As long as prisoners have access to cookers, they will find a way to fat up their enemies.

GLASGOW KISS

A **Glasgow kiss** is a headbutt to the face, given this name because of its popularity in the city.

JERKING

Jerking is stabbing somebody very seriously so as to cause the utmost damage, and takes its name from the body's reaction to it. In prison, these stabbings will usually be done with half a pair of scissors or a sharpened six-inch nail set into a wooden handle (known as a 'jerker', or **chiv**).

JUGGING

Jugging is a very violent prison punishment. Every prisoner is issued with a two-pint plastic jug to keep drinking water in when they are locked up in their cell. This jug can be used as a weapon (usually reserved for sex offenders and informers, though not exclusively so) if it is part-filled with sugar and then topped up with boiling water from the wing's communal waterboiler. The mixture is stirred until it becomes a boiling syrup and then thrown in the face of the victim. The syrup clings to the skin and burns like acid, often leaving the victim permanently scarred.

See Teabagging, Wetting up

MATTRESS JOB

A **mattress job** is a beating, usually given by the police to a prisoner in a police cell. Each police cell contains a thin blue mattress for prisoners to sleep on. If a prisoner is a bit leery or causes problems, is violent or won't admit to crimes, the police will enter the cell **mob-handed** and knock him to the floor. They will then throw the mattress over him and proceed to stomp and kick him all over his body. The blows will hurt very much but leave no tell-tale cuts or bruises because of the mattress. Mattress jobs are also sometimes used in prisons by prison officers in the punishment block.

See Blanket job, Mob-handed, Sheeting

MILLWALL BRICK

A **Millwall brick** is a makeshift weapon popularized by the hooligan element of Millwall Football Club. It is a normal newspaper that has been folded several times until it's the size of a housebrick; it's then a solid block that can be used to **cosh** rival hooligans. It's a very effective weapon in the right hands (though it usually isn't). The Millwall brick became popular when police searches were introduced at football grounds in order to prevent hooligans bringing weapons in. A newspaper would attract no suspicion.

SHANK

A **shank** is any kind of bladed instrument used for cutting or stabbing. It's an Americanism that has found its way into common British usage via films and rap music.
See Blade, Chiv

SHEETING

In recent years, particularly among prisoners in Young Offender Institutions (though not exclusively so), **sheeting** has become a common punishment. It involves prisoners throwing a bed sheet or duvet over the victim from behind and then beating (or, in extreme cases, stabbing) the victim while they are wrapped in it and unable to see. This method of attack has three advantages: the victim won't be able to identify the assailants; the cover will stop blood or other DNA evidence from splashing on to the attackers; and the sheet or duvet will muffle the screams of the victim.
See Blanket job, Mattress job

STABBERS' ALLEY

Almost every prison wing will have a blind spot where there are no screws or cameras. These spots are known as **Stabbers' Alley**, originally after a short, dark corridor in HMP Winchester used as a location for 'hits' on other prisoners. If you venture into Stabbers' Alley, the chances are you'll be stabbed, beaten or cut, or see it being done to someone else.

STRIPE

To **stripe** someone is to slash them with a **chiv** or razor, usually across the face, leaving a stripe. Striping is a pretty common punishment in prison, particularly in young offenders' jails, and is often dished out to drug debtors and informers. A stripe from ear to mouth is called a **telephone line** and is the mark usually given to informers.

TEABAGGING

Teabagging comes from the Tetley teabag adverts that boasted of the bags having a thousand perforations. I now realize that the term has a very different connotations in the outside world, but in prison it is a serious stabbing, usually by two or more assailants. It can happen anywhere, but the favourite location is the shower block, preferably when the victim is naked, with shampoo in their eyes and at their most vulnerable, or in the meal queue, when there are very few screws about. (There are no Marquess of Queensberry Rules governing jail violence.) A teabagging relies on speed: the assailants attack quickly then melt into the background, leaving the victim in a pool of blood.

Teabagging is usually reserved for sex offenders or informants but can also be a punishment ordered by a dealer because a prisoner owes him a serious amount of money. The average price for hiring a hitman in prison is around £50 worth of heroin.

TELEPHONE LINE

A prisoner or criminal with a scar that runs from his mouth to his ear is usually one to be avoided. This kind of scar is called a **telephone line** and it is usually inflicted to show that the victim has informed.

TRAM LINES

Prison violence is brutal and bloody. One method that causes serious injury to an enemy is to melt two razor blades into the handle of a prison-issue plastic toothbrush, usually with a good gap between the blades, and use this as a weapon, a **chiv**. The reasons for using two blades are, firstly, because they will make a distinctive scar and, secondly, the wound will be very hard to stitch up. The strip of skin between the cuts will also be affected and so the attack will leave a broad scar. It's known as handing out the **tram lines** because the two cuts resemble a tram track.

WET UP

To **wet** someone **up** in prison is to attack them using a mixture of boiling water and sugar.
See Jugging

8. *Drop Me Out, You Lemon!*

In the criminal and prison world many extremely offensive and often racist insults are thrown around. You have to remember that criminals and prisoners generally do not class themselves as part of conventional society; for them, rules are made to be ignored or smashed to pieces. Whereas in straight society there are boundaries around the sort of things you can say (and rightly so), in the criminal world those boundaries are either very different or do not exist. A straight-goer might worry about causing offence or hurting somebody's feelings by using certain words or phrases but, most of the time, a criminal will only worry about a physical comeback. When it comes to insults and racial epithets, the slang of the criminal world is a law unto itself. There are very few polite criminals and, though the denizens of this world are not all die-hard racists and forever insulting each other (although a lot of that does go on), they are very casual about what most people would call offensive language.

British adult prisons and juvenile jails (in the male estate) are, as one might expect, extremely macho environments. Politeness, political correctness and decency hold no sway. It's all about showing how tough you are through the way you speak as well as the way you act, and if this means you have to use offensive and insulting language, then that's the law of the jungle. There is an official prison rule against prisoners using offensive words and behaviour, but if prison staff were to nick everyone eligible for a **nicking** under this rule, they'd have no time for anything else and the queue of prisoners waiting to receive **adjudication** would take longer than most prison sentences! The only time prison staff nick a prisoner under this rule is if the offence has been directed at them – though sometimes this doesn't work out as the officer might have planned.

Some years ago a pal of mine was nicked for calling a screw a 'big fairy'; he was a tall, skinny officer, quite effeminate, and he spoke with a lisp. The governor heard the evidence from his officer, then turned to my pal and asked, 'Why did you call this officer a big fairy?' To which my pal replied, 'Well, look at him, Governor; what would you call him?' The governor glanced at the officer, then lowered his head over the paperwork, trying to hide a grin. He found my pal guilty but gave him a suspended sentence instead of seven days' solitary confinement.

It must also be noted, for the sake of balance and honesty, that a majority of prison staff are not shy about using offensive and abusive words and phrases themselves. As for racism, it has been well documented (the Woolf Report; *Loose Screw* by Jim Dawkins, *Screwed* by Ronnie Thompson, numerous news reports, among others) that a culture of racism certainly existed up until the 1990s amongst prison staff. Personally, I can remember certain prison officers wearing National Front pins in their ties, or 'gollywog' badges, quite openly in the 1980s.

You do hear some pretty entertaining insults in the world of crime and punishment; I've used some of them in my short stories. Some of the bon mots I've heard border on the surreal: 'When she smiled her teeth looked like a bowl of Sugar Puffs!'; 'If I had a face like that, I'd shave my dog's arse and teach him to walk backwards!'; 'She looked a bit like Winston Churchill licking week-old Nazi piss off a broken bottle!'; 'If he'd had one white tooth in his mouth, he'd have had the full snooker set!'. These are just some of the things I've heard over the years, and most of them in all seriousness. When it comes to slagging people off, you can't beat the criminal world for offensiveness.

Some insulting words and phrases fall out of use with time, and others become popular. For example, nowadays, you rarely hear a lot of the racist expressions of the 1960s and '70s – words such as 'wog', 'sambo', 'jigaboo', 'spade' and 'darkie'. You might think this is because criminals, along with people in general, are more enlightened and less racist than they were in the past, but this, in my experience, is sadly not the case. Criminals come from every race, country and cultural background, but I would say they are usually more casually racist than the general population. Many criminals of different racial origin will work together to commit crime, sometimes out of necessity. Different races in the criminal world tend to specialize in different crimes, though there is a large crossover. For example, if a criminal is dealing in heroin, they will as a matter of course have to deal with criminals from Turkey, Afghanistan or China. Heroin comes into the UK from these three countries and the trade is all but controlled by criminals who come from there. Pickpocketing, once the preserve of UK criminals, is now almost completely in the hands (no pun intended) of Eastern Europeans. Drug smuggling has broadened the horizons of some UK criminals, who now deal with the Dutch, the Germans, the Iranians and Afghans (or 'cheese-eaters', 'krauts' and 'rag-heads', to give them their racist alternative names). I'm quite sure that people from these countries also have offensive names for the UK criminals they deal with. It's the way of the criminal world and, as far as the criminals are concerned, as long as the cash flows in, it's nothing to lose sleep over. So, to make it quite clear: if you look at the language of insults in the criminal world, you have to be prepared to be offended.

ADIDAS SEX-CASE

Adidas sex-case refers to prison-issue plimsolls: blue, with a thick sole, a white stripe and white laces, primarily for wearing in the gym but often worn by some undiscerning prisoners as everyday footwear. There are many names for this footwear and all are derogatory. A lot of sex offenders and weirdoes will wear them, but most self-respecting prisoners would rather go barefoot. The use of 'Adidas' is ironic because Adidas make real training shoes.

See Baccy tins, Fila c***s, Jack the Ripper, Nigerian Nikes (p. 233)

BABYLON

To West Indians, **Babylon** can be anything they don't like or consider ungodly. So England itself can be Babylon, or the police, or prisons. The term was brought into use in prison by Rastafarians, who consider Babylon to be their great enemy. To some Rastafarians, white people are Babylon.

BACON

Bacon is offensive slang for a sex offender. It comes via a pretty convoluted phrase of rhyming slang (bacon bonce = nonce = sex offender). The thinking behind this is that a good and nasty name to call sex offenders is 'bacon bonce', which translates to pig's head ('bonce' being slang for 'head') and rhymes with 'nonce'.

See 86 (p. 138), Beast (p. 157), Biff/Biffa (p. 157), Nonce (p. 235)

BALLOON (1)

In Scottish prisons a **balloon** is a very stupid person, someone whose head is full of nothing but air, as in 'Get te fuck, ye fuckin' balloon'.

BAM POT

Bam pot is Scottish slang for a complete idiot or imbecile, as in 'Get te fuck, ye bam pot!'.

It has found its way into common criminal usage due to the amount of Scottish prisoners in English prisons.

BANDIT

A **bandit** is a criminal who will try their hand at most crimes: 'anything to earn a pound note,' as the old criminal adage goes. Bandits are serious criminals, in that they commit crime for a living rather than as a one-off or a hobby. It seems they just love to commit crime and usually have long criminal records and numerous prison sentences behind them. But 'bandit' is also an offensive term meaning a homosexual (**bum bandit**), or just a dishonest person who will try to rip you off.

THE BARRY

If someone tells you to 'stop giving it **the Barry**', they mean for you to stop acting so flash or cocky (rhyming slang: Barry McGuigan = big un). Barry McGuigan was a World Boxing Association featherweight champion. To give it the 'big un' means to act in a flash or cocky way.

BATTY MAN

Batty man is an insult much used by young men of West Indian origin to denote a homosexual. 'Batty' is a patois version of 'bottom', so a batty man is a homosexual who enjoys buggery.

See Bumba Claat, Raas Claat

BEAST

Beast is usually reserved for those who commit crimes against children. To be labelled a beast means that, wherever you go in prison, you have to keep looking over your shoulder in case of attack. Beasts are detested by ODCs (Ordinary Decent Criminals) and even by other sex offenders who may feel their crimes are not as bad as those of a beast.

See Beast man

BEAST MAN

Beast man is a West Indian slang term for the police, as in 'Man was strapped but when the beast man rushed him he couldn't get his ting out in time'. It can also be used to describe a sex offender.

See Beast

BILLY BULLSHITTER

There are many **Billy Bullshitters** in our prisons – prisoners who can't tell the difference between reality and their own outrageous fantasies and spend their time spinning stories, usually about how many Ferraris they have, or how they were in the SAS but were thrown out for being so vicious. One particular Billy Bullshitter who comes to mind from my own time in prison was always banging on about his time in the Parachute Regiment and the great battles he'd fought in. Eventually, I grew tired of listening to his fantasies and told him to prove he'd been in the Paras or not talk to me again. A few days later he turned up with a book about the history of the Parachute Regiment and pointed to a picture in it of a heavily equipped and masked parachutist freefalling from a plane. 'There you go!' he said triumphantly. I pointed out that the caption gave the name of the parachutist, and it definitely wasn't his name. Quick as a flash, he smiled craftily and said, 'Yeah. But who do you think took the picture!?' What can you say to bullshit like that?

See Jackanory

BLOGGS

Joe Bloggs has long been a pseudonym for the 'man in the street', or the 'man on the Clapham omnibus', or any man whose name is unknown to the speaker, but in the 1990s a special unit was set up in HMP Parkhurst in order to hold supergrasses away from the rest of the prison population, who, for obvious reasons, would be intent on doing them harm. Each of the prisoners on this unit was given a number, preceded by the name Bloggs, for example, Bloggs 1, Bloggs 2, etc. So now, if someone in prison calls you a **Bloggs**, it means they suspect you of being an informer.

BOO-BOO

A **boo-boo** is a derogatory term for an African, usually used by young West Indians. West Indians think that Africans are stupid and not very streetwise and, particularly in prison, class them as inferior. The term is a play on how the conversations of Africans (though mainly Nigerians) sound when they talk in their own languages, as in 'They're talking that fucking boo-boo shit again'.

BOY/BOY OFF

To **boy** someone **off** – that is, to call them a boy or treat them as if you think they are less than a man, to challenge their manhood – is a bad insult, and is seen as very disrespectful, particularly among the young. Much of the violence in young offender institutions results from someone being boyed off: it denotes a lack of respect, which is bound to trigger it. 'Boy', when used as an insult, has connotations of slavery; in the American Deep South, even old men (if they are black) are still referred to as boys. In prison the word is used only by someone prepared to act with violence.

However, in another context, it has less potency and is used almost as a term of endearment. For example, if someone were to say, 'Clean my cell, you fucking boy,' this would be very insulting, but if they said, 'Me and you is **bredrins**, you're my boy,' it wouldn't be a put-down. As with a lot of slang, context is everything.

BREAD (1)

To be described as a **bread** in prison or criminal circles means that you are a bit of a violent maniac (rhyming slang: bread and butter = nutter.) If a prisoner is having trouble getting their money or drugs from debtors, or someone is threatening them, it's handy to have a friend or associate who is 'a bit of bread' to call in to help them out.
See Crank, Radio Rental

BROWN TONGUE

Anyone who hangs around the screws or works for them as a tea boy is known as a **brown tongue**, which means that they have been metaphorically licking the system's arse. Brown tongues are usually ostracized by the rest of the prison population and can become targets of violence for fraternizing with the enemy. Sucking up can also be known as 'brown-nosing', as the nose of the toady will be stuck firmly into the backside of the authorities.

BUBBLE

A **bubble** is a Greek person or person of Greek origin (rhyming slang: bubble and squeak = Greek), as in 'I sold it to some bubble firm over in North London'. Bubble and squeak is a dish made with leftover potatoes and cabbage, which are fried up, and is often served as breakfast; the name comes from the noises the ingredients make when they are put into a hot pan.

In London, 'bubble' is also used for someone who gives information to the police or other authorities. So a **grass** can also be known as a bubble in some quarters and this has nothing to do with the Greek explanation but is due to the fact that the rhyming slang 'bubble and squeak' can also mean 'speak'. If someone calls you a bubble and you're not of Greek origin, then you'd better watch your back.

BUDGIE SYNDROME

Budgie syndrome is what a lot of prisoners who regularly use the prison gym seem to suffer from. It's a disease that makes them pose or parade up and down in front of the full-length mirrors, preening and chirping at their own reflection. Every prison gym will have a large quota of bodybuilders who act as though they're on Muscle Beach, grunting and stretching and working out, but always with one eye on themselves in the mirror. It's called budgie syndrome because these prisoners ape the behaviour of budgerigars locked up in cages with only a mirror for company. Many men in prison make use of the gym in order to build themselves up, and a lot of them take it very seriously. In some prisons there's a roaring trade in steroids and a lot of gang members will hit the gym, which is classed as neutral territory – very few people will cause trouble in a prison gym, as they know they'll be instantly banned and that means more time locked up in their cell. The way to make a bodybuilder turn into a paranoid quivering wreck is to ask casually if they're losing weight – as the bodybuilder's target is to bulk up in order to look bigger, the thought that they may be losing weight is, to them, as the crucifix and garlic are to the vampire.

BUMBA CLAAT

Bumba claat is a West Indian insult in common usage in Jamaica. Its literal meaning is 'bum cloth'. Before the invention of toilet paper (and even in some poor countries today), you would clean yourself after defecation with a piece of rag. The sound of the words 'bum cloth' in Jamaican patois is drawn out, creating the expression 'bumba claat'. It's also called a **raas claat**. 'Pussy claat' is very similar in origin, and is also used as an insult in Jamaican patois.

BUM BANDIT

A **bum bandit** is a predatory homosexual who will try to force himself on vulnerable or unwary males. In essence, they are sex pests and rapists who target men and boys. Ronnie Kray was a notorious bum bandit.

CABBAGE

A **cabbage** is anyone dimmer than a 20-watt light-bulb. Before the advent of in-cell television in prisons, there was a communal TV set, usually at the centre of the wing, where prisoners on **association** could get their daily diet of soap operas. This was commonly known as the 'cabbage patch' or **vegetable patch**, because only those with not much going on between their ears would gather there.
See Hobbit hole, Vegetable patch

CARDBOARD GANGSTER

A very common insult, particularly in prison: a **cardboard gangster** is someone who likes to pretend to be a real gangster, though in reality they are no such thing. 'Celebrity gangsters' are a prime example of this, posing with fake guns and pretending to be major criminals when they have no such pedigree as a 'working criminal'. Some people are attracted to the dubious glamour of the criminal world, in much the same way that certain women are attracted to the worst kind of serial killer.

CARE BEAR

Care bear is a disparaging term used by some prison officers to describe the minority of their colleagues who try to help prisoners with their problems. The world of prison officers is, overall, a macho one, where daring to show that you care about doing your job properly is frowned upon by the majority. If a prison officer gets a reputation among his fellows as a care bear, he can expect to be sneered at and treated like an idiot. Some prison officers pride themselves on how little they can get away with doing during their working day and treat all prisoners like shit. Being a care bear in this culture and environment is a bit like being a fart in a spacesuit.

See Dog screw

CAT'S ARSE

Cat's arse is rhyming slang for **grass**, so another name for an informer, as in 'I don't like that new bloke on C wing, I heard he's a bit of a cat's.'

See Grass, Lolly, Midnight

CELL SOLDIER

A **cell soldier** is a prisoner who is full of mouth when locked in his cell, shouting insults and threats at other prisoners through his cell window during lockdown, but who is as meek as a kitten when the cell doors are opened and they are faced with the people they have been abusing. 'Cell soldier' can also be used to describe somebody who remains in solitary confinement, usually in the punishment block of a prison, and shows no signs of concern – somebody who can handle their **bang-up**.

See Bang-up, Cardboard gangster, Window warrior

CHARLIE BIG SPUDS

Charlie Big Spuds is the generic insult for anyone who walks around giving it **the Barry**, a bully who may have a tendency to fold when confronted. It's particularly used in prisons, where some criminals try to reinvent themselves. Other forms are Billy Big Bollocks or **Jack the Biscuit**.

CHIEF

To young people, **chief** is a dire insult and to call someone it is to invite violence: you cannot 'chief someone off' and expect to get away with it. The word has African connotations and relates mainly to Nigerians, who are considered by some to be stupid, greedy and ruthless enough to inform on anyone in order to save their own necks. It comes from the fact that many Nigerian criminals will falsely boast that they are the chief of their tribe or village in order to perpetuate fraud. Nigerians have a reputation unparalleled around the world as major fraudsters, so much so that, in 1989, the Nigerian Government, embarrassed by a report which claimed that Nigerians made up the highest population of foreign prisoners in most of the prisons in Europe, decreed that any Nigerian national who had been convicted of crime or served a prison sentence abroad would be deported back to their homeland and face an immediate five-year prison sentence.

See Boy

CLEAN-AND-JERK

Clean-and-jerk is rhyming slang for a Turkish national and is used quite extensively in the parts of the criminal world in which there are a lot of Turks involved, in particular, the heroin trade. In British prisons, Turkish prisoners are known as big gamblers and provide a great income for the prison bookies. A clean-and-jerk is a weightlifting exercise used in competitions; it involves lifting a heavy weight to waist level and then jerking it up above your head in one clean movement.

See Gon-bee

CRACKHEAD

A **crackhead** is someone addicted to the semi-solid form of cocaine known as crack. Once known as freebase, crack is made from powdered cocaine which is cooked, or 'washed', and turned into a rock that can be smoked in a pipe. It's very addictive, as the initial high doesn't last very long; addicts can go downhill fast in the search for cash to fund their addiction. Crackheads are avoided by serious criminals. They generally have to become prolific thieves to feed their habit but, usually, the only people who will work with them are other crackheads. Even **skagheads** look down on crackheads.

See Skagheads

CURRY MUNCHER

Curry muncher is a derogatory term for anyone of Asian origin but particularly Indians and Pakistanis. It's taken, obviously, from the fact that curried meat and vegetables are the staple diet.

See Half-ounce, Joe Daki

DABBLER

A **dabbler** is a prisoner with no, or very little, history of drug use or abuse who will start to use heroin whilst in prison. Unfortunately, heroin is a drug that is cheap and widely available in UK prisons and a lot of prisoners take their first hit whilst behind bars. Dabblers usually think that if they only smoke the drug, rather than injecting, and use it every few days rather than daily, they will not get addicted. Sadly, they are usually wrong. The large majority of dabblers will leave prison with a habit to feed and only one way to get their hands on the money to do it – stealing. It is dabblers who are more likely to die of an overdose once released from prison. This is because they have become addicted to prison heroin, which is weaker than street heroin as it has been further cut in order to maximize profit behind bars. As soon as the dabbler has their first hit of strong street heroin they will realize the difference, but by then, it may be too late.

DIDIKOI

A **didikoi** is a Gypsy of mixed blood, not strictly a Romany. The word is used as an offensive term or insult by criminals to describe an amateur who can't be fully trusted. In the Gypsy world the didikoi was never fully trusted by full-bred Gypsies as he was 'neither here nor there'.

DIS

Dis is a word frequently used by the young to mean 'disrespect'. The concept of respect is a broad one for most youngsters nowadays. If you make a face at someone, if you stand on someone's toe or even just disagree with them, you are showing a lack of respect for them. Most of the postcode gang wars in London and other major cities start with one person dissing another.

DIV/DIVVY

Div is a very common insult in the criminal and prison world. Meaning a stupid person, it comes from the Romany word *divvio*, meaning a little bit mad. A form of the word is also used as an adjective, **divvy**, as in 'I ain't sure about Tony, he seems a bit too divvy to deal with the alarms on his own'.
See Fraggle, Mong

DODGY

If something or someone is described as **dodgy**, it usually means that there's something decidedly suspect about them: risky, not quite right, fake, as in, 'That kettle looks very dodgy, you sure it's a Rolex?'. It's probably derived from 'dodge' (to avoid or evade, moving swiftly and shiftily). Street traders and fly pitchers sell the dodgiest of dodgy gear to the public.

DOG SCREW

Prison warders are traditionally known as screws, but if a screw is classed as a particularly bad bastard, one who detests the prisoners in his charge and behaves towards them accordingly, then they will be known as a **dog screw**, that is, one who should not be approached as they will behave like a rabid dog, snarling at you as if you had tried to snatch a bone from them. In my estimation, and speaking from thirty-two years' experience of the prison

system, the ratio of dog screws to regular screws in the UK prison system is about 1:10.
See Care bear

DO ONE

If someone were to tell you to **do one**, it would mean you are to go away and attempt to procreate with yourself. It's a relatively polite way to tell someone to fuck off, widely used by criminals, and often followed by the word **mug**, as in 'Do one, you mug, or I'll rip your head off and piss down your neck'.

DOSSER

A **dosser** is a down-and-out, or homeless person, who will sleep wherever they can. The word is used as a mild insult, especially by young Travellers.
See Paraffin

DRY LUNCH

Dry lunch is an East End expression for someone who is particularly tight-fisted with money, and refers to the fact that even when having a meal this person will not buy a drink.

DRY SNITCHING

This is to inform on someone indirectly by talking loudly or performing suspicious actions when screws are around. **Dry snitching** is an Americanism mainly used by younger prisoners; 'snitching' is American slang for informing or grassing. There is a popular saying in American jails, which has now made its way into the British penal system: 'Snitches Get Stitches.' This means that if you inform on anyone to the authorities and you are found out, you will be seriously cut, usually around the face or across the buttocks, though not exclusively so. **Sweetgrassing** is the British version of the dry snitch, and it pertains to someone who informs in a roundabout manner rather than directly. For example, you might say to an officer, 'How come so-and-so has got his own jeans on but the rest of us have to wear prison-issue jeans?' To someone on **The Out** that might sound like a perfectly reasonable enquiry, but in prison it is seen as grassing so-and-so for not wearing prison-issue jeans. For this you can get in serious trouble, but it depends on who hears you and whether so-and-so then has his jeans confiscated by the staff because you have pointed them out.

See Grass

EEJIT

Eejit, meaning a very stupid person, is an Irish corruption of 'idiot', though it is now quite extensively used by English people with the same meaning and context.

FEARGAL

'Darkie' as a description of a black person has long fallen out of vogue in both the criminal and civilian worlds but racism is never far away at any time and it has made something of a comeback, albeit in a disguised form, in the last decade, particularly in prisons. **Feargal** sounds quite inoffensive, on the face of it, compared to some slang for ethnic minorities, but the full explanation is not quite so innocent. It comes from rhyming slang: Feargal Sharkey =

darkie. (Feargal Sharkey was the lead singer of 1970s new-wave band The Undertones and went on to have a solo career.)

FIRE

Fire has the same meaning as **hot**, but it is used more by people of West Indian origin, as in 'Keep well away from me, man, you is fire, blood!'
See Heatwave, Hot

FRAGGLE

Fraggle Rock was a children's television show featuring weird little puppet creatures that spoke in a strange language. To be called a **fraggle** is a mild insult; the word was casually bandied about in the 1980s and '90s, though it has now fallen out of vogue. A fraggle was somebody who was obviously mentally ill. The word was so popular in prison at one time that the infamous hospital wing at HMP Brixton where seriously mentally ill prisoners were held was nicknamed Fraggle Rock, after the island where the TV fraggles lived. Even prison staff referred to the hospital wing like this.

FRIDGE

Fridge is rhyming slang (fridge freezer = geezer). It's not really insulting as such, although 'geezer' does imply someone old. It's possibly a corruption of 'geyser' – ancient natural landmarks, holes in the ground, which shoot out hot water and air.

FUGLY

Fugly is used to describe somebody who is a bit more than ugly, and is a mix of two words, 'fucking' and 'ugly', as in 'That bird I saw you with last night was fugly, mate'.

GOBSHITE

Gobshite is a slang word of Irish origin and means somebody who talks shit; nothing they say is to be taken at face value or trusted.

GON-BEE

Gon-bee is slang for a Turk (rhyming slang: gone berserk = Turk), as in 'Fuck me, I got in the warehouse an' it was full of gon-bees all waving AK47s'. Gon-bee is quite prevalent in London prisons and manors, whereas the use of **clean-and-jerk** is spread more widely across the country.

GRASS

To be called a **grass** (grasshopper = copper) in criminal or prison circles is a serious matter, as people who inform are a danger to other criminals and are dealt with severely, and sometimes fatally. Probably the most infamous grass in British criminal history was Derek Creighton 'Bertie' Smalls, who became the first supergrass in the early 1970s and gave evidence against dozens of his confederates whilst securing freedom for himself.
See Cat's arse, Lolly, Midnight

GRASSHOPPER/COPPER

HALF-OUNCE

A **half-ounce** is someone who hails from Pakistan (rhyming slang: half-ounce of baccy = Paki), and is often used by white criminals to describe anyone of Asian origin. Half an ounce is smallest weight of rolling tobacco (baccy) you can buy. In the old borstal system the slang was 'quarter-ounce', because the wages were so low that canteen staff would cut a half-ounce packet straight down the middle and sell it to the trainees for half the price. This process has now been banned in UK prisons, for reasons of 'health and safety', apparently.
See Curry muncher, Joe Daki

HANDBAG

To be described as a **handbag** in criminal circles is to have your manhood called into question. A handbag is an effeminate or drippy person, someone not to be trusted in a fight.

HEAD-THE-BALL/HEADER

A **head-the-ball**, or **header**, is someone who is a bit **divvy** and not to be trusted, as in 'He's a proper fucking header so don't bother trying to explain anything complicated to him'.

The term comes from the idea that, when playing football, if you head the ball too much, it will scramble your brain and make you dim.
See Div

HEATWAVE

If a prisoner is described as a **heatwave**, it means they are hotter than a £50 shotgun. They will be hotter than **hot**, meaning that even to be seen in their vicinity will be dangerous. This can be because the prisoner is behaving in an obviously suspicious manner, or because they are obviously under surveillance by the authorities. Avoid them at all costs.

HOBBIT

A **hobbit** is a **mug** of no importance, or someone who is always sucking up to the screws. Calling someone a hobbit, unless they actually are a hobbit, is an insult and can sometimes lead to fisticuffs. The word has been used as an insult in prison since the 1970s and is of course taken from the J. R. R. Tolkien book of the same name.

HOT

If someone is described as **hot**, it usually means that the authorities are on to them, or watching them, and that if you approach them you run the risk of being implicated by association. For example, there may be a raving junkie on the wing who has lost all discretion and is going from cell to cell, prisoner to prisoner, asking who will sell them heroin. This person will be considered hot, or even a **heatwave**, and will be avoided by all sensible cons and dealers. Prison staff know very well that as long as they can identify the drug users in prison – and their demeanour makes this easy – all they have to do is watch which cells they visit on the prison wing and the odds are good they'll be able to identify who's dealing drugs. Also, in the criminal rather than the prison context, if a criminal is described as hot then it means they are too risky to work with, due to being under the attention of the police or another authority; they may be under constant surveillance. Or it could be that they are suspected of cooperating with the authorities. Either way, if someone is described as hot, they are best avoided.

See Heatwave

HUNGRY C***/HUNGRY BASTARD

A **hungry c*****, or **hungry bastard** is someone who wants more than their fair share. The term can be applied to a criminal but is usually used for bent officials who demand large bribes in order to lose evidence or supply information to criminals. The Flying Squad had this reputation in the 1960s and '70s when they were known to take bribes and demand part of the loot stolen by certain robbery firms. They became known as 'the firm within a firm' after Detective Sergeant John Symonds was covertly taped in 1969 by two undercover reporters working on a police corruption story for *The Times*. He told the reporters that he could fix any police matter for a price and, if he couldn't, then he would know someone in the force who could, as they were 'a firm within a firm'. Proper **hungry bastards**!

See Noble cause corruption, Operation Countryman (p. 114), *The Sweedy*

ICE CREAM

If you were to describe someone as an **ice cream**, you would be seriously questioning their courage. Back in the 1970s and '80s the hooligan element of West Ham United Football Club in East London were known as the ICF (InterCity Firm) because of their habit of using InterCity trains to get to away matches. The ICF had a terrible reputation as brutal tear-up merchants but were very proud of it, and their name. Their West London rivals, Chelsea Football Club, had an equally violent hooligan element known as the Headhunters. In order to goad their East London rivals, the Headhunters nicknamed the ICF the Ice-Cream Firm, meaning they would melt in the face of stiff opposition. This slur on the ICF led to many pitched battles between the two sets of fans. In criminal circles, to have a reputation as an ice cream is a serious hindrance, as no sensible criminal will want to work with you.

JACKANORY

A **jackanory** is a liar or someone who tells outrageous stories. It comes from the children's television show *Jackanory*, in which a presenter reads stories. To mutter 'jackanory' when someone is speaking is an indication that you don't believe a word that is being said.
See Billy Bullshitter

JACK THE BISCUIT

Jack the Biscuit is someone who acts hard or tough when they are no such thing, and is an insult applied to any flash or cocky prisoner or screw. Jack the Biscuit will walk around with both arms stuck out as though he has an imaginary roll of carpet under each armpit, trying to give off an air of being hard. But nine times out of ten Jack is as thick as two short planks, although he may very well be able to bench-press his own bodyweight. Despised by most as a **mug** or a **div**, he will nevertheless continue to have an overinflated sense of his own importance, handsomeness and fighting skills, even when faced with evidence to the contrary. But, like a biscuit, the fake hard man will disintegrate when in hot water.
See Cardboard ganster, Charlie Big Spuds

JAFAKEN

A **jafaken** is a white or Asian person who affects a Jamaican accent in order to make themselves seem more windswept and interesting. A lot of young prisoners develop a ridiculously accented patois, despite the fact that the closest most of them have been to the Caribbean is hearing a Bob Marley track on the radio. Many young British blacks also put on a West Indian patois, even if they were born in this country and have grown up in Peckham. When questioned, they'll tell you they do this because their parents speak in this way, which is a bit like a British kid with Italian parents giving it plenty of '*Mamma mia!*', or someone with Irish parents talking in a thick brogue and shouting 'Top o' the morning to ye!' every five minutes. The jafaken is usually held in contempt by other people of white or Asian origin. Jamaican patois seems to have replaced estuary English and mockney as the accent and language of choice for many young people. Such people used to be called **wiggers**.
See Wigger

JAFFA

A **jaffa** is someone who is impotent, because Jaffa oranges are seedless, but it's also cockney slang for a complete idiot. The word has fallen out of favour with criminals due to its heavy usage by Del Boy Trotter, the character played by David Jason in the BBC comedy series *Only Fools and Horses*.
See Div, Jules, Melt, Mug

JAMMY

If someone is described as **jammy**, it means that they are having a run of good luck or are getting rewards they do

not truly deserve, as in 'I see that jammy bastard just won a grand on the lottery'.
See Spawny

JESSIE/NANCY

Jessie or **Nancy** is old-fashioned slang for a man who is effeminate though not necessarily homosexual, as in 'What do you mean you don't like football? Are you some kind of fucking Jessie?' To be labelled a Jessie or Nancy means that you're a bit suspect and not to be trusted.

JOCKNEY

A **jockney** is a person of Scottish origin who has spent too long in London and starts to talk with an accent that is a mix of Scottish and London (cockney). The term is seen as offensive by true Scots, but not as offensive as **sweaty**.

JOE DAKI

Many cockneys call anyone of Pakistani origin a **Joe Daki** (rhyming slang). As far as I know, there was never anybody whose name was Joe Daki; in that way, it's a bit like 'Joe Bloggs'.
See Curry muncher, Half-ounce

JULES

A **Jules** is somebody who is a little bit effeminate and not very bright, and comes from the 1960s BBC radio show *Round the Horne*, with Kenneth Horne, in which Hugh Paddick and Kenneth Williams play a couple of flamboyant homosexuals, Julian and Sandy.

KAPPA SLAPPA

Kappa slappa is a mainly northern term for a female of loose morals who will invariably be wearing a cheap tracksuit or any other item of clothing by the sports clothing company Kappa. Kappa clothing is considered the cheap and tacky end of 'designer name' wear. It's a very common term, particularly in the north-east.

KNOBHEAD

Knobhead, meaning complete idiot, is a common insult in criminal and prison circles but has also come into popular usage in some sections of straight society. If you clench your fist and place it on your forehead, that is the 'sign' for a knobhead.

KNOB JOCKEY

A **knob jockey** is a homosexual, the term fairly evidently taken from the action of riding a penis. It's used frequently as an insult in prison, particularly in the Northern nicks.

KNOCKER/TILBURY

A **knocker** or **Tilbury** is someone who does not pay their debts (rhyming slang: Tilbury docker = knocker). Tilbury was once a thriving port with many huge container ships, and the dock workers employed there were known as Tilbury dockers. 'Knocker' for someone who does not pay their debts comes from the game of dominoes, where a player will knock on the board or table if they aren't able to take their go. If a player knocks, they miss a go, and their opponent gets the chance to lay their domino. If a debtor misses a payment, particularly in prison, then they become known as a knocker, but instead of missing a go they might be assaulted, sometimes very seriously, as a 'lesson' to pay their debts promptly. Once a prisoner has a reputation as a knocker, no one will allow them to bet or gamble on anything, which can be a problem, as gambling is a big part of life in British jails. Gambling in prison is officially banned, but it is so endemic that prison staff find it impossible to enforce this and usually turn a blind eye.

LAG

A **lag** is a convicted and serving prisoner, from the nineteenth-century word meaning to steal and be caught, as in 'He's done about a twenty-stretch in shovel; he's an old lag now'.
See Lag Boat

LAG BOAT

Having a **lag boat** means having a tired, grey, haggard face, as though you had spent years in prison. It's a combination of **lag** and the rhyming slang for 'face' ('boat race').

LEMON

As with the majority of slang words, **lemon** has more than one meaning. The first dates from the old **borstal** system. Fred Lemon was a confirmed criminal who served many prison sentences before, apparently, meeting God Himself in HMP Dartmoor in the early 1950s. He then dedicated his life to preaching the Gospel and wrote a book about his experiences, *Breakout*. This book was heavily pushed on borstal trainees by the chaplain's department as a sort of 'guide to going straight', and Fred's surname became slang for a **mug**, for someone gullible, or someone who professed a belief in religion. If you were called a lemon in borstal, it meant that you weren't very bright and you believed in fairy tales. The second use in criminal slang is to describe the face people pull when they are annoyed, that is, as though they have been sucking a lemon, as in 'Don't get lemon with me or I'll give you a smack in the jaw'. It's also slang for cocaine, or charlie (lemon barley = charlie). These days, the most common use of 'lemon' is the second one, a facial indicator of displeasure.

LOLLY

At one time, back in the 1950s and '60s, **lolly** was used by criminals to describe the loot or money they had stolen, but that use has now fallen out of favour. These days, a lolly is someone who has been giving information to the police or prison authorities (rhyming slang: lollipop = cop). To be called a lolly in the criminal or prison world is a serious matter and can mean that your health and well-being is in imminent danger.
See Cat's arse, Grass, Midnight

LUCOZADE

Lucozade is rhyming slang for 'spade', meaning a black person.

MALT

Between the First and Second World Wars there was an influx of Maltese citizens into the UK, and many of them settled in London. Crimes that the Maltese criminal was particularly attracted to were gambling and prostitution. Some Maltese criminals became pimps, but were known as **ponces**, because what they were doing was seen as poncing off women. Poncing was frowned upon by a lot of the more macho and violent London criminals, so the Maltese were held in contempt by them. In the 1950s and '60s **Malt** was an offensive word on a par with 'nigger' or 'Paki'.

MANKY

If something or someone is considered **manky** it means it is or they are dirty or unwashed. The word is believed to be a corruption of the Italian word *mancare*, meaning to be lacking something (in this case, hygiene). It came into usage via Polari, the secret language of homosexuals, in the 1950s.

MATEY

Matey is south-coast slang (particularly in Portsmouth and Southampton) for any male whose name you don't know, as in 'I just about had the patio doors open when some matey stuck his head over the fence and said he'd called Old Bill' or 'I was minding my own business when a couple of mateys jumped me'. The word has a naval connotation, which is probably why it is more popular in coastal towns.
See Mush

MELT

A **melt** is an idiot who cannot be trusted – as thick as cow shit (cow's melt) and liable to **grass** you up at the earliest opportunity. Melts are to be avoided for your own safety.

It's mainly a South London word, though it is also widely used elsewhere.

MICKEY MOUSER

Mickey Mouser is mainly used by Londoners for someone from Liverpool (rhyming slang: Mickey Mouser = Scouser).

MIDNIGHT

If someone accuses you of being a **midnight**, they are calling you a **grass** or an informer (rhyming slang: midnight mass = grass). It's a word that was used a lot in the 1960s, and is also currently used in Irish prisons (where the prison population is more religiously minded, and the accent works better).
See Cat's Arse, Grass, Lolly

MONG

A very common insult meaning that someone is not the brightest spark in the fuse box. It's a corruption of both 'mongol', which used to be used in connection with people who have Down's Syndrome, and 'mongrel', meaning a mixed-breed dog, not a pedigree. The meaning of **mong** depends entirely on the context of its use.
See Monged out

MUG

A **mug** is anyone who is not a criminal and some people who are! Mugs are targets for criminals, and being a mug generally means you'll get no respect from those who commit crime. The original meaning of the word was 'face', because of the popularity of Toby jugs, which featured short-bodied figures with over-large faces, but these days **boat** is more commonly used for 'face', and 'mug' has become a person who doesn't deserve respect.

See Toby

MUPPET (2)

Once a commonly used casual insult in the criminal world to describe anybody who was stupid or strange-looking, as in 'That fucking **muppet** forgot to cut the main wire to the alarm'. It has fallen out of favour because it's now overused by straight-goers, having been featured in director Guy Ritchie's mockney gangster films. Once a word comes into common public use it usually falls out of the criminal lexicon. The original Muppets were created by Jim Henson, who coined the word 'muppet', a mix of 'marionette' and 'puppet'.

MUSH

A **mush**, a Gypsy word for a man, is any male person whose name you don't know, as in 'I was just about to set me jook on a hare and some mush pulled up in a jam jar' or 'You know that mush with the twin lurchers, him from Lonesome Depot?'. It can also, however, be used as slang for the face, as in 'I hit him right in the mush with a right hook'. It was very common in the 1960s and '70s but has now rather fallen out of vogue except for Travellers and Gypsy folk.

See Matey

NARK

A **nark** is someone who will get busy around your business in the hope of finding information about you which they can sell to the police, so it's a paid police informer. The word comes from the Romany word *nak*, meaning nose, so by extension it's a nosey person. In America, the word is connected to the police narcotics (drugs) squads who would harass hippies in the 1960s and go undercover on college campuses and at music festivals in order to catch them using or dealing drugs.

NUMPTY

A **numpty** is a complete idiot. It's Scottish in origin but came into criminal usage via the many ex-armed forces bods who take up crime or end up in prison for violence after they are discharged. It's used not only by criminals and prisoners but also by the majority of prison officers, a high proportion of whom are also ex-armed forces personnel.

NUT JOB

A **nut job** can be a mentally ill prisoner, a seriously violent criminal or a method of execution. The 'nut' is the head. In the first case, the word refers to the odd behaviour of mentally ill prisoners – they are **nutters,** or nut jobs. An active criminal who is referred to as a nut job is someone who is very violent and willing to commit violence for money, as in 'I want this bloke taught a proper lesson – get one of the local nut jobs to pay him a visit.' In the world of professional assassins, a nut job is a bullet in the head. Once again, context is everything.

See Double tap (p. 352), *Nut nut*

NUT NUT

A **nut nut** is how young, crazy people are described, meaning that there seems to be something wrong in their heads. 'Nut' being slang for head and also for being mad, a nut nut is someone who is not right in the head.
See Nut job

NUTTER

A **nutter** is somebody who isn't quite right mentally but, in the context of prison, it can also be a very violent or ferocious person, someone who will do anything and fight anyone just for the fun of it.
See Nut job

ODD MARK

In criminal circles an **odd mark** is somebody strange or not quite right, either because of something to do with their appearance or the way they act. It comes from the world of confidence tricksters and scam artists, who call their victims **marks**.

PARAFFIN

Were someone to call you a **paraffin**, they would be intimating that you are a **dosser**, or tramp, or someone scruffy and not very well dressed (rhyming slang: paraffin lamp = tramp). It's a mild insult in criminal and prison circles.

PIG

Pig is an offensive word for the police which was very widely used in the 1970s but isn't so much these days, having been largely replaced by the more offensive 'filth'. It was used a lot in Northern Ireland during the Troubles, not only to describe the police (who are also commonly known as **black bastards**, because they wear black uniforms) but also for the Saracen armoured vehicle used by the police and the British Army.

PIKEY

In the sixteenth century 'pike' meant 'to go away from', as in 'You had better pike or there will be trouble', and was connected to the words 'turnpike' (a toll road) and 'pike-man' (the man who collected the tolls). It is not until the publication in 1847 of J. O. Halliwell's *Dictionary of Archaic and Provincial Words* that **pikey** is applied to Gypsies. In general, a pikey was 'a turnpike traveller; a vagabond; and generally a low fellow'. **Pikey** in the twenty-first century is usually used to describe any group of people or individuals who are deemed an underclass of thieves, tramps or Travellers. Romany Gypsies use the word to describe Irish Travellers and non-Roma Gypsies. It is classed as an insult to most people but particularly to Roma Gypsies. In the criminal world, the word is used to describe petty thieves and **ponces** in the lower reaches of the criminal underworld. East London gang boss Ronnie Kray once described his South London rivals the Richardson gang as 'just a bunch of South London pikeys'. *See Ponce*

PILCHARD

Pilchard is old cockney slang for someone who is not very bright, 'not the full shilling', because pilchards are classed as particularly stupid fish who will swim straight into a net in great numbers.

PLUM

To be labelled a **Plum** in the old borstal system was to be a stupid person of very little importance. It originally came from the *Beano*, in which there was an American Indian character called Little Plum who was as thick as they come. Borstal boys usually came in three categories: **chaps**, the top tier; saps, run-of-the-mill middle dwellers; and plums, the victims at the bottom of the pecking order.
See Pilchard

PONCE

A **ponce** is someone who lives off others because they do not have the balls to put themselves on offer by committing their own criminal activities; they are held in contempt by 'real' criminals. Infamous twentieth-century criminals the Kray brothers were known as 'thieves' ponces' because they would bully and seriously assault other criminals to steal their ill-gotten gains. In prison, a ponce is someone who is always looking to 'borrow' or get something for nothing. The majority of **skagheads** are ponces. Nobody likes a ponce.

PURE MENTAL

Pure mental is an expression, mainly used in Scotland, to describe someone who is very 'hard' or a particularly violent person. It can also be used as a term of admiration for someone's fighting prowess.
See Nutter

RAAS CLAAT

Rass claat is a Jamaican expression along similar lines to **bumba claat**, also literally translated as 'arse cloth'. It's a mild insult or cover-all expression mainly used by West Indians and **jafakens**.

RADIO RENTAL

If someone is described as **Radio Rental** it means they are not all there mentally (rhyming slang: Radio Rental = mental). The original Radio Rentals company was popular from the 1930s (when it rented out radio sets to the public) up through to the 1990s (when it rented out TVs and video recorders), but it went out of business in 2000, as electronic goods had become cheaper and people could afford to buy their own.
See Bread, Crank

RAVING IRON

A **raving iron** is a flamboyant homosexual (rhyming slang: iron hoof = poof). Before 1998 it was sometimes shortened to 'raver', but after the 'acid summer' when raves became popular the meaning became blurred as young people attending raves were known as ravers. The balance was soon restored, however, when rhyming slang took up the slack and ravers became known as cheesy Quavers (after the snack), then as just cheesys, and raving irons went back to being known simply as ravers.

SCROTE

This is a typical insult used for criminals and prisoners, a favourite with uniformed authority, so also big in the armed forces. Examples would be 'Let's get all these **scrotes** banged up in their cells' or 'You're nicked, you fucking scrote!'. It originated in America and came to the UK via US films and TV shows. The word is a corruption of 'scrotum'.

SCRUBBER

A **scrubber** is a young woman or girl of loose or dubious morals; also, classically, a female prisoner, so called because of the amount of scrubbing done in female prisons. In 1980 a film called *Scrubbers* was made about the British female **borstal** system in response to the 1977 film about the male borstal system, *Scum*.

SI /SYE

A **Si**, or **Sye**, is someone who can't be trusted, is gullible and not very bright. It comes from the old children's rhyme 'Simple Simon met a pie man . . .' in which Simple Simon basically gets mugged off.

SIZZLER

A **sizzler** is a **nonce** or sex offender. It's an evolution of **bacon**, in that bacon sizzles in the pan.

SKAGHEAD

A **skaghead** is someone who is addicted to heroin and has lost their moral compass. Skagheads are usually despised and mistrusted in the criminal and prison world. It's thought that they will do absolutely anything to get their hands on a fix of heroin, so they are avoided by unaddicted criminals. Heroin is known as skag by a lot of people, hence the word skaghead; it is also known as 'tackle', so to be called a 'tacklehead' is an insult on par with being called a skaghead.

See Crackhead

SKANK

A **skank** is an ugly, dirty female of dubious sexual morals. The word was originally used for a Jamaican dance performed to ska music. It's also a word of West Indian origin that means to cheat someone or take something without paying for it. In Rochester **borstal** in the 1970s the local newsagent who visited the institution once a week in order to supply tobacco and confectionery that the borstal trainees could spend their weekly wage on was known as 'Fred the Skank'. He gained the 'skank' tag because he would constantly try to rip the trainees off, for a penny here and a penny there.

See Borstal

SLAG/SLAGGING/SLAG OFF

Slag started life as a slang word for a girl or woman of loose or dubious morals. Possibly, it comes from mining communities in the Midlands and the North where slag is the all-but-useless by-product of coal, so something extremely cheap. London villains have made the word an insult that isn't gender specific but usually means a bad, nasty person, as in 'That slag blew the whistle on the blag'. As a verb, it's also used as a means of putting something down, **slagging** it **off**, and similarly, it can also mean to give someone a severe dressing-down, as in 'I gave him a right **slagging**!' It's been widely used in prisons since the 1950s.
See Slapper

SLAPPER

A **slapper** is a female of very loose morals inclined towards sexual promiscuity. The word is believed to have come either from the amount of slap (make-up) a woman wears when out on the pull, or, more likely, from the sound of naked bodies slapping together during sexual intercourse.
See Slag

SPAGHETTI BENDER

A **spaghetti bender** is anyone of Italian origin. The British seem to have a deep-seated ditrust of Italians and this can perhaps be traced back to the Second World War, when the Italian Fascist Party under Benito Mussolini formed an alliance with the Nazis. The Italians were quick to surrender and change sides when things began to go against them and this led to the myth that all Italians were cowards and to a lot of jokes, for example, 'What is the smallest book in the world?' '*The Italian Book of War Heroes*'; or 'Italian tanks have only got two gears, reverse and surrender', and so on. The British people were quick to forget that the Roman army, who conquered a lot of the known world, were of course Italians. But then, racism is a lot about choosing what to remember and what to forget. It's a form of selective amnesia.

SPAWNY

Spawny has the same meaning the same as **jammy**, and is a Northern word that came into common usage in southern prisons because of a character in the early *Viz* comics called Spawny Bastard. Spawny Bastard, no matter what outrageous situation he got into, would end up better off and smelling of roses. A lucky, jammy, spawny git!

STOOLIE

Stoolie is an Americanism that has found its way into the British lag's lexicon via film, TV and music; it means a **grass** or informer. It comes from the old practice of tying a pigeon to a stool and leaving it out in the open (much the same as a tethered goat) to attract other birds or predators while the hunter waits in the undergrowth with their gun at the ready. The stool pigeon is considered a traitor because it's a decoy luring in others, so any criminal who is working for the police to help them to catch other criminals was labelled a stool pigeon, and this is shortened to stoolie. It's used extensively by younger British criminals and prisoners.
See Grass

SWEATY

There is nothing more guaranteed to elicit violence from a Scotsman than to be called a **sweaty** to his face (rhyming slang: sweaty sock = Jock).
See Jockney

SWEETGRASS

A **sweetgrass** is an informer who grasses by mistake, or by design disguised as mistake. For example, if someone in prison goes to the staff in secret and gives them information that so-and-so has an unauthorized item, say an extra visiting order which he may have obtained by illegal means, then that person is no more than a **grass**, plain and simple. But if that same person were to speak to the staff out in the open and within hearing of other prisoners, and say, 'How come so-and-so can get an extra visiting order and I can't?', that would be construed as sweetgrassing. The person would still be informing the authorities about something, but because they are doing it openly it would be perfectly legitimate in some people's eyes, although others would see it as being against the prisoners' code. Sweetgrassing is such a grey area that the sweetgrass will not usually suffer violence from other prisoners as a result of it but they will, most of the time, be ostracized by 'proper' cons – depending on the temperament and capabilities of the person who has been sweetgrassed. To be known as a sweetgrass is pretty bad, but it's not as dangerous as being known as a plain **grass**.

TORY JUG/MUG

TART

When it's used to describe a woman, **tart** usually means a sexually promiscuous girl or woman (rhyming slang: merry heart = tart), but when it's used to describe a male, it usually means someone with effeminate tendencies or suspect courage, as in 'I told him to smack the fella right in the mooey, but the tart just let him get away with a **slagging**'. It can also be used as a term of endearment towards a girlfriend, as in 'Me tart came up yesterday and brought me a pukka **elephant**', though, understandably, it's not usually used within the hearing of the girlfriend.

TIDDLY

A **tiddly** is anyone of Chinese origin (rhyming slang: tiddlywink = chink). 'Chink' is an offensive word for Chinese people and comes from the shape of their eyes, which are said to 'only open a chink'; Tiddlywinks is a game played with counters that must be flipped into a central container.

TOBY

A **toby** is somebody who is very gullible and ripe for ripping off (Toby jug = **mug**). A Toby jug, also known as a fillpot or philpot, is a pottery jug usually in the form of a seated man. Some people believe they were named after Sir Toby Belch in Shakespeare's *Twelfth Night*, but the term has come into general criminal slang through the blurred borders between street traders and criminals. It's usually used to describe the customers who buy from the former, as in 'I've got a suitcase full of pissy water ramped up as designer perfume and a box of brass rings with

9-carat-gold stickers all over them – the tobys will lap them up.' Sellers of stolen goods and illegal street traders are constantly on the lookout for tobys.

See Hedge (p. 80)

TOSSER

Tosser is old-fashioned slang for somebody who masturbates, so a **wanker**. It's used as an insult for anyone who goes out of their way to make life difficult for others; the implication is that they are too **fugly** or useless to get a girlfriend.

VEGETABLE PATCH

Some prisons do not have a specific room for the communal television and so it is placed centrally on the wing and prisoners must bring their cell chairs to sit on around it during **association** periods. This spread of chairs around the TV is usually known as the **vegetable patch** because it's where the 'vegetables' (those who want to sit, slack-jawed, in front of a TV watching soap operas) sit. When a prisoner ends up in the vegetable patch they are classed by other prisoners as a **cabbage** or Cabbage Patch Kid (after the freaky-looking American dolls of the 1980s), or as a **hobbit**, meaning they have given up and accept their imprisonment. 'Real' prisoners never accept their imprisonment.

See Hobbit hole (p. 208)

WANKER

A **wanker** is somebody who masturbates. The terms wank and wanker originated in British slang in the late nineteenth and early twentieth centuries, and they have been widely used both in prisons and in the Royal Air Force since at least the 1920s. In modern usage, it is usually a general term of contempt rather than a commentary on sexual habits. The sign language for it is to curl the fingers of the hand into a loose fist and move the hand back and forth to mime male masturbation, usually to an audience out of hearing range, which is equivalent to saying, 'You're a wanker.'

See Tosser

DOING BIRD

WIGGER

A **wigger** is a white or Asian person who acts and speaks as though they are black, particularly Jamaican or West Indian. The word is a combination of 'white' and 'nigger' and has been in use since the 1970s.

See Jafaken

WINDOW-LICKER

To be a **window-licker** means that you are mentally deficient. It comes from the myth that whenever you used to see a blue bus (the favoured mode of transport for days out from mental institutions), at least one of the passengers would have their tongue on the window. The insult is on a par with **mong**. Some criminals class all of straight society as window-lickers, in the belief that straight-goers are idiots and must be mentally ill for going to work and doing things the hard way.

WINDOW WARRIOR

A **window warrior** is a prisoner who is either on drugs, unable to read or write, or bored and wishing to stir up trouble during a lockdown period in prison. The window warrior will try to disguise his voice and shout threats and abuse at other prisoners through his cell window, hanging on to the bars and trying to wind up other prisoners in order to get them shouting threats back. Before the introduction of in-cell television in British jails, window warriors were a big problem, causing untold aggravation with their verbal antics and creating a dangerous and violent atmosphere, as, when the cell doors were unlocked, most prisoners would go looking for whoever had been dishing out the verbal abuse and try to physically assault them. Prisoners are volatile enough without all this abusive prompting. The introduction of televisions has meant that window-warrior behaviour has all but died out now, as even the dimmest con can't be bored when there are soap operas by the dozen and daily documentaries on killer sharks or Nazis to keep them occupied.

9. *Drugs*

The drug world is littered with slang, both obscure and well known, as you would expect. The trouble is that it changes so quickly: no sooner does someone think up a code for a product than the authorities crack it and everyone goes back to square one. Most street-level dealers now call their product 'food', which implies that it's something users can't live without. This section of the book would be as long as the Bible if I were to list every single slang word there has ever been for drugs and drug dealers, so I'll limit myself to the more common and perhaps more interesting ones connected to the denizens of this shady world.

ACID

Acid is LSD (lysergic acid diethylamide), a hallucinogenic drug that was very popular in the 1960s and '70s. It had a renaissance in the late 1980s due to the acid-house craze, where young people would gather in fields and empty warehouses to take acid and ecstasy and dance the night away.

See Bumbles, Cheesy Quaver

BALLOON (2)

A **balloon** is a packet of drugs that has been placed inside a rubber balloon and swallowed. Cocaine and heroin are the main drugs smuggled in this fashion, as they come in powdered form. The smuggler will normally double or triple up on the parcel, so the drugs will be put inside the first balloon and then two or more put over the first. (Rubber can be corroded by stomach acid and the balloons have to be held in the smuggler's stomach, sometimes on very long journeys halfway around the world.) Smuggling drugs in this way is very dangerous; if even one balloon bursts inside the body, it can lead to death. Some people use condoms rather than balloons, but the principle is the same.

BILLY

Billy is amphetamine sulphate, or speed, a drug, usually in powder form, that is a powerful stimulant and appetite suppressor. The term is taken from a character in *The Beano*, Billy Whizz, who moves so quickly he leaves clouds of dust behind him.

BILLY RAY

To a lot of intravenous drug users the prospect of contracting **Billy Ray** (rhyming slang: Billy Ray Cyrus = The Virus (AIDS)) is very real. Billy Ray Cyrus is an American country singer who had a big hit in 1992 with a song called 'Achy Breaky Heart'.

BOMB

In the drug world a **bomb** is powdered speed (amphetamine sulphate) wrapped in a cigarette paper and dropped into a drink. This means that the drug enters the blood system more quickly; the practice is known as 'bombing' it.

BOOT

Boot is a word you will hear a lot in our prisons, given that approximately 70 per cent of the prison population are heroin users. It's rhyming slang for smoking heroin off a piece of foil (bootlace = chase, as in 'chase the dragon'). Needles are quite hard to get hold of in prison, so most heroin users will put the powdered drug on a piece of tinfoil and light a taper under it, causing the drug to liquefy and run along the foil. The resulting fumes are sucked from the foil using a 'tube', also made from tinfoil. First-time users of the drug (it has been estimated that up to 60 per cent of users have their first taste of heroin in prison) prefer to smoke rather than inject, as they believe it is harder to get addicted if the drug is smoked. This is nonsense.

See Jimmy, Skaghead (p. 304)

BOTTLE (1)

To **bottle** something is to secrete it in your anus for later retrieval. This is quite common in prison, where there are many rub-down searches for contraband.

BROWN (1)

Some criminals and drug users refer to Afghan heroin as **brown**. This is to distinguish it from Chinese heroin, which is white in colour and is referred to as **China white**. In 1981 the punk/new wave band The Stranglers released a song called 'Golden Brown' about the joys of Afghan heroin, and it became a hit all around the world. Initially the band said the song was about Marmite, and it wasn't until songwriter Hugh Cornwell released a book about The Stranglers' songs in 2001 that he finally admitted publicly that the song was about heroin.

See China White

BUMBLES

Bumbles is Ecstasy (rhyming slang: bumble bee = E), as in 'Send another thirty bumbles, the **cheesy Quavers** are up for it'. Ecstasy is usually taken in pill form and contains MDMA. It made its debut on the acid-house rave scene of the late 1980s and became the drug of choice for people who fancied a wild weekend of dancing. The drug had many nicknames – disco biscuits, the love drug, E – but the criminals who dealt them called them bumbles.

See Acid

CHEEKING

Cheeking is a popular prison method of smuggling or concealing drugs. It involves placing the **elephant** (parcel of drugs) between the buttocks so it won't be found in a rub-down search. It's used as a temporary measure for people who normally **bottle**, but also by those too squeamish to force something up their anus. The standard prisoner search involves a rub-down or pat-down search over the clothing on the outside of the body. It is only during a full strip search that prison staff might force the prisoner to squat and visually inspect their buttocks. If you have an illicit item cheeked, the odds are good that it will pass a rub-down search, but it will rarely pass a strip search.

See Dry bath (p. 190), Elephant

CHEESY QUAVER

This rhyming slang was in widespread use during the acid-house dance craze and is still in use today. The people who went to illegal raves (all-night drug and dance parties) were known as ravers initially, but in London and the south-east 'ravers' had homosexual connotations so was preferred.

CHINA WHITE

China white is high-grade Chinese heroin that is white in colour, as opposed to Afghan heroin, which is brown.
See Brown

CLUCKING

To be **clucking** is to be suffering withdrawal from any drug, but particularly heroin. It's taken from the jerky movements and cries that junkies – and chickens – make. Those addicted to heroin find it hard to bear when they don't have any, and this is when they cluck. Also, when they are coming off heroin, voluntarily or involuntarily, clucking is part of the process.
See Roger

COLOMBIAN NECKTIE

A **Colombian necktie** is a pretty extreme and bloody method of dealing with suspected police informers. Pioneered by Colombian drug cartels in the 1970s and '80s, it involves cutting the person's throat and then reaching into the wound to the base of the tongue and dragging the entire tongue through the gaping wound so that it hangs down on to the chest like a gruesome necktie. This is a warning to anyone else who might think of informing.

COP

Cop has several meanings, but the one related to drugs is a verb – 'to cop' – meaning to obtain drugs.

CRACK

Crack is a form of cocaine. The powdered cocaine is 'cooked' with various chemicals until it forms a solid lump, which will then be broken down into small rocks for sale by street dealers. Crack cocaine is much more addictive than powdered cocaine and the high only lasts a couple of minutes, meaning there is an immediate need for more. Crack is usually smoked in a pipe. In the 1970s this way of cooking the drug was known as free-basing, but it was an expensive habit as some of the powder was wasted in the process. In the 1980s the Colombian drug cartels and the Jamaican yardies found a cheaper way of creating the drug and it became a relatively inexpensive way to get seriously addicted.

See Crackhead

DEVIL'S

A **devil's** is a measure of drugs, usually a quarter of an ounce (rhyming slang: devil's daughter = quarter), as in 'Give me a devil's and I'll pay you on Friday when I get my **elephant**'.

DREADLOCK HOLIDAY

A **dreadlock holiday** is a trip to Jamaica in order to pick up and smuggle drugs back into the UK. Many drug dealers will pay single mothers to take one, asking them to pick the drugs up from one of the dealer's accomplices in Jamaica. Cocaine is usually liquefied and put into bottles of suntan lotion, shampoo or even champagne, which the **mule** packs into their luggage for the return trip. Some ruthless dealers will pay several people to smuggle the drugs on each trip and then inform the authorities that one of them is carrying drugs in the hope that the rest of the smugglers get through with their parcels and the authorities will be kept happy, thinking they're doing a great job of guarding the borders. The term comes from a 1976 number-one hit by 10CC.

See Mule

ELEPHANT

An **elephant** is a parcel of drugs that can be concealed on the person (rhyming slang: Elephant and Castle = parcel). Elephant and Castle is an area in South London. A typical example of the incomprehensibility of prison slang can be found in this statement: 'Got me Richard on a v this avvy with a pukka elephant, I'll be off me tits by six bells bang-up!' (Translation: 'My girlfriend's coming to visit me this afternoon and she's bringing me a parcel of drugs, so I should be high as a kite by six o'clock lock-up!'). If someone in prison tells you that they have an elephant coming, do not automatically assume a pachyderm is visiting the prison!

HALF-OUNCE DEAL

Between the 1960s and '90s cannabis was the main black-market currency in British prisons and the **half-ounce deal** was the standard unit of that currency, the amount of cannabis given for a half-ounce packet of tobacco. For this you would get enough to make two spliffs. Almost every item on the prison black market was priced in half-ounce deals or multiples of it. For example, a litre of good **hooch** would cost three half-ounce deals, and a well-made **chiv** might cost five half-ounce deals. Before cannabis became popular in prison, tobacco was the king of prison currency. Since the introduction of Mandatory Drug Testing the new currency is £10 bags of heroin.

See The Naughty

HEP

Hep is short for hepatitis, a disease that is fairly prevalent in British prisons. This isn't surprising, given the high number of intravenous drug users.

ICKLE PREPS

Used mainly in the juvenile prison system and of West Indian patois origin, **ickle preps** is a small amount of cannabis usually given for free. It's usually enough for a joint or a 'one-skinner' and the term is a corruption of 'little preparation'.

See Return

JACK UP

To **jack up** is to inject drugs intravenously, usually heroin. A prison refinement is that the 'syringe' is usually homemade, from the outer casing of a ballpoint pen, and far from being sterile: both syringe and needle will be kept, when not in use, up the prisoner's anus. As any kind of disinfectant is banned in prison (as well as syringes), these homemade syringes are passed from person to person with only a cursory attempt at cleaning them. The British prison system is awash with heroin, though most prisoners prefer to smoke it rather than inject. For obvious reasons . . .

The younger criminal element, enamoured of all things American and heavily influenced by gangsta rap, use the term in another context. To them, a jack-up is a street robbery or the theft of a luxury or expensive car. Jacking is stealing, usually with threats or force.

See Billy Ray, Boot, Bottle, Jag, Skaghead (p. 304)

JAG

To **jag** yourself is to inject drugs intravenously. The word is of Scottish origin and refers to the jag of the needle as it enters the vein.

See Jack up

JIMMY

A lot of heroin users believe that smoking the drug, rather than taking it by intravenous injection, makes it less likely that they will become addicted. This is quite wrong: heroin is an addictive drug no matter how you take it. The criminal world and UK prisons are full of heroin addicts and they have their own language for their habit. **Jimmy** is rhyming slang: Jimmy Boyle = foil. When smoking heroin ('chasing the dragon') the user will empty the powdered drug on to a strip of jimmy and then hold a lighted taper under it to build up enough heat to liquefy the drug. The liquefied heroin, or 'beetle', is 'chased' up and down the foil with a 'tube' and the fumes are sucked deep into the lungs. It's ironic that heroin users have adopted this term, named after infamous Scottish hard-man prisoner Jimmy Boyle, as he is notoriously against heroin and has campaigned against the drug in his native Glasgow.

See Boot, Skaghead

MONGED OUT

To be **monged out** is to have taken a lot of drugs and as a consequence be sitting around staring into space and dribbling. People who take heroin will usually have a period soon after taking the drug where they are monged out. It's also known as gauching, or nodding, as the drug taker's head tends to droop. Some drugs seem specifically designed to mong you out, in contrast to those that make you very active, such as cocaine or speed.

See Mong

MULE

A **mule** is someone who is paid, usually a pittance, in order to transport drugs on their person. Quite often they are people living in poverty in countries where the drugs are produced. Drug mules carry the drugs either on their person or internally, by swallowing packets of them. There are many drug mules serving long sentences in the British prison system. Mules are the lowest rung on the illegal drug ladder.

THE NAUGHTY

The naughty is heroin. It got this name because up until the heroin revolution in British prisons in the late 1980s, mainly caused, I would say, by then Home Secretary Michael Howard's introduction of Mandatory Drug Testing (MDT), heroin was considered to be a dirty drug, used only by hippies and scumbags (according to the serious-criminal fraternity). It was believed that any criminal who used it could be a liability, as the police would be able to manipulate them into **grassing** by withholding the drug. No serious criminal would openly admit using heroin or **having it** with anyone who used it.

It was only after the introduction of MDT in prisons that heroin really took hold in the criminal fraternity. Cannabis had been the drug of choice for the majority of prisoners up until then, but heroin can be flushed through the body in forty-eight hours, whereas traces of cannabis can remain for up to fifty-six days, so using heroin lowered the risk of proving positive for drugs. If a prisoner proves positive for drugs, they may lose remission, privileges, be placed on closed visits or in solitary confinement – usually for a period of fourteen days. These days, prisoners who do not take heroin are seriously outnumbered by those who do, and it's the non-users who are viewed with suspicion.

NECKING

To **neck** something is to swallow it in order to retrieve it later. This is a popular method of smuggling drugs into prison. A prisoner can then either 'chuck it up', usually by swallowing obnoxious potions such as washing-up liquid and toothpaste (whatever happens to be available) or have

a 'cave in', brought on by taking large amounts of laxatives. Necking parcels of drugs can be very dangerous, particularly if they are opiates, which is why prisoners are in a hurry to get them out of their bodies rather than waiting for nature to take its course. Most necked drug parcels will be wrapped in several layers of clingfilm and then tied into a condom or rubber balloon for extra safety.
See Balloon (2), Bottle

RETURN

A **return** is an exchange of drugs between prisoners. If two prisoners have social visits on alternate weeks, they may help each other out, with one giving the other a small amount of drugs with no charge, with the proviso that the other does the same the following week. A return can be mutually beneficial and assure a supply of drugs for both users for the bulk of the time. The problems come when one of the parties misses a visit for any reason, or fails to **cop**; then they have to pay for the drug return or suffer the consequences. This can be anything from being blanked and losing the beneficial arrangement to actual physical assault, depending on the relationship between the two parties.

ROGER

If you use drugs like heroin, crack or powdered cocaine, then the chances are good that you will end up with a **Roger** (rhyming slang: Roger Rabbit = raving habit), after the cartoon character in the 1988 film *Who Framed Roger Rabbit?*. Once someone is addicted, they can spend days and nights in pursuit of the drugs themselves or the money to buy them.
See Clucking

STASH

A **stash** is something illegal, usually drugs, that is being stored or stockpiled. To stash something is to hide it for later retrieval. Drug dealers have a stash of drugs which they sell portions of at a time.

See Lodge (p. 362)

WEED

Weed is herbal cannabis. 'Have ya got a weed, lad?' is a common question in northern prisons, meaning 'Are you selling cannabis?'.

Giving It All That

10. *Old Bill, Persians and Rabbiting the Script*

As well as specialist words for crime and criminal acts, there are also everyday slang words which have become the norm for a lot of people, whether they're connected to the criminal world or not. Many of the following may be quite familiar to the straight-goer, having crept into day-to-day language. Words and phrases such as **bung** or **bang to rights** have entered the straight-goers' consciousness through their use in tabloid newspapers and popular television programmes and, often, phrases fall out of favour with the criminal fraternity just because they have become so widely accepted.

ABRAHAM LINCOLN

A term meaning smelly (rhyming slang: **Abraham Lincoln** = stinking), sometimes shortened to 'Abes', as in 'That khazi is absolute Abes!'
See Reels of

ACKERS

Ackers is old-fashioned cockney slang for money, taken from the Egyptian currency the akka and possibly brought into British usage by returning servicemen. A lot of slang words were brought into popular usage by ex-service personnel.
See Jank

ADAM

A synonym for 'believe' (rhyming slang: Adam and Eve = believe), as in 'Would you **Adam** it?' Mainly used by cockney criminals and prisoners and often heard on television and the radio throughout the 1970s and '80s in such programmes as *Only Fools and Horses* and *Minder*. Some people use the full rhyme, as in 'Would you Adam and Eve it!', usually as an expression of disbelief or exasperation.

ALL RIGHT?

All right? is the universal greeting among criminals and prisoners, who tend to be paranoid by nature and always want to be reassured that everything is okay.

ALMONDS

A word for socks (rhyming slang: almond rocks = socks), as in 'When is **kit** change in this **nick**? These **almonds** are **reels of**' or 'I need to change my almonds, they're proper Abes'. *See Reels of, Abraham Lincoln*

ANCHORS

The **anchors** are the brakes of a vehicle, as in 'I saw the security van in me rear-view mirror, so I slammed on the anchors'.

ANKLE-BITER

An **ankle-biter** is any small child that can't yet walk, as in 'Yeah, I've got a visit on Sunday; me missus is bringing the ankle-biters'.

APPLE

An **apple** is £20 (rhyming slang: apple core = score; twenty is a score), but the more common usage among criminals and prisoners is as a coverall for knowledge or information, as in 'What's the apple?', meaning 'What's going on?' or 'Tell me the news'. It can also be used as the opener to a threat: for example, 'You know the apple, now pay up or nasty things will happen' (or words to that effect). Screws tend to use it a lot in a mildly threatening context in order to solicit compliance from mouthy prisoners, particularly when they're about to carry out some routine indignity like a strip search or piss test. The subtext is that if you argue or kick off in any way, the screw will be forced to get nasty. In the past tense, it's used to imply that a victim is to blame, as in 'He knew the apple. If he didn't want his face slashed then he should have kept his nose out.'

ARCHER

An **archer** is £2,000 in cash, and is named after the amount of money paid to prostitute Monica Coughlin by lying toad and piss-poor plotmeister Jeffrey Archer in order to ensure her silence. Archer eventually went to prison for perjury and spent his time there writing three volumes of prison memoirs. Three volumes is quite a feat, considering he only spent two years of a four-year sentence in prison, and the majority of this was at HMP Ford, an open prison sometimes known as 'the country club' because it's such an easy regime. It's the prison where those with fame, money and clout go when they're sentenced. A 'double archer' is £4,000.

BABY MOTHER/BABY MUDDAH

A **baby mother** is any female who has had a child by someone. The term is of West Indian origin, particularly Jamaican, and is widely used by young black males to describe the mothers of their children, as in 'Later, **bredrin**, man haffa go an check my baby muddah'.

BACK-UP

If you were going on a dangerous criminal mission, to front another criminal or to collect on a debt, then you would take at least one other person to back you up in case things got naughty. The people who go with you are known as your **back-up**, but it can also be a term for a weapon hidden about your person for use in emergencies.

BAG MAN

A **bag man** is a member of a professional robbery team whose job it is to gather up the cash and bag it. Each member of the team will have a specific task, and the bag man will normally be unarmed. The bagman will also carry the **happy bag**, which is the slang name given to the bag or holdall armed robbers use to transport guns and disguises (masks, gloves, etc.) to and from robberies.
See Happy bag (p. 60)

BAIL BANDITS

Bail bandits are serious criminals who are granted bail on a case and then decide that there's a good chance they'll be found guilty at trial so they commit more crimes in order to keep them and their families going financially while they are serving their sentence. Before the PACE (Police And Criminal Evidence) Act was introduced in 1984 it was quite common for criminals to bribe the police, or offer them details about other criminals, to ensure that they raised no objections at a bail hearing in front of magistrates, no matter how serious the charge. If someone is on bail for armed robbery and it looks as though there's a chance they'll be found guilty and jailed, it becomes worth the gamble to go out and commit more armed robberies. If they're caught for these robberies, it will add very little time to the eventual sentence, and if the criminal gets away with them, he's quids in.

BAKE

Bake means I'll see you later (rhyming slang: baked potato = later). It only works due to the cockney pronunciation 'potater'.

BANGER

A **banger** is a gun, though it can also be stun and fragmentation grenades, which are increasingly being used by criminals for hits and armed robbery. It's taken from the sound a gun makes when it's fired. Although this is a fairly obvious word for gun, a lot are less so: criminals must be secretive when talking about firearms as just being in possession of one without a licence is cause for an immediate prison sentence.

BANG TO RIGHTS

To be caught **bang to rights** means to be caught in a situation in which you have little or no room to manoeuvre. For example, if the police surround you when you're coming out of a newly robbed bank, clutching a firearm and a bag of money, you've been caught bang to rights. Some criminals will throw in the towel and plead guilty when something like this happens, but others will fight the case by running a cut-throat defence. In the example above, you could say that you did it under duress, under threat of violence. This is really the only defence under British law for the crime of armed robbery.

BARNEY

To have a **Barney** is to have a fight or argument (rhyming slang: Barney Rubble = trouble). Barney Rubble is a character from *The Flintstones*, a cartoon about a Stone Age family very popular with the baby-boomer generation. 'Barney' has the same meaning in Polari slang.

BEEF

To have a **beef** with someone is to have an argument or fight. It's an American word that has made its way into the lexicology of young criminals and prisoners. Many young gang members who have been jailed for crimes of violence against rival gang members consider it their duty to carry on their beef while they're incarcerated.

BELL

A **bell** is a telephone call, as in 'Give Eric a bell and see if he's up for a bit of wet work', and is taken from the days when telephones actually had a bell. It was used a lot in the past and is now making something of a comeback as more people download old-fashioned bell ringtones on to their mobile phones.

BENT

To be **bent** means to be dishonest or corrupt, or homosexual. It all depends on the context. A bent **copper** is one who will take bribes from criminals in order to weaken a case, or 'lose' vital evidence for a price. A bent brief is a solicitor who will commit illegal acts in return for payment from criminals. If you're as 'bent as a nine-bob note', you are totally corrupt, as there is no such thing.
See Hooky

BERK

Despite the origins of **Berk** (rhyming slang: Berkshire Hunt = c***), it has been a favourite term of abuse on family comedy shows since the 1950s and still is up to the present day.

BIG UP

Big up is a West Indian/Jamaican phrase meaning to praise someone or boost their ego, short for 'big up your chest', meaning you should feel pride in something and stick your chest out. Similarly, to 'big up yourself' means to boast or make outlandish claims about yourself. At one period in the 1990s 'big up' became a greeting amongst West Indian youths.

BINS

Bins was originally slang for binoculars but in recent years has come to mean spectacles or glasses, as in 'Get on the geezer in the bins; I think he might be **Old Bill**'.

BIT OF WORK

Serious career criminals describe armed robberies or any other criminal enterprise that nets an illegal profit a **bit of work**, as in 'I see Fingers had that bit of work over in Luton: nice few quid there'. Career criminals class their activities as their job, so it's only natural for them to describe such goings on as work.

THE BLACK

The black is blackmail, a criminal offence involving unjustified threats to make gain or cause loss to another unless a demand is met. It can be coercion, involving threats of physical harm for example, and is a form of extortion. To put the black on someone is to threaten to expose something they would rather keep hidden in order to obtain money.
See Strong-arm

BLANK

To **blank** someone is to act as though they are not there, something done by criminals and prisoners to people they don't like: screws, informers, sex offenders, and so on. It can also mean a refusal, as in 'I was up for **jam roll**, but the Board gave me a right blank' or 'I pulled the shooter but the bank staff gave me a blank and ducked down behind the counter.'
See Jam roll

BLAZE

Blaze is mainly used by the young to describe the act of smoking cannabis or crack cocaine, as in 'Yeah, man, I stayed in my crib blazing ganja wid me **bredbins**', after the blazing end of a joint or crack pipe.

BLITZING

Blitzing is committing lots of crimes in a short space of time, after the Blitz. To 'go on a blitz' means to really go to war with robbing or thieving. The term is very widely used by those addicted to heroin or crack cocaine who need to feed their habits every day. Life becomes one big long blitz as they strike hard and fast to get money for drugs. *See On the UPS* (p. 46)

BLUEY

Lead sheeting from church roofs is known as **bluey** from the blue sheen of the metal, as in 'If they catch you nicking that bluey from the church roof, the beak will give you a **carpet** and God will not forgive'. It's also slang for a £5 note, which used to be blue.

BOAT

A **boat** is someone of rank and importance in the criminal world. It's an extension of 'face' (rhyming slang: boat race = face).

BOD

Short for the word 'body', and widely used by criminals and prisoners to describe any male person whose name they don't know, as in 'I went over to B wing and some **bod** started giving it **the Barry**.'

BOLLOCKING

To give someone a **bollocking** is to give them a severe talking to; it's the next best thing to a kick in the **bollocks**. It's now mainly used by uniforms, such as the police or prison officers, so it's fallen out of favour with criminals.

BOLLOCKS

Usually used to refer to the testicles but also to describe something that is untrue or crappy, as in 'That stereo is a load of old bollocks; it don't work' or 'Stop talking bollocks, you **mug**, it's boring me'.
See Pony (1)

BOOK

A synonym for 'rate' taken from the motor trade, as in 'I **book** him as an iron'. There's a book, *Glass's Valuation Guide* (now an online service) that's known as the bible of the motor trade and gives prices for all makes and models of used cars. When traders buy used cars they will see what the vehicle is 'booked as', i.e. the list price, by looking in *Glass's*. If you think a car is worth less than what the seller is asking, you'd tell him at what price you 'book it'. Criminals now commonly use it to add weight to their own opinion, as in 'Charlie reckons the geezer's okay, but I book him as a slippery bastard'.

BOOTS

There's a black-market trade in stolen spare wheels and tyres, and it became known as **boots** because they're the part of the vehicle that touches the ground.
See Boot Burglar

BO PEEP

Bo Peep is rhyming slang for sleep, as in 'That guard didn't even see me coming, I sent him Bo before he knew what was happening'.

BORASIC

To be **borasic** means to have no money (rhyming slang: borasic lint = skint). (Borasic lint is a medical dressing made from surgical lint soaked in acid and glycerine.)
See Polo

BOSH

Bosh is an all-purpose word and widely used, for example as an exclamation of surprise – 'I opened the peter and *bosh!* There was the cash!'; or as the sound of hitting someone – 'I gave him the right-hander, *bosh!*'; or to mean adding filling agents to illegal powdered drugs like heroin or cocaine – 'How many times has this parcel been boshed?'.

BOTTLE (2)

Bottle can have many meanings. The first, or original, meaning is from rhyming slang: bottle and glass = arse. This then led to 'Aris' (rhyming slang: Aristotle = bottle). From here, it became a slang word for courage, as in 'I hope you've got the bottle for this **bit of work**'. It can also mean to attack somebody with a glass bottle, as in 'Terry jumped in to stop the fight and somebody bottled him', as a warning that you are being followed, as in 'Here, do you know you've got **Old Bill** on your bottle?', and as slang for followed someone, as in 'Yeah, I bottled him all the way to the **jug'** (as in following closely behind, on someone's arse, hence bottle). In the 1970s it became slang for **dipping** or picking pockets – 'to go out on the bottle' – because most men carry their wallet in a rear pocket. In prison, it means to smuggle drugs or other items in your anus, as in 'Yeah, I've got the parcel bottled' and, finally, it can be used as a word for male homosexual prostitutes.

BOUNCE

Bounce is West Indian slang meaning to go or leave, as in 'It's getting late, man's gotta bounce.' It refers to a particular walk sometimes referred to as 'the Brixton bounce', bouncing on the balls of the feet and moving with loose hips.
See Bake

BOUNCER

In the days before all nightclub doormen had to be registered with the police, and before they were renamed 'crowd control technicians', they were known as **bouncers**. It comes from the fact that if a customer caused a problem they would be 'bounced' from the premises – thrown out without ceremony. Aggressive punters would be bounced off the walls and the pavement in order to subdue them.

BRAHMS

To be described as **Brahms** means that you are very drunk (rhyming slang: Brahms and Liszt = pissed). Both Brahms and Liszt were classical composers so it seems a shame that they should end up as rhyming slang for the modern inebriated.
See Elephant's

BRASS

A **brass** is bit of northern slang for a prostitute that has made its way down south over the years, so-called because you need brass (money) in order to pay one.

BRASS KNUCKLES

Brass knuckles are knuckledusters, heavy metal weights, sometimes spiked, that are worn over the fingers and can do terrible damage to an opponent in a fight. For a lot of violent criminals knuckledusters are their weapon of choice. Being hit by a pound of spiked brass on the end of someone's fist will knock someone out if they're hit in the right place. Before **bouncers** had to be registered with the police and licensed, some of them would carry a set of brass knuckles for dealing with leery punters.

BREAD (2)

Bread is money (bread and honey = money), initially from London at the turn of the twentieth century when you'd count yourself lucky to have a meal of bread and honey, but it also became very popular in America during the hippy era and beyond.

BREAD-AND-JAM-EATERS

Bread-and-jam-eaters is a disparaging Romany term for the children of the *gorja* (non-Gypsies). The message is that Gypsy children are better fed, better looked after and have a greater sense of family than the children of non-Gypsies.

BREDRIN

A West Indian word used primarily by the young, and meaning brother or brothers. A lot of West Indians are brought up in strongly religious households where the Bible is required reading, so the word 'brethren' is not uncommon. Young black criminals and prisoners use the word to describe anyone who is a member of their gang or family or a friend, as in 'Boy, man's looking to go Pentonville; I got nuff nuff **bredrin** there.'

BREK

Brek is **borstal** and prison slang for breakfast. When calculating a prison sentence the con will have to take into account the breakfast on the last day of the sentence, as they will not be released from prison until after, so a trainee or prisoner coming to the last couple of weeks of a sentence might say, 'I've got ten and a brek left to do.'
See Carpet (p. 172)

BROMLEYS

To have it on your **Bromleys** means to run away or escape (rhyming slang: Bromley by Bow = toe), as in 'I just about had the lock off the peter when **Old Bill** crashed the door and I had to have it on my Bromleys.'
See Have it Away

BROWN (2)

In the criminal world, if you describe someone as **brown** it means they are dead (rhyming slang: brown bread = dead). The nickname of one of the most infamous South

London criminals of the 1960s, Freddie Foreman, was Brown Bread Fred, because it was said that if you crossed him you would end up dead. Even though he was from South London, Brown Bread Fred had a long association with the equally infamous East End Kray Brothers. Brown Bread Fred was arrested along with the Kray gang in 1966 and charged with the murder of Frank 'The Mad Axeman' Mitchell and disposing of the body of Jack 'The Hat' McVitie.

BROWN (3)

To **brown** someone is to perform anal sex on them, as in 'Jimmy is a **raving iron**; that's how come he had the **black** on those MPs, he was browning both of them' ('Jimmy is a blatant homosexual; that's how he was blackmailing those Members of Parliament, he was sodomizing both of them').
See Raving iron

BROWNS

Browns is the brown-coloured two-piece prison uniform that used to be worn by unconvicted remand prisoners while awaiting trial or sentence in British prisons.
See Blues

BUNCE

Bunce is money (rhyming slang: Bunsen burner = earner), as in 'I'm going to see if Knuckles has got that bit of bunce he owes me.' An 'earner' is usually illegal money that has been 'earned' through skulduggery. The word bunce became quite popular in the 1970s when it was used in the television series *The Sweeney*. The programme used a lot of criminal and police slang which then came into public usage and was subsequently abandoned by criminals.

See Bung, Nelsons

BUNG

A **bung** is a purse or moneybag. The word dates back to Elizabethan times when there were no wallets and men tended to carry their money in a cloth bag attached to their belt. In the 1950s the word became slang for a bribe, often to the police, as in 'Sergeant Plod is willing to lose the evidence if we give him a bung'. In the 1960s 'earner' (a sum of illegal monies) was added to 'bung', as in 'I'll see if we can bung Plod an earner'. By the 1990s 'bung' was in common usage, particularly in the tabloid press and often in the context of football managers and agents taking bribes. It's rarely used by criminals these days.

See Bung nipper

BUNG NIPPER

A **bung nipper** (also called a cut-purse) was one of a pickpocket team in the eighteenth century who would carry scissors or a sharp blade in order to cut purses and money bags from the belts of their victims while they were being distracted by other members of the team. The original bung nipper died out when wallets were invented and men no longer carried their money in a bag tied to their belt, though in the early 1990s a form of bung nipping made a bit of a comeback in the armed robbery trade. Security guards were issued with a radio alarm device that was strapped to their belts and would emit a powerful alarm if the cash box was taken from them. In order to counter this, armed robbers would carry a Stanley knife to cut the radio from the belt and take it with them when they took the cash. As long as the device stayed in close proximity to the cash box, the alarm wouldn't be activated.

See Dipper (p. 38)

BURN

In prison slang a **burn** is a roll-up or a bit of tobacco, quite literally describing the act of burning tobacco to smoke.

See Bible pages (p. 156) *Civvy* (p. 114) *Tailor-made* (p. 252)

BUSY

To be **busy** is to be nosey or to involve yourself in things that don't concern you. Criminals have a particular hatred for people like this as they, understandably, like to keep their actions quiet and secret.

BUTCHER'S

To be asked to have a **butcher's** at something is quite common in the underworld (rhyming slang: butcher's hook = look). If you are going to rob a bank, for example, you would definitely go and have a butcher's at the premises before committing yourself.

See Dekko

BUZZ

The **buzz** is the addictive feeling some criminals get from committing crime, and this is particularly true of armed robbers or others who put their lives and liberty in jeopardy in the pursuit of crime. To some, it's like a drug high, and some professional criminals describe it as an addiction. It's a feeling of euphoria generally felt during the commission of the crime, followed by an emotional 'crash' when the crime is over.

CAKOBAKO

To be **cakobako** with something means that you've got more than enough of it. It's from 'caked', meaning to be heavily covered with something, and is used quite a lot by North London heroin addicts when describing someone with a lot of drugs or money, as in 'The geezer's cakobako with tackle but his prices are **bollocks**'.

THE CALI

The **Cali** is a run-down area of council estates around Caledonian Road in North London, now infamous for its **hoisting** teams, just as parts of South London are notorious for their armed robbery crews. The favourite shop of choice for the Cali mob is Gap, because it is so easy to get away with stuff and it always has a resale value. In fact, going hoisting in the Cali is now known as 'going out on the Gap' or 'Gapping'. One refinement to the hoisting genre was introduced by a little firm in Bermondsey (also, coincidently, junkies), and this was known as **the bird game**.

See Blitzing

CANISTER

In East London **canister** is slang for backside, though it probably started out as a mishearing of *keister*, which is from the German word *kiste*, meaning a chest or box. So if someone from the East End offers you a kick in the canister, they intend to kick you in the rear. However, in South London your canister is your head, as in 'Oh yeah, he's definitely brown **bread**, he took three from a .45 in his canister'.
See Bottle (2)

CARVE-UP

A **carve-up** is a share-out of stolen loot, as in 'We had fifty large off the van and then went down to Freddie's **slaughter** for the carve-up'.
See Slaughter

CHAP

In the old **borstal** system the **chaps** were the trainees with the power, up-and-coming criminals who weren't afraid to fight either the system or other borstal boys. Borstal was very black and white as far as the trainees were concerned: if you weren't one of the chaps then you were a sap. The chaps were usually career criminals in the making and many went on to commit bigger crimes and to serve longer prison sentences.
See Boat

CHORE

To **chore** (a Gypsy/Traveller word) something is to steal it or get it by other nefarious means, as in 'I went three fields over and chored a nice trailer'. To Gypsies and Travellers anything that is 'choredy' is stolen and should be kept out of sight. *See Pinch (2)*

CLARET

Claret is blood, because they are of a similar colour. It's a word beloved by football hooligans, as in 'We done the ICF good and proper; there was claret all over the **gaff**'.

CLOCK

To **clock** someone is to see them, as in 'I clocked you up at Freddie's **gaff** last week'.

CLUMP

A **clump** is a punch or a hit, taken from the sound of a fist or boot on flesh, as in 'Talk to me like that again and I'll give you a right clump'. In the old **borstal** system a 'clumper' was a screw who was liable to give you a dig for any reason or no reason.

CORNED BEEF

Corned beef is rhyming slang for teeth, as in 'Check out the corned beef on the geezer, they look like a bowl of Sugar Puffs'. Teeth are also known as 'railings' or 'tombstones'.

COREY

Corey is a Travellers' word for penis but is also used to describe security guards who work in the cash-in-transit industry. Any guard who delivers or collects cash tends to wear a crash helmet so is known to criminals as the corey because of their resemblance to a walking penis.

See Pony bag (p. 46)

CREPES

A slang word for footwear but for trainers in particular, used mainly by youngsters, as in 'Nice **crepes**, blood, they is sick!' The word comes from the crepe-soled shoes worn by Teddy Boys in the 1940s and '50s.

DEKKO

To have a **dekko** at something is to look at it, as in 'Have a dekko at these diamonds, they're top of the range'. The word is possibly from the Urdu for to look or spy.

See Butcher's, Clock

DOG END

A **dog end** is what remains of a cigarette after it has been put out, or 'dogged out'. They're usually collected and smoked by prisoners who have no access to funds to buy tobacco.

See Swooper (p. 250)

DOG'S BOLLOCKS

To describe something (or someone) as the **dog's bollocks** is to class it as something very good indeed. The phrase is sometimes shortened to 'the dog's', and it's taken from the fact that a good fighting dog has big balls.

DOING ME NUT

If someone says 'You are **doing me nut**,' it means you are annoying them greatly and they're almost at the point of doing you violence. 'Nut' is slang is for head, so if you are doing someone's nut it means you are getting into their head in an annoying way.

See Doing me swede in

DOING ME SWEDE IN

Doing me swede in means to annoy someone a lot, 'swede' being slang for the head, as it is usually a large round vegetable.

See Doing me nut

DOUBLE TAP

The **double tap** is the killing method adopted by professional killers. Favoured by assassins and the Special Forces, it means to shoot one bullet into the chest or heart, and the second bullet into the head in order to ensure death. It's sometimes also known as 'belt and braces'. For **one in the nut**, a large-calibre bullet has to be used to ensure the death of the target, which, unless the killer is using a suppressor or silencer, means a loud bang but, with the double tap, a smaller and quieter calibre, such as a .22, can be used, which means a quick and quiet killing.

DWELL THE BOX

To **dwell the box** is to hang around somewhere for way too long, resulting in you getting arrested, as in 'Jimmy's a fool to himself, if he hadn't dwelled the box he never would have ended up nicked'. It can also mean to stay at home and not go out, as in 'I don't see him much nowadays; all he wants to do is dwell the box'.

ELEPHANT'S

To be **elephant's** is to be under the influence of alcohol (rhyming slang: elephant's trunk = drunk), as in 'I only went out for one pint but ended up elephant's'.
See Brahms

FANNY

Fanny can be either female genitalia or lies and bullshit. If someone says you are 'talking a load of old fanny' it usually means you are lying or making things up. The word could come from an earlier slang phrase, 'sweet Fanny Adams', which has come to mean 'nothing at all'.

The original sweet Fanny Adams was an eight-year-old girl who was murdered in Alton, in Hampshire, in 1867. She was butchered by her killer, a solicitor's clerk named Frederick Baker, and parts of her body were strewn around, including her eyeballs, which were thrown into a nearby river. The trial was well reported and Frederick Baker was publicly hanged outside Winchester Prison, the last public execution there, attended by over five thousand onlookers. Two years later, the Royal Navy introduced new rations of tinned mutton and the meat was so bad it became a standing joke that the tins were filled with the butchered remains of Fanny Adams, so the term became slang for something worthless, and then for nothing at all: 'sweet FA'. With time, sweet FA changed to 'sweet fuck all', meaning nothing and plenty of it. Now it has evolved further to mean a lie.
See Fuck All

FIVER

A **fiver** is usually taken to mean a £5 note, as in 'Yeah, he gave me a tenner but he still owes me a fiver'.
See Bluey

FIX UP

Fix up is a common expression used by young tearaways, usually, though not exclusively, of West Indian origin. It's an instruction, usually issued in the form of a threat, to sort yourself out and stop acting like a fool, as in 'You better fix up before I see you next, or man will get **vex**'.
See Vex

FLASHER

A **flasher** is a sex offender who exposes his genitals to people in order to get a sexual thrill. They're known as flashers because they will usually just give a quick flash of the goods before making their getaway.

FRIDGE

A **fridge** is a man (rhyming slang: fridge freezer = geezer), usually one with criminal connections or tendencies, as in 'Yeah, I see the fridge with the **hooky** currency and he's willing to **have a trade**.'
See Having a Trade

FUCK ALL

Absolutely nothing, as in 'I spent eight hours cutting my

way into that peter and when I got it open there was **fuck all** in there.' Can also be shortened to its initials 'FA' or to 'sweet FA'.
See Fanny

GAFF

A **gaff** is a place and can be used in many contexts, as in 'I was up at me bird's gaff having a cup of rosy [tea]' or 'I hate Bricko [Brixton nick], it's a fucking terrible gaff'.
See Dwell the box

GET RUSHED

To get **rushed** means to be attacked by several assailants at once. It's usually used by younger criminals or prisoners to describe an attack, as in 'Yeah, man, I punched one screw boy in his face and the rest of them rushed me.' It can also be used to mean **steaming**, as in 'Twenty of us rushed the jewellery shop and got nuff nuff gold'.

GOING THROUGH THE SLIPS

Going through the slips is getting out of a tight or dangerous situation. It means you have found a clever way out. It can also be used in an insulting manner in order to imply cowardice or cooperation with the authorities, as in 'Funny that, weren't it? All the lads got collared but you managed to go through the slips.'

GOLD WATCH

This is quite an old-fashioned piece of rhyming slang,

usually used by old-time villains to mean a large scotch, as in 'Two pints of mild and a **gold watch** please, barman'.
See Pig's ear

GRAND

A **grand** is £1,000, also known in rhyming slang as 'a bag of sand'. The word is taken from the fact that it is a grand amount of money, particularly back in the 1920s, when it was first used.
See Monkey, Pony

GROWLERS

Growlers is an eighteenth-century criminal word for pistols, as in 'I'd have been taken by the watchman if I'd not had my growlers with me'. Pistols were also known as 'barkers' because of the noise they made when discharged. In those days, even burglars tended to carry at least one pistol while committing a crime, and some of them weren't shy about using one, as homeowners tended to dish out their own brand of justice if they caught criminals in the act.

HALF-INCH

To **half-inch** something is to steal it (rhyming slang: half-inch = **pinch**), as in 'Yeah, I'm doing a three-stretch for half-inching a van load of pussies.'

HAVE IT AWAY

To **have it away** means to escape from prison or from a criminal venture that has gone wrong, as in '**Old Bill** turned up so I had to have it away'. It can also mean to have sexual intercourse, as in 'I had it away with that little barmaid from the Red Lion last night'.

See Bromleys

HEAVY

There are two meanings to **heavy** in the criminal world. The first is a way of describing the crime of armed robbery – the heavy – so-called because of the seriousness of the crime and the fact that it attracts heavy sentences. The second is to describe someone who uses violence and intimidation in order to achieve their ends, as in 'Then the Twins turned up with their heavies and I had no choice but to hand over the protection money'.

See Strong Arm

HENCH

A word used by youngsters to denote great body size and a hard demeanour, taken from 'henchman', as in 'Bwoy, I don't really fancy going up against him; have you seen how **hench** he is?'.

HITTING THE PENNY

Hitting the penny is slang for being knocked out or knocked down. It is rhyming slang – Penny Draw = Floor. Also known as 'hitting the rory' (Rory McGraw = Floor). Back at the turn of the twentieth century tobacco was sold loose and you could buy a 'penny draw' of tobacco – the tobacconist would draw a handful of loose tobacco from his bundle and wrap it up in paper for you and for this you would pay 1 penny. Still a very popular slang phrase, as in

– 'I gave him one knuckle sandwich and he hit the penny', or 'As soon as the flying squad jumped us, Tony hit the penny like a sack of spuds!'

HOOKING (2)

Hooking is a method of operation used by car thieves which involves putting a fishing rod or any long, thin stick through the letterbox of a home in order to 'hook' car and house keys from a hallway. Traditionally, most householders would leave their keys on a table or ledge in the hallway, and thieves knew this. It used to be a simple matter to spot a nice expensive car parked in a driveway, then creep up to the front door of the house and peep through the letterbox to see if the keys were close by.

HOOKY

If something is considered **hooky**, it is probably stolen, from the saying 'By hook or by crook', as in 'Hide that telly, Doris, **Old Bill** are on their way round and that set is definitely hooky'.
See Bent

HOOTER

Your **hooter** is your nose, so called because you blow it, as in 'Keep giving me grief, mate, and you'll get a punch in the hooter'.

HUMP (1)

To have the **hump** with someone means you are annoyed with them, as in 'That **mug** is giving me the right hump'.

Taken from the action of hunching up your shoulders in annoyance or irritation.

HUMP (2)

An Irish Travellers' word for a pensioner or elderly person, **hump** is taken from the humped back or stooped posture of some old people. Unfortunately, despite their talk of honour, a lot of Travellers and Gypsies actively target the elderly in their crimes and have no compunction about leaving vulnerable old people with no money and in a state of terror.

JACK

Jack is the female genitals (rhyming slang: Jack and Danny = fanny; **fanny** is slang for vagina), as in 'Stop moaning or you'll get a swift kick in the Jack'.

JACK JONES

If somebody tells you that they prefer to be on their **Jack Jones**, it means they want to be on their own (rhyming slang: Jack Jones = alone). Jack Jones is an American pop crooner who had several hits in the 1960s and '70s, including 'Sons and Lovers'.

JACK'S

A **jack's** is a £5 note (rhyming slang: jack's alive = five). The term 'jack's alive' is used in the card game blackjack but has come, in criminal usage, to mean five of anything, but particularly money, as in 'I'll lend you a jack's until canteen day'. In Irish slang, 'the jacks' are the toilets.

JACOBS

If someone threatens to give you a kick in the **Jacobs**, it would be a good idea to cross your legs (rhyming slang: Jacobs cream crackers = knackers; 'knackers' is slang for the testicles). *See Niagaras*

JAIL BAIT

A sexually active and attractive girl under the legal age of consent but looking older is **jail bait**. Any sexual activity with a girl like this, if discovered, will lead to jail for the perpetrator.
See Nonce (p. 235)

JAMES

If someone calls you a **James**, they are in fact calling you a c*** (rhyming slang, from James Blunt). A pretty recent arrival in the slang lexicon and much loved by youngsters.
See Berk

JANK

If something is described as **jank**, it means it's no good, rubbish or unacceptable, as in 'This fucking **nick** is jank' or 'I can't use this razor, it's jank!'.
See Pony (1)

JIGGLER

A **jiggler** is a homemade key or skeleton key that has to be jiggled in a lock in order for it to work. Somebody who is **mustard** at picking locks is known as a jiggler.

JOHNNY CASH

The name of **Johnny Cash**, a world famous country and pop singer who started out at the small Sun studios in the early 1950s, is now used as rhyming slang for a medical complaint: Johnny Cash = rash.

JUMP

The **jump** is any counter in a bank, building society, post office or any other building where cash and valuables are held. 'Going over the jump' is an old expression for robbery and comes from the act of physically jumping over the counter in order to snatch the prize. It's not so common nowadays, when most banks have bulletproof screens to stop robbers from getting over counters.
See Across the Pavement

KITE/KITER

A **kite** is a cheque (it's as light as a kite), and a **kiter** is someone who passes bad or fake cheques. To go out 'flying kites' is a criminal expression meaning you are passing stolen or forged cheques. The heyday of kiters or kite flyers was the 1980s and '90s, when security around fraud was still pretty lax. The average price a thief could get for a cheque-book and guarantee card would be a 'ching' (£5) per page, and the average chequebook had thirty-two pages, so stealing and selling them was pretty good business. As might be expected, forged or stolen cheques were used for criminal acts such as cashing them for money or using them to pay for goods which could then be sold on for cash. At one stage there was at least one London firm that was paying burglars to break into small building society branches out in the country to steal the company chequebooks. With a company cheque or building society cheque you could buy larger, more valuable items and the London firm was using the cheques to buy things like cars, speedboats and Rolex watches from the pages of *Exchange and Mart* and paying with building society cheques, which are as good as money in the bank. The items bought with the stolen cheques would then be sold, creating 100 per cent profit.

KNACKERED/KNACKER

To be **knackered** is to be tired out after severe exertion. The word is probably Irish in origin, as Gypsies and Travellers are known as **knackers** and buy old horses and cattle; tired-out horses end up in the knackers' yard. To call an Irish Traveller a knacker is definitely fighting talk and will inevitably lead to violence; it's as offensive as calling a black man a nigger. Often extended into rhyming slang: cream crackered = knackered.
See Jacobs

LARDY

A **lardy** is a cigar (rhyming slang: la-di-da = cigar).

LODGE

To **lodge** something or someone is to hide it for later retrieval, as in 'Old Bill came up the street so I had to lodge the tools' or 'I lodged Jimmy in the lock-up until the heat dies down'.
See Stash

MAN DEM

Man dem is a West Indian expression meaning 'us', particularly when referring to a gang. For example, one of the most notorious gangs in North London is known as the Tottenham Man Dem, meaning the men of Tottenham.
See Boy Dem, (p. 98)

MERRY HEART

Merry heart means girlfriend (rhyming slang: merry heart = tart). It's been in use since the 1950s and replaced **Richard** (Richard III = bird). The term is mainly used between men, as in 'I'm taking my merry heart to the pictures tonight', but rarely to a girlfriend's face.
See Richard

MOB-HANDED

To be **mob-handed** means to be in a group intent on crime or violence. It's used quite a lot in prison when referring to beatings by the screws, who always come mob-handed. It comes from the football hooligan days of the 1970s when, if you turned up at an away ground with your gang or mob, you were said to be 'going mob-handed'.

MONKEY

A **monkey** is racecourse slang for £500. The word was brought back by servicemen returning from India and used in civilian life when some of these men ended up working as bookies or enforcers at UK racecourses between the wars. This sum of money was called a monkey because the Indian banknotes had pictures of animals on them, and the 500 rupee note featured a monkey. These slang words for money were quickly adopted by criminals and are still in constant use today.

See Pony

MOOCH

To **mooch** is to move about in a sly manner. If you are going to 'case a job' or if you are just going out on spec, then you might say you are 'going for a mooch'. The word possibly comes from the old French word *muchier*, which means to hide or skulk. In America, apparently, a moocher is someone who is on the **ponce**, begging or looking for a handout. In 1931, jazz 'scat' singer Cab Calloway recorded a song called 'Minnie the Moocher', which sold over a million copies. The song is heavy with drug references, although the word 'mooch' has little connection with the drug world.

MUCKER

In the criminal world, just like in the straight world, a **mucker** is a good friend, someone who will muck in with you when things start getting difficult or dirty.

MUSTARD

To be called **mustard** is a good thing, as it means you are red hot at what you do, as in 'Wow! Fingers is mustard at the con game!'.

NELSONS

To be holding **Nelsons** means that you are in possession of cash (rhyming slang: Nelson Eddy's = readies). (Nelson

Eddy was an early film star and singer who had hit duets with a female singer/actor called Jeanette McDonald.)
See Bunce

NIAGARAS

If someone offers you a kick in the **Niagaras**, it would be best not to take them up on the offer as it involves a blow to the testicles (rhyming slang: Niagara Falls = balls). Sometimes shortened to 'Niags'.
See Jacobs

NICKER

A **nicker** is one pound. The origin of this is unknown, but the word is widely used even today. It used to refer to the old £1 note, but with the introduction of the pound coin, one pound is also now known as a 'bar' or a 'nugget'.
See Two Bob (p. 252)

ONE IN THE NUT

To get **one in the nut** means to be shot in the head – executed. If you are ordered to give someone one in the nut, there can be no mistake that the instruction is to kill them. Also known as a 'lead injection behind the ear', this is the favoured method of killing by criminal hitmen, usually by way of a large-calibre bullet.
See Double tap

ON THE COBBLES

If someone invites you **on the cobbles,** they are suggesting that you should go outside for a fistfight. It comes from the days when the roads were made from cobblestones, and means to fight out in the open. A cobbles fight is generally deemed to mean a fair fight with no weapons involved. Cobbles fighters are much respected in the criminal world as real hard men of courage and skill. Many infamous criminals were also great on the cobbles, the most infamous of them all being armed robber Roy Shaw. Shaw was rumoured to have been the one that got away from the Eastcastle Street Ppost Office robbery in 1953, which netted over £200,000 in cash, the biggest cash robbery in the UK before the Great Train Robbery of 1963. The raid was said to have been planned by 'King of the Underworld' Billy Hill, and Roy Shaw escaped a police ambush by hanging underneath a lorry and escaping unnoticed in the mêlée. Roy Shaw went on to become one of the greatest bare-knuckle and unlicensed fighters in the UK.

See Straightener

PAGE 16

Page 16 is the page of a prisoner's official wing record used to make comments and observations on the prisoner for later reports. Some prison staff will use page 16 to record their suspicions or any rumours they have heard about the prisoner. Red ink on your page 16 means bad reports. This information will be taken into account when the prisoner applies for any privileged job, for home leave or parole.

PAPER

Paper is modern youth slang for money. It originated in America and was made popular by gangsta rappers.

PIG'S EAR

Pig's ear is beer in rhyming slang, as in 'I had a few pig's ears and lost track of the time.'
See Gold Watch, Vera

PINCH (1)

To **pinch** something usually means to steal something small, as in 'I pinched a bit of his baccy when he wasn't looking.'

PINCH (2)

It can also mean to be arrested, as in 'He was loitering so he got pinched by the **rozzers**.'
See Chore

PISSED

In British slang to be **pissed** usually means to be very drunk, but in America being pissed means you are in a bad mood or angry about something. The Americanism is coming into popular usage by the young criminal who sees anything American as glamorous, including their slang.
See Brahms, Elephant's

POLO

If someone tells you they are **polo**, it means they have no money (rhyming slang: Polo mint = skint).
See Borasic

PONY (1)

If someone says they are 'going for a **pony**' it means they are going to defecate (rhyming slang: pony and trap = crap), but it is also widely used in the criminal world to mean anything that you might describe as crap, as in 'That fucking motor you sold me is absolute pony!' or 'Don't go to Dartmoor **nick**, mate; the weather down there is pony.'

See Jank

PONY (2)

In racecourse parlance a **pony** is £25 and this was soon adopted by the criminals who frequented the races in order to extort money from the bookmakers for 'protection'. It comes from the old Indian rupee notes which featured pictures of animals; the twenty-five rupee note featured a horse.

See Monkey, Pony bag (p. 46)

PORKIES

To tell **porkies** is to tell lies (rhyming slang: pork pie = lie).

PRANG

Prang is a word widely used by youths of West Indian origin and means to be frightened or nervous, as in 'He knew I was strapped cos I could see him getting prang'.

See Bottle (2)

PUNTER

A **punter** is a customer or someone willing to buy something stolen. It was originally used on the racetracks and was used to describe a person who will have a punt (small bet on an outsider), and then adopted into the criminal world via prostitution. The clients of prostitutes became known as punters because not only were they paying but they were also taking a gamble that they weren't going to get venereal disease from any of the girls and boys they had intercourse with. The term is now generally used by criminals for amateur buyers of stolen goods, i.e. the general public. A professional buyer of stolen goods is known as a **fence**.
See Toby

READIES

Readies is cash, from the expression 'ready cash', as in 'He will sell the whole parcel, but he wants readies for it' (as opposed to getting goods or services 'on bail', that is on loan).
See Bunce, Nelsons

REELS OF

If someone says you are **reels of** it usually means you are dirty and smelly (rhyming slang: reels of cotton = rotten), as in 'Have you washed that shirt? It's reels of'.
See Abraham Lincoln

RIB

A **rib** is a ribbed dirigible boat used for smuggling drugs, weapons or other contraband across relatively short stretches of water, for example, across the English Channel or the Straits of Gibraltar. These boats are ideal because they are light, low to the water and fast enough to evade customs patrols. The rib boat is a boon for drug smugglers and no smuggler worth his salt would be without a fleet of them. The boats can be deflated and folded up so as to take up very little space in storage.

RICHARD

A **Richard** has two meanings and both come from rhyming slang. In the original rhyming slang of the 1800s a Richard was a turd, but in the middle of the twentieth century **pony** became a popular term for excrement and Richard became rhyming slang for one's girlfriend (Richard III = bird.

See Pony (1)

RING IT

If somebody says they are trying to **ring it**, it means they are trying to fake something or pretend they are something they are not. It comes from the illegal and stolen car trade, where vehicles will be rung – from 'ringing the changes' – meaning to change all the VINs (Vehicle Identification Numbers) and plates in order to disguise the identity of a stolen vehicle for resale. For example, if you are committing fraud by using somebody else's identification, you would say, 'I'm going to ring it.' The term is sometimes used in sport: when a 'ringer' is put in place it means a different horse or fighter has been substituted for the original one, which is likely to up the odds for a loss or win.

See Ringers and Clones

RUBBER CHEQUE

A **rubber cheque** is a fake cheque proffered for goods or services in the knowledge that there are insufficient funds to cover it. It's also known as a 'bouncer', and is used widely by **kiters**.

See Kite/Kiters

SAFE

An expression of reassurance used by the young, as in 'Yeah, blood, I know him, he's **safe**.' It can also be used in reply to a greeting: 'Yo, whassup?' 'Safe, man.'

See Sweet

SALMON

Salmon refers to tobacco (rhyming slang: salmon and trout = snout; snout is slang for tobacco), as in 'Gi's a salmon, mate, I've left mine in my cell'.

See Desperate Dan (p. 182)

SAVVY

To be **savvy** is to be in the know, to have your finger on the pulse and know what's going on, from the French *savoir faire*, as in 'I'd get Georgie to do the alarms, he's very savvy around that stuff'.

SCALLY

Scally is a Liverpool or Scouse word for a criminal or ne'er-do-well, derived from 'scallywag', a deceitful and unreliable scoundrel. A lot of Liverpool criminals take pride in their scally status.

SCAM

A **scam** is a confidence trick or other large-scale criminal enterprise that involves parting a victim from their cash without the use of violence. The word is of American origin and could be a carnival term (a lot of carnival workers, or 'carnies', have their own slang words and phrases). Some believe it's related to the British word 'scamp', someone who cheats.

See Mark (p. 82)

SCRATCHER

Scratcher is Dublin slang for 'bed' (rhyming slang: scratch yer head = bed). It's sometimes used by British criminals to describe their cell, which is basically a small room with a bed taking up most of the space. The word is also slang for signing on the dole, as in 'I've just been down to the scratcher but my giro wasn't there'. Signing on at the Job Centre is also known as 'scratching on'.

SEND-OUT

A **send-out** is a lackey or inferior member of a gang who will be sent to do the gang's bidding, for example, to pick up guns or drugs.

SICK

If a youngster describes something as **sick** it means it's exceptionally good. The slang of the modern young, like all previous slang, is designed to be confusing, but then, that's the whole idea of it.

See Boo yakka! (p. 165)

SLASH

If someone tells you they are just going for a **slash**, you should not assume that their intention is to cut themselves or someone else. It's slang for urine, from the way a stream of hot urine seems to slash through snow, dust and dirt. It's also known in rhyming slang as Harry Dash, as in 'I'm just going for a Harry Dash, me back teeth are swimming!'

SLAUGHTER

A **slaughter** is a place where criminals keep stolen or fake goods and also a place where they share out the proceeds after a crime has been committed. It's called the slaughter because it is where proceeds are cut up and distributed to those involved in a crime.
See Carve-up

SLEEVES

Sleeves are cartons of smuggled cigarettes, so called because they are packed in cardboard sleeves. Each sleeve will contain 200 cigarettes with the name, logo and brand of the legitimate maker. Because of the large amount of tax taken by the government on tobacco and cigarettes, cigarette smuggling is a very lucrative criminal enterprise and the money generated by it is sometimes used to fund larger criminal enterprises. A case of the government aiding the criminal fraternity in their endeavours!

SPANISH ARCHER

Spanish archer is breaking up a relationship. It's a play on words, as a Spanish archer could be said to be 'El Bow'.

STEAMERS/STEAMING

In Ireland, a **steamer** is a homosexual, but in the UK steamers are usually young, violent thieves and robbers. Originating in inner-city shopping centres in the mid-1980s, **steaming** was the practice of running into shops **mob-handed**, and proceeding to steal or 'lift' every item of value on display. Steaming gangs usually consisted of twenty or more teenagers (sometimes up to fifty) who would descend on shopping centres, usually high on drugs and alcohol, and **rush** into the targeted shops (those that sell high-value items), creating mayhem and stealing valuable property. Because of the aggression of the gangs and their sheer numbers it was almost impossible for shop owners or members of the public to stop them. Once the premises had been looted, the gangs would quickly disperse in different directions in order to make pursuit all but impossible. Steaming fell out of favour in London due to the 'postcode wars', in which young gang members were busy shooting and stabbing each other in turf wars and disputes. Having a gang of teenagers on the high street now will almost certainly attract a large police presence. Steaming has been replaced by the slightly more sophisticated crime of motorized **smash-and-grab**, or 'steals on wheels', as it is also known.

STRAIGHTENER

A **straightener** is a fair fight arranged between two people in order to settle a difference or dispute. The rules are that no weapons should be used and no other person should get involved, but anything else goes. Opponents can use fists, boots, head and teeth in order to inflict damage on each other.

See On the Cobbles

STRAIGHT UP

A verbal qualifier often used in conversation by criminals and prisoners, meaning 'This is the unvarnished truth', as in 'There's twenty **grand** in that safe, straight up'. It's also sometimes used to question the truth or seriousness of a comment or statement, as in 'What? Straight up?'.
See Billy Bullshitter

STRING VEST

Rhyming slang for pest, and frequently used in prison as a light insult where there are plenty of people with enough time on their hands to become **string vests**, as in 'That Freddie is becoming a right string!'.

STRONG-ARM

To **strong-arm** someone is to intimidate and put pressure on them in order to achieve your own ends. Strong-arming on **The Out** can take the form of the 'protection game', where violent or heavy criminals threaten to cause trouble in pubs and clubs and demand a regular payment in order to 'protect' these establishments from anything untoward happening to them. The Kray Twins were experts at this sort of strong-arm tactic in the 1960s. The law would call it demanding money with menaces. In prison, and particularly in youth prisons, there's a lot of strong-arming – putting pressure on and inciting fear in weaker prisoners in order to steal their canteen, food or other property. Strong-arming in adult prisons is frowned upon by ODCs (Ordinary Decent Criminals) and is classed as bullying. In some of the top-security jails a strong-armer will be given a good talking to by other prisoners and, if they persist, then they will pay the price for their actions either by being seriously assaulted or being run off the wing by way of threats. In these cases, some of the strong-armers will seek the safety of the protection wings, where, no doubt, they will have an even weaker bunch of prisoners on which to practise their dubious behaviour. Like all bullies, strong-arm men who throw their weight about in prison get their comeuppance. On the other hand, strong-arming of the public on the outside is seen by some criminals as a perfectly legitimate crime. Some strong-arm men are in demand as debt collectors for criminals who cannot use the law in order to retrieve what they are owed by other criminals.

See Heavy

SWEET

Sweet is a word much overused in prison and means that everything is good. It can be used as an enquiry, as in 'Sweet?', or as an instruction: 'Keep him sweet' ('Do not upset him'). It can also be used to describe your own state of wellbeing, as in 'Don't worry about me, I'm sweet'.

TENNER

A **tenner** is £10 cash. A £10 note is known as a tenner or a 'cockle' (rhyming slang: cock and hen = ten). 'Cock and hen' has been shortened and corrupted over time to become 'cockle'.

TICKLE

To 'have a **tickle**' is to be involved in a successful and lucrative criminal activity or enterprise. It comes from the fact that tickling makes people smile or laugh, as in 'I see

Tommy had a right tickle on that bank job in Fulham, fifty large all in **readies**'.

See Readies

TON

A **ton** is £100. The word was originally used in the motor trade and then adopted by criminals, many of whom used their ill-gotten gains to invest in used-car fronts – before drugs became such a lucrative investment, and comes from a ton being a measurement of a hundred cubic feet.

UP THE ROAD

Up the road is Scotland, so any Scottish criminal who talks about 'going up the road' is talking about going back to Scotland.

See Jockneys (p. 291)

VERA

If you walk into a pub and ask for a **Vera**, you'll be ordering a gin (rhyming slang: Vera Lynn = gin). Vera Lynn was a British singer and actress who had a 1940 hit with 'The White Cliffs of Dover' and became known as the Forces' Sweetheart.

See Vera and Phil, Veras

VERA AND PHIL

A **Vera and Phil** is rhyming slang: Vera Lynn and Philharmonic = gin and tonic.

VERAS

Modern slang for cigarette rolling papers, which are also known as 'skins' (rhyming slang: Vera Lynns = skins). The phrase came into popular use during the acid house/rave craze of the late 1980s when **Veras** were used to 'skin up' cannabis joints.

VEX

Vex is a youth slang word, from 'vexatious', for getting annoyed or angry, as in 'Don't get me vex, blud, or I'll be coming strapped'.

WEBBED UP

To be **webbed up** with someone means that you are very close to them professionally, as in 'I see Charlie's webbed up with that Russian firm who are doing the dodgy MOTs'. People you may be webbed up with as a criminal are not necessarily people you would class as close friends. It can also be used in the negative as a description of being stuck with something or somebody, as in 'I got webbed up with those poxy Betamax video cassettes that nobody wanted', meaning you are stuck with something you do not want. *See China* (p. 173)

WIND-UP

A **wind-up** is a practical joke carried out in order to make somebody look foolish. Wind-ups are very common among prisoners, as they have plenty of time on their hands. It can also be used as an expression of disbelief and incredulity, as in 'Is this some sort of fucking wind-up?'.

YOG

A yog is a gun, from Romany, as in 'Dik ere, **mush**, I'll fight you fair an' square, no need for no yogs.'
See Corp the Feen

YOU FUCKING WANT SOME?

The battle cry that has led to violence outside every pub, club and football ground and on every prison landing. It means, of course, 'Would you like me to nut you or punch you in the face, 'cos I'm ready for action?' It's a warning not to be ignored as violence is bound to follow. The 'some' mentioned in this phrase is violence.
See You Fucking Want Some, or What?

YOU FUCKING WANT SOME, OR WHAT?

Again, a possible precursor to violence, but this time with a get-out clause. By adding 'or what?' the antagonist is revealing the fact that, while he is ready and willing to offer up violence, he may also be looking for a way out and be open to a bit of verbal being the end result – as long as the target for this question is suitably contrite and does not reply with exhortations to violence himself.
See You Fucking Want Some?

Acknowledgements

Writing this book was a long and arduous process that seemed dogged by bad luck every step of the way. Three times I lost the whole manuscript, once by leaving my laptop on a train, and had to start again from scratch. I am delighted that the book is finally finished and I would like to thank a few people for their help and encouragement. My agent, Will Self, and my publishers and editors at Penguin, who have been very patient and supportive. Big thanks to Justin Rollins, Freddie Lunn, Chris Hawes, Brian Stead, Alan Ward, John Shelly, Ray Bishop and Ricky Abbott for their helpful contributions. I would also like to thank my lovely wife, Caroline, for all her love and support and for getting me motivated when I was at my lowest. And to all my readers – be lucky!